AF598755

Luther as a Spiritual Adviser

The Interface of Theology and Piety in Luther's Devotional Writings

Luther as a Spiritual Adviser

The Interface of Theology and Piety in Luther's Devotional Writings

Dennis Ngien

Foreword by Timothy George

WIPF & STOCK · Eugene, Oregon

Wipf and Stock Publishers
199 W 8th Ave, Suite 3
Eugene, OR 97401

Luther as a Spiritual Adviser
The Interface of Theology and Piety in Luther's Devotional Writings
By Ngien, Dennis and George, Timothy

ISBN 13: 978-1-55635-481-6
Publication date 1/24/2011
Previously published by Paternoster, 2007

This Edition Published by Wipf and Stock Publishers
by arrangement with Paternoster

To
the Centre for Mentorship and Theological Reflection friends
who forge the interface of theology and piety
as the primary focus of my life and career

Contents

Foreword

Martin Luther is well remembered for posting his *Ninety-five Theses* on the door of the castle church at Wittenberg on 31 October 1517, and also for having an important debate with Johannes Eck at Leipzig in 1519. Midway between these two famous events, however, Luther made a long trip across central Germany to the Rhineland for a disputation at the university town of Heidelberg in 1518. It was here that he articulated clearly for the first time his 'theology of the cross'. Rejecting the triumphalist 'theology of glory' that exalted human reason and sought to domesticate the biblical God to the schemes of scholastic dialectics, Luther claimed that the cross was the place where the heart of God was most clearly revealed. *Crux probat omnia*! – everything is challenged and tested by the cross, Luther said.

The *theologia crucis* was not only an affirmation of the centrality and objectivity of Christ's atoning work at Calvary, though Luther certainly believed in that, but it was also a statement about the context for doing theology. Luther would later say, 'I did not learn my theology all at once, but I had to follow where my temptations (*Anfechtungen*) led me. It is not by reading, writing, or speculating that one becomes a theologian. It is living, dying, nay, being damned that makes one a theologian.' The God we are given to know in Jesus Christ, the one and only true God, is the God who saves us and damns us, the God who knows us, confronts us, and 'will not let us go'. He is at once the awesome God who flung the galaxies into existence and the baby of Bethlehem who lies muling and puking in Mary's lap. Call it paradox, mystery, antinomy, or whatever you like, for Luther the only way to talk about such a God is in the midst of struggle, from the abyss, out of the depths – *de profundis*.

Luther was trained as a scholastic theologian and never renounced his doctoral degree (unlike his monastic vows), but, as this book shows so well, Luther was from first to last a pastoral theologian. He preached regularly in the Wittenberg parish church and was deeply involved in the care of souls. Indeed, it was primarily concern for his flock that prompted him to expose Tetzel's indulgence scam in the first place. He was thus caught up in the high drama of the Reformation and drawn into the fray of papal politics, imperial power maneuvers, and princely rivalries.

But Luther never lost touch with the common people nor forsook his pastoral vocation. He published catechisms for children; he gave spiritual advice to barbers; he wrote a letter to a father who had lost a young son; he sent counsel to a woman who had suffered a miscarriage. It is a mark of Luther's genius that he could have an exchange with the best-trained theologians of Europe in the morning, preach to the townspeople of Wittenberg at noon, laugh and drink with his students over dinner, and still have time to pray with his children and love his wife at night. In all of this, he remembered the counsel his mentor, Johannes von Staupitz, once gave him when he was troubled about the fate of his own soul, 'Look at the wounds of Christ and the blood that was shed for you.' The last sermon Luther preached in Wittenberg in

1546, just three days before he died, was on the words of Jesus, 'Come unto me, all you who labor and are heavy laden' (Matt. 11:28).

Dennis Ngien is the author of a fine book on Luther's understanding of the suffering of God. In this volume he extends his study of Luther's *theologia crucis* into Luther's pastoral and devotional writings. Karl Barth once said that one could not have dogmatics without polemics, and no doubt Luther would have agreed! Luther lived in an argumentative age and knew both how to give and receive invective on a grand scale – Luther against Erasmus, against Zwingli, against the Anabaptists, against Roman Catholics, against Jews, etc. But there is another Luther, or, perhaps, another side of Luther, often obscured in the crossfire of polemics. Dennis Ngien shows us Luther up close and personal, Luther at the bedside of the sick, Luther kneeling to pray, Luther laughing at a wedding, Luther consoling the bereaved, Luther singing lustily in worship, Luther joyous at the table of communion.

Although Luther continued to give lectures at the University of Wittenberg till the end of his life, he always knew that his calling was to be a theologian in the service of the church. Luther is a teacher of the church whose work we can best honor today by hearing and heeding what he has to say.

Timothy George
Dean of Beeson Divinity School of Samford University
and an executive editor of Christianity Today

Acknowledgments

This book emerges out of the time I spent with scholars, pastors, and students, associated with my Centre for Mentorship and Theological Reflection. Their insights, concerns, and prayers have fostered in me the importance of making theology relevant to piety, and seeing piety as inherently connected with theology. I am grateful to them for animating me towards the production of this book that reflects the interface between the two. I return to the Reformer Martin Luther for two reasons, that his life exemplifies such a coherent unity, and he is such 'an ocean' (Paul Althaus's description) from which one continues to draw ample resources for faith and practice. It is written with the hope that the Reformer's insights will water the roots of faith, prick the conscience, and nurture the soul.

Special thanks must be extended to the acclaimed Reformation scholars Drs. Timothy George of Samford University, for writing a generous foreword, and Carl Trueman of Westminster Theological Seminary, for his enthusiasm about this subject. Both have invested long hours of reading and provided helpful pointers that have made this book much better. I am also indebted to notable scholars such as Drs. Jeff Greenman, the Associate Dean of Wheaton College, Michael A.G. Haykin, the Principal of Toronto Baptist Seminary, Toronto, Victor Shepherd, the renowned Calvin scholar, Professor of Historical and Systematic Theology at Tyndale Seminary and Centre for Mentorship and Theological Reflection's Senior scholar, for spurring me on to write more about Luther's works, Dr. John Kessler, Professor of Old Testament at Tyndale Seminary and Dr. Ken Gamble of Missionary Health Institute, for their unfailing encouragement, the library staff at Tyndale University College and Seminary, for their endless assistance in securing relevant sources, Priscilla Chan, my research assistant, for her hearty effort in text formatting at the initial stage, and Peter Andrews, for his laborious work in copy-editing.

With minor variations, Chapter 1 – 'Reaping the Right Fruits' – appeared in *International Journal of Systematic Theology* (Fall 2006); Chapter 3 – 'Gems for the Sick' – appeared in *Trinity Theological Journal* (Fall 2005); Chapter 5 – 'The Theology and Practice of Prayer' – appeared in *Luther-Bulletin* (Fall 2005). I am grateful to these journals for allowing me to reuse them here.

Last but not least, much appreciation belongs to my love, Ceceilia, for taking my son away so that I could concentrate on writing, and for forging in me not only a love for scholarship but also for God, his word and his people.

Praise Be Unto God!

Dennis Ngien,
Research Professor of Theology,
Tyndale University College and Seminary,
Toronto, Canada,
26 July 2006.

Introduction

Most Luther scholars have focused on the polemical side of the Reformer, with occasional allusion to his *Devotional Writings* in volumes 42 and 43 of the American edition of his works.[1] So far, these writings have not been studied as a separate monograph. August Nebe's *Luther as Spiritual Adviser*, published in 1894, was merely a scanty presentation of Luther's pastoral advice, quite remotely related to these volumes.[2] The aim of *Luther as a Spiritual Adviser: The Interface of Theology and Piety in Luther's Devotional Writings*, is to unfold the pastoral, not the polemical, side of the Reformer, drawing on the spiritual insights he offered to people of high and low estate. These writings are devotional and catechetical in shape and intent, yet not devoid of rich theological substance, the fruit of his rigorous reflections. They are the exercises of Luther's basic calling as a theologian-pastor, and are concrete illustrations of the interface of theology and piety, the former being the abiding presupposition and logical cause of the latter. Through them, readers are informed not only of the Reformation theology of justification, but also introduced to a distinct expression of the Christian faith in which Christ and his cross occupy the center stage. What is noticeable is the single overarching theme – God's ways with people – that the Reformer sought to relate to the events of his day.

Luther's entire calling as a professor and reformer involved the exercise of his pastoral vocation in three distinct areas: (1) in the classroom; (2) in pulpit ministry; and (3) in personal counsel and assistance to his flock.[3] His devotional writings portray him not as a theologian detached from the world but as a theologian concerned with the Bible on the one hand and pastoral issues on the other. Most of his theological writings are dominated by polemics, but not so his devotional writings, wherein we observe his pastoral and irenic style, which frequently escapes his readers.

Despite his heavy workload, he was very much in touch with life at the most mundane as well as the most ethereal levels. People of all sorts frequently called upon him for advice, and even arbitration. As such he was a spiritual adviser in many important areas of the Christian life: how to meditate aright on Christ's passion; how to prepare to face the terror of death; advice for the sick; how to

[1] The primary source for this study is the English translation of Luther's works, volumes 42 and 43. References from the original language will be cited where helpful. Abbreviations used in this book: *LW* = *Luther's Works* (American Editions, 55 vols: ed. J. Pelikan and H.T. Lehman; St. Louis: Concordia; Philadelphia: Fortress Press, 1955–67). *WA* = *D. Martin Luthers Werke: Kristische Gesamtausgabe* (100 vols; Weimar: Hermann Bohlau Nachfolger, 1883–). *WABr* = *D. Martin Luthers Werke: Kristische Gesamtausgabe, Briefwechsel*. *WATr* = *D. Martin Luthers Werke: Kristische Gesamtausgabe, Tischreden*.

[2] See A. Nebe, *Luther as Spiritual Adviser* (trans. C.A. Hay and C.E. Hay; Philadelphia: Lutheran Publication Society, 1894).

[3] *LW* 42, x.

approach the sacrament of the altar correctly; why and how to pray aright; the benefits to be gained from the Lord's Prayer; and how to live out a life of discipleship under the cross. Although academically and religiously far in advance of his audience, Luther exhibited a distinct restraint when responding to these issues. In a rapid, repetitive, and epistolary style, he made use of the forms, terminology, and imagery of his era to communicate the gospel without compromising it.

Luther's ability to remain focused upon believers' concerns and not to allow any external pressures or personal circumstances to obstruct his pastoral vocation is praiseworthy. These writings, especially volume 42 of the American edition, were written during the crucial years from 1519 to 1521, the period between the posting of his 95 Theses and his stay in the Wartburg. However, he neither spoke nor alluded to the specific historical events and controversies he was facing. During those years of crises and upheavals, when his own life was at stake, he remained faithful to his call as the preacher-pastor, who yielded himself and his struggles to the message with which he was entrusted. Martin Dietrich comments, 'Perhaps it is precisely this very absence of personal and contextual references which adds strength and vitality to what he has to say.'[4] In the year 1520 alone, he produced some of his most inflammatory treatises including his *Treatise on Good Works*,[5] in which he dismantled the medieval doctrine of righteousness by works, *The Christian Nobility of the German Nation*,[6] in which he indicted ecclesiastical and social errors and abuses and made proposals for reform, and *Babylonian Captivity of the Church*,[7] in which he attacked the sacramental system of the Roman Church. In contrast, his devotional writings show no trace of polemics, for these were works not forged on the iron heat of controversy but borne out of his devotion to the gospel and his people. They did not demonstrate the external techniques by which Luther applied his theology; rather they showed the faith out of which his theology emerged. Furthermore, the contents of volume 43, ranging from 1522 to 1545, the year before Luther's death, represent the mature and distinct expression of Reformation theology, the exact opposite of the external devotions of late-medieval piety.[8]

These literary pieces also reflect the seriousness with which Luther took his doctoral oath and office as teacher and preacher. This he declared in his 1532 treatise *Infiltrating and Clandestine Preachers*:

> I have often said and still say, I would not exchange my doctor's degree for all the world's gold. For I would surely in the long run lose courage and fall into despair if, as these infiltrators, I had undertaken these great and serious matters without call or commission. But God and the whole world bear me testimony that I entered into this

---

[4] *LW* 42, xiv. Martin Dietrich is the editor of this volume.

[5] *LW* 44, 15-114.

[6] *LW* 44, 115-217.

[7] *LW* 36, 3-126.

[8] See S.H. Hendrix, 'Martin Luther's Reformation of Spirituality', in T.J. Wengert (ed.), *Harvesting Martin Luther's Reflections on Theology, Ethics, and the Church* (Grand Rapids: Eerdmans, 2004), 240-60 (244).

> work publicly and by virtue of my office as teacher and preacher, and have carried it on hitherto by the grace and help of God.[9]

This oath and office helped liberate him from the shackles of detached academic pursuit, and imposed upon him what was essentially required of his pastoral vocation. The chief function of theology, and thus of the theologian which Luther was, was not to speculate about the naked being of God, but to lead people into faith in God through Jesus Christ. As he wrote, 'True theology is practical, and its foundation is Christ, whose death is appropriated to us through faith ... Accordingly speculative theology belongs to the devil in hell.'[10] In contrast to the modern divorce of theology from pastoral concerns, they were one for Luther. This unity is evident in his devotional writings, where he informed his readers of the importance of the minister as a theologian, not an academic theologian detached from real issues of life but a pastoral theologian engaged with people's struggles. The true minister of the gospel was indeed the true theologian in action, not as a speculative theologian circumscribed by the walls, procedures, customs, and language of the university but a practical theologian, whose primary task was to lead people and strengthen them in faith. Ascribed to the theologian-pastor was the significant role he played as the womb of the Lord Jesus, whereby Jesus is revealed to believers, and who carried the people by means of the word of God to faith and love of neighbor, and ultimately to solace in Christ.[11]

For Luther, nothing was as important as our relationship to God. Concomitantly, today there is no greater duty or higher vocation than the call to preach and teach the word of grace, and hold out God's marvelous ways with people as revealed in the gospel. By virtue of that, theology ought not to be a discursive discipline of the university but is itself a matter of life and death. The theological curriculum ought to be taught differently, that is, in a way that takes seriously the spiritual formation of a theologian, since his primary vocation is to preach and teach the gospel of Jesus. This accords with Luther's emphasis on the theology that has Jesus Christ as its foundation.

In his advice to young theologians, he spoke of three essentials which might form a kind of theological paradigm for the formation of a theologian-pastor: *oratio* (prayer), *meditatio* (meditation), and *tentatio* (struggle). Following Augustine and basing his teaching on Psalm 119, Luther proposed a correct way for studying theology, in his preface to the 1539 edition of his German works:

> Herein I follow the example of St. Augustine, who was, among other things, the first and almost the only one who determined to be subject to Holy Scriptures alone, and independent of the books of all the fathers and saints ...

---

[9] *LW* 40, 387-88.

[10] *LW* 54, 22.

[11] *LW* 28, 219.

> Moreover, I want to point out to you a correct way of studying theology, for I have had some practice in that. If you keep to it, you will become just as good as those of the fathers and councils, even as I (in God) dare to presume and boast, without arrogance and lying, that in the matter of writing books I do not stand much behind some of the fathers. Of my life I can by no means make the same boast. This is the way taught by holy King David (and doubtlessly used also by all the patriarchs and prophets) in the one hundred nineteenth Psalm. There you will find three rules, amply presented throughout the whole Psalm. They are *Oratio*, *Meditatio*, and *Tentatio*.[12]

Behind these rules is the unity of the word and the Holy Spirit – the Reformer's theological prolegomena, that is, his starting point for doing and living theology.

> Thus you see in this same psalm how David constantly boasts that he will talk, meditate, speak, sing, hear, read, by day and night and always, about nothing except God's Word and commandments. For God will not give you his Spirit without the external Word; so take your cue from that. His command to write, preach, read, hear, sing, speak, etc., outwardly was not given in vain.[13]

Henceforth prayer is ineffectual apart from God's word and his promise. This follows the pattern of David, who, although he was aware of the text of Moses and other books, still humbly prayed, 'Teach me, Lord, instruct me, lead me, show me.' This he did in order to lay hold of 'the real teacher of the Scriptures himself.' A true theologian should not allow human reason to rise above the real teacher and become his own teacher. Such was the practice of the factious spirits who deluded themselves into thinking that the Scriptures were subject to them and could be easily grasped by their human reason, as if they were human productions likened unto *Markolf* or *Aesop*'s Fables, for which no Holy Spirit nor prayers were needed. Meditation (study) is a form of obedient prayer: 'But kneel down in your little room (Matt. 6:6) and pray to God with real humility and earnestness, that he through his dear Son may give you the Holy Spirit, who will enlighten you, lead you, and give you understanding.'[14]

Luther encouraged the young to recite repetitively the words of the Bible with diligence and reflection until the Holy Spirit should open their eyes to the real meaning behind the words. Thus meditation is not the conjuring up of human opinions about Scripture, but rather is a thoughtful reflection on God's word and his work for us (*pro nobis*). *Tentatio* (*Anfechtung*), which can be variously translated as 'temptation,' 'trials,' 'tribulation,' 'afflictions,' 'assaults,' 'the cross,' or 'inner struggle,'[15] is the reason for prayer and meditation. 'This (*tentatio*) is the touchstone

---

[12] *LW* 34, 285.

[13] *LW* 34, 286.

[14] *LW* 34, 286.

[15] See R. Kelly, '*Oratio, Meditatio, Tentatio Faciunt Theologium*: Luther's Piety and the Formation of Theologians', *Consensus* 19 (1993), 9-27; Y.J. Won, 'The Work of the Holy Spirit and the Charismatic Movements from Luther's Perspective', *Concordia*

which teaches you not only to know and understand, but also to experience how right, how true, how sweet, how lovely, how mighty, how comforting God's Word is, wisdom beyond all wisdom.'[16] Through suffering and assaults in life, as in Jesus' life, the believer is led to seek God's word, and, together with it, love the gospel message. Consequently this touchstone crucifies all attempts at speculation about God on the part of the self-confident rationalist, and eliminates all achieving of fellowship with God on the part of the self-confident moralist. By *tentatio*, Luther avowed that he was made a 'real doctor', and a 'fairly good theologian'.[17]

These rules provided by the Holy Spirit for the correct reading of theology and Scripture, which Luther sought to inculcate in the young, were constitutive of Luther's entire life. This triad – prayer, meditation, and struggle – when properly used, would enable a theologian to preach and teach a practical theology of justification. This was precisely what Luther did as he implemented the triadic rule in the production of his devotional writings, where he instructed people how to meditate aright, pray aright, bear the cross with patience and with spiritual benefits, etc., ultimately leading them to a deeper apprehension of God's salvific ways with them in the gospel. His spiritual advice, interlaced with scriptural citations, displays a tight causal connection between what he held to be the unshakable foundation (word of grace) and how that foundation affected the religious life and shape of the Church. Undeniably, theology grounded in the word of God is of utmost importance for the theologian-pastor, if he is to take seriously his calling to nurture the soul. Pastors and Christians of all denominations and persuasions could reap considerable fruits from the Reformer's theological insights on practical issues.

Chapter 1 of my book deals with Luther's *Meditation on Christ's Passion* (1519), where he taught that to meditate aright is not to arouse in us an emotive piety for the crucified, but to be acquainted with the knowledge of our sinful nature, and be devastated by it. To the Reformer, there is no natural knowledge of sin. Knowledge

---

Journal 11 (1985), 204-13 (208-209). The German word *Anfechtung* corresponds to the Latin *tentatio*. David Scaer, in his article 'The Concept of *Anfechtung* in Luther's Thought', *Concordia Theological Quarterly* 47 (1983), 15-30 (15), points out that there are various translations of the word: F. Pieper's *Christian Dogmatics* (4 vols; St Louis: Concordia, 1950–62), uses 'temptation'; H.J.A. Bouman in his translation of W. von Loewenich's *Luther's Theology of the Cross* (trans. H.J.A. Bouman; Minneapolis: Augsburg, 1976) favours 'trials'; Ewald M. Plass in Plass (comp.), *What Luther Says: A Practical In-Home Anthology for the Active Christian* (St. Louis: Concordia, 10th edn, 1994), uses 'afflictions'; the American translation of *Luther's Works* uses the above three, but adds 'tribulation.' However, the American translation also uses 'assaults.' Timothy J. Wengert, in his 'Introduction', in Wengert (ed.), *Harvesting Martin Luther's Reflections*, 16, favours 'struggle.' Kelly prefers 'the cross'; Yong Ji uses 'inner spiritual struggle and affliction.' See Kelly, '*Oratio, Meditatio, Tentatio Faciunt Theologium*', 16; Won, 'Work of the Holy Spirit', 209. The aforementioned are related terms, and the word *Anfechtung* or *tentatio* can be variously translated. It is a multifaceted concept, and has various sources – devil, flesh, the world, and even God and his alien work.

[16] *LW* 34, 286-87.

[17] *LW* 34, 287.

of sin comes when believers compare themselves with Christ whom Luther called 'the earnest mirror.'[18] This mirror causes sin to surface in our conscience so that it might cause it to disappear from it. This is made possible through Christ's atonement, where Christ, after exposing our sins, appears to us as the bearer of our sins, the one who suffers on account of our sins but defeats them by means of his cross and resurrection, if only we believe. The mirror then leads us beyond Christ's heart to the friendly heart of God, the one and same heart, which from eternity beats with such earnest love for us. Thus to grasp God aright, as the mirror reveals, is to grasp him not in his power and majesty, which might be terrifying, but in the opposite, that is, in his weakness and humility. God's way of being 'most himself' is by being for us (*pro nobis*), bearing and suffering the judgment of sin, and eventually dying on the cross.[19] Then our faith and salvation stand immovably certain.

Chapter 2 focuses on Luther's *Sermon on Preparing to Die* (1519), in which he counseled those preparing to die to ponder on the three 'glowing pictures' of Christ – 'life, grace, and heaven,' and the affective sign of the sacrament to drive out the three counterpictures of the devil – 'death, sin, and hell.' The proper time for contemplating death and the proper prospective of clinging to Christ and his merciful acts on the cross enable the sufferer to face death with confidence and hope. Before the saving image of Christ, the trilogy of evil vanishes of itself without a battle, which consequently incites faith and praise of God at the last hour. The annihilating knowledge of the negative images may be useful, causally useful, if it drives us into the arms of Christ. This is intrinsically tied to Luther's distinction between law and gospel: God performs an alien work in the law of damnation through the terrifying images of the devil, from which we must flee and cleave to his proper work in the gospel of redemption by means of the victorious pictures of Christ.

Chapter 3 deals with Luther's *Fourteen Consolations* (1520), in which he taught the sick (especially Frederick the Wise) how to reap consolation from contemplating aright seven images of evils and seven images of blessings. In all these consolations the image of Christ looms large, before which all earthly things – pleasure or pain – pale into insignificance. Through the eyes of faith, we see how with such eagerness Christ was willing to die so that he might conquer death and render it impotent for us. Contemplating aright these images would strengthen the pious heart. The whole treatise is geared towards renewing our vision that, in Christ, we are truly his beloved, despite the state of our life. As a theologian of the cross, Luther peeled away the masks of all evils, and named evils for what they really are, and simultaneously named the corresponding remedies for them. By sheer grace, evils may be transformed into blessings, if only we but believe this.

Chapter 4 deals with Luther's *Sermon on a Worthy Reception of the Sacrament* (1521), in which he taught people how to receive the Lord's Supper with profit. This sermon was devoid of polemics and Aristotelian metaphysics, but the major

---

[18] *LW* 42, 9.

[19] *LW* 21, 331; *WA* 7, 577; 26 (The Magnificat, 1521).

constituents of Luther's sacramental theology are found in it. The sacramental causality lies not in our worthiness or unworthiness, but solely in the majesty of God's word. Luther's view of the justifying word as God's deed saturates his thinking. He conceived of the mass through the concept of a 'testament', of which Christ is the very content. Central to this idea is that Christ, moved by love, writes our names into his last will so that upon his death all his designated inheritances are bestowed upon us, his appointed heirs, thereby fulfilling what he has promised. God's promises are effective, since they emanate from God and point to him, and in this sense are to be grasped purely by a personal act of faith, without any human accretions. In lieu of the position that saw a sacrament as a work we perform to achieve our righteous standing before God, the Reformer saw it purely as God's work, and therefore God's gift. Faith grasps God's own action performed for us according to the efficacious words of institution so that his divine idioms – righteousness, life, and salvation – are communicated to believers in exchange for human idioms – sinfulness, death, and damnation. This sermon illustrates how Luther's sacramental theology governs the religious life and shape of the congregation.

Chapter 5 seeks to articulate systematically Luther's theology and practice of prayer, based on his *An Exposition of the Lord's Prayer for Simple Laymen* (1519), *Personal Prayer Book* (1522), his *Small* and *Large Catechism* (1528–29), and *A Simple Way to Pray* (1535). The structure and content in which prayer is done corresponds to the manner in which God's revelation of himself comes to us, proceeding from the crushing power of the Ten Commandments (law), to the creedal fulfillment of it (the gospel), and ending with the Lord's Prayer, the appropriation of the creedal benefits by prayer. Authentic prayer relies on the strength of God's command, God's promise, the words, and faith – all are God's gifts. These four modalities, which make up Luther's understanding of prayer, are intended to move us to God, so that we seek what we need from him alone, not from ourselves. Thus in prayer, the proper position in which we stand before God (*coram deo*), is revealed, that we are the recipients of what he gives with extravagance and generosity.

Chapter 6 deals with a selection of writings of consolation, in which Luther furnished six basic principles of comfort. In dealing with temptation (*Anfechtung*), Luther relied on the efficacious word of God, and the communion of saints, follows Christ's obedience to his Father's will, resorts to praising God as a remedy, recognizes the hiddenness of God's benefits in such assaults, and lays hold of the constancy and reliability of God in fulfilling his promises. In varied forms these principles are interwoven into the counsels that Luther offered to those assaulted by temptation and evil. Above all, the majesty of God's word predominates. The unquenchable thirst for the word of God is a positive proof of a genuine faith, but the resultant persecution because of it is a negative proof of a genuine faith. Yet faith knows that the Lord will avenge the faithful, and clings to God's unsurpassing goodness, even against appearances to the contrary.

These pieces are concrete exercises of Luther's theology of the cross. What makes him worthy of the name of 'a true theologian'[20] is his ability to perceive God's blessings hidden in experiences of suffering, and to maintain a paradoxical tension between the comfort that the tempted derive from God's word and the agonizing mystery of pain which defies human scrutiny. The experience of temptation is God's creation, his alien work as in the law, through which believers are led to teach and practice pure doctrine – the justification of faith. As alien work, temptation effects in believers despair of self-justification; as proper work, it effects in them faith in God's word and the gospel promises. The distinction between the hidden God and the revealed God corresponds to the distinction between his alien work in the law and proper work in the gospel, the former leading to the latter, yet both being functions of the one and same word in securing justification for us.

[20] *LW* 31, 52-53; *WA* 1, 362, 18-19.

CHAPTER 1

Reaping the Right Fruits: Meditation on the 'Earnest Mirror, Christ'

What impelled Luther to write the treatise *Meditation on Christ's Passion* (1519) was not his polemical responses to Prierias's attacks upon him at the time when he wrote it.[1] Rather the momentum came from his pastoral concern with ordinary believers who struggled in their search for peace and salvation. It became so widely read that, by 1524, a total of twenty-four editions had been printed in various cities, a Latin edition having appeared at Wittenberg in 1521. To underscore the human reality of Christ's Passion, most of the early editions were illustrated with woodcuts of the crucifixion scene, showing Mary and John standing at the foot of the cross. Other woodcuts showed scenes such as Christ with an unidentified man kneeling before him, Christ at prayer in Gethsemane, Christ sitting on a rock surrounded by the instruments of the Passion, Christ and those instruments, with a chalice in his left hand.[2] This treatise Luther called 'his very best book', which he included in the *Church Postil* of 1525 as the sermon for Good Friday.[3]

Although medieval tradition provided Luther with the form which meditations on Christ's suffering took, the thoughts expressed here represented the early fruit of his evolving theology of grace.[4] Drawing insights from St. Augustine of Hippo and St. Bernard of Clairvaux, Luther taught how a proper meditation on 'this earnest mirror, Christ' would lead Christians to an experience of justification by faith. He wrote, 'This earnest mirror, Christ, will not lie or trifle and whatever it points out will come to pass in full measure.'[5] Both the knowledge of our sinful nature and Christ's

---

[1] Silvester Prierias was a member of the Roman Commission who introduced canonical proceedings against Luther in the Spring of 1518. See C. Lindberg, 'Prierias and His Significance for Luther's Development', *Sixteenth Century Journal* 3.2 (1972), 45-64.

[2] *LW* 42, 5; T.F. Lull (ed.), *Martin Luther's Basic Theological Writings* (Minneapolis: Fortress Press, 1989), 151.

[3] *WA* 10, I, 1-2; 17, II, 21-22, as cited in *LW* 42, 5.

[4] Marc Lienhard pointed out that the two major works of the Middle Ages, which Luther evidently knew, were the *Meditationes vitae Christi* and the *Rosetum exercitorium spiritualium et sacrarum meditationum*. See his *Luther: Witness to Jesus Christ* (trans. E.H. Robertson; Minneapolis: Augsburg, 1982), 101.

[5] *LW* 42, 9. For a study on St. Bernard's influence on Luther, see F. Posset, 'St. Bernard's Influence on Two Reformers: Johannes von Staupitz and Martin Luther', *Cistercian Studies* 25 (1990), 175-87. It is Posset's argument that Luther's

role as Saviour as the cure for it flowed directly from Christ, not from us or any other creature. It is in his capacity as the bearer of our sin that Christ exposes the reality of our sinfulness. The outcome of this revelation corresponds to the alien work of the law and the proper work of the gospel: both belong to the one God who kills in order to bring life. The paradox of this 'earnest mirror' is that it condemns, and truly condemns, so that we might be saved. Both acts proceed from the same love of God. The mirror performs the alien work of taking us down so that we might despair of our own righteousness *coram deo* (before God), and cling to the proper work of Christ, the bearer of our sin, as the way out of the torments of sin. The mirror acquaints us with the horror of our nature as sinners, which can be healed only by Christ's act of atonement on the cross. In a joyous exchange Christ becomes sin for us, while we obtain the righteousness of God. The mirror, then, drives us beyond Christ's heart to the Father's heart, so that we might be grasped by that same heart which, from eternity, beats with such burning love for us. The mirror teaches us how we may grasp God aright, not in his power, glory, and majesty but in the weakness, shame, and lowliness of the cross, where God is most divine humanly. Only by revelation do we get a real picture of God's inner life and the loving relationship that exists between the Persons of the Trinity. Finally, to embrace Christ as Saviour is to embrace his example, the former necessarily leading to the latter. Christ as sacrament precedes Christ as model, and this proper order, which was distinctive in Augustine's Christology, must be observed in order to meditate aright. Intriguing, too, in this treatise is Luther's emphasis not only on Christ's cross but also on his resurrection, a frequently neglected aspect, as ontologically constitutive of Luther's doctrine of justification.[6]

Erroneous Ways of Contemplation

Meditation on Christ's Passion was a common practice in the time of Luther. Such meditation, he wrote, 'is a very laudable thing.'[7] However, he wrote of three groups of false meditators, who practised meditation for the wrong reasons. The first group meditated on Christ's Passion, focusing though on the Jews and the 'wretched Judas.' Luther denounced this false usage, and regarded their singing and ranting as

---

Christological spirituality agrees with Bernard's, while acknowledging that he owes 'everything' to his fatherly confessor, Johannes von Staupitz, who mediates Bernardine thoughts to Luther. B. Lohse, *Martin Luther's Theology: Its Historical and Systematic Development* (trans. R.A. Harrisville; Minneapolis: Fortress Press, 1999), 47-48, observes that Augustine's sacrament-example Christology finds favor in Luther.

[6] On the relationship between Christ's cross and his resurrection in Paul's doctrine of justification, see R.B. Gaffin, 'Redemption and Resurrection: An Exercise in Biblical-Systematic Theology', *Themelios* 27 (2002), 16-31; M.F. Bird, 'Justified by Christ's Resurrection: A Neglected Aspect of Paul's Doctrine of Justification', *Scottish Bulletin of Evangelical Theology* 22 (2004), 72-91; J. Stott, *The Cross of Christ* (Downers Grove, IL, and Leicester: IVP, 1986), 238.

[7] *WA* 1, 342, 16, as cited in Lienhard, *Luther*, 144, n. 19.

'meditation on the wickedness of Judas and the Jews, but not on the sufferings of Christ.'[8] The second group meditated on Christ's Passion in order to acquire protection for themselves. They followed blindly a saying attributed to Albert Magnus (1193–1280) that it was more meritorious to ponder Christ's Passion just once than to fast a whole year or to pray a psalm daily, etc.[9] This was apparent in those who carried pictures and booklets, and crosses as charms in order to advance their own interests and to safeguard themselves from all sorts of perils. Luther rejected using Christ's Passion 'to effect in them a lack of suffering', for such action was 'contrary to Christ's being and nature.'[10] He denounced this false meditation, for it did not reap the fruit of Christ's Passion.

The third group exhibited a sentimental way of considering the Passion of Christ, nourishing an emotive piety dominated by pity for the crucified, 'lamenting and bewailing his innocence.'[11] This was to repeat what the women of Jerusalem did, whose tears Jesus publicly forbade. Related to this group were those who believed that the Mass is '*opere operati, non opere operantis*, that it is effective in itself.'[12] Luther was against those who rested for their salvation on the mechanical performance of the Mass. Later, in his sermon *On the Sacrament of the Body of Christ* (1526), he attacked all usage of the Mass, which was linked to the *opus operatum* (automatic effectiveness), but neglected the *opus operantis* (the need for faith).[13] For him, the Mass was not for its own sake, but was meant to remind us of Christ's Passion for our sake. Not until we appropriated the *pro me* (for me) of the cross as the right fruit did our participation in the sacrified body of Christ remain anything but strictly external. Luther asked, 'of what help is it to you that God is God, if he is not God to you?'[14] His Christological emphasis on the *pro me* reflected the personal aspect of faith, which Luther himself experienced. Accordingly, he put participation in the Mass under the sign of faith that one has to be touched inwardly by the cross of Christ in order for Masses to be fruitful. He juxtaposed the emotive actions of the women of Jerusalem and superficial participation in the Mass. In both cases, those concerned did not seek the right fruit because they were not confronted by the *pro me* of the cross. They had not appropriated the work, which the person of Christ performed, and the right fruit, which he reaped for them. Only when believers realize that Christ had been given for them have they discerned the import of Christ's

---

[8] *LW* 42, 7. Luther was not an anti-semitic. At the beginning of his career he had high hopes of seeing the Jews converted to Christianity. This is reflected in his treatise *That Christ was born a Jew* (1523) (*LW* 45, 195-229). However, over the years his position changed, mainly because of the Jews' refusal to accept his invitation to confess Christ. See his treatise of 1547, *On the Jews and Their Lives*, *WA* 53, 412-552.

[9] *LW* 42, 7.

[10] *LW* 42, 7.

[11] *LW* 42, 7.

[12] *LW* 42, 8.

[13] See 'The Sacrament of the Body and Blood of Christ – Against the Fanatics, 1526', in Lull (ed.), *Martin Luther's Basic Theological Writings*, 314-40; *LW* 36, 335-61.

[14] *LW* 42, 8.

accomplishment. More profoundly, for Luther, the suffering and dying of Jesus is not simply something that happens in history, but happens 'for me'.

Correct Ways of Contemplation

In paragraphs 4-11 of the *Meditation on Christ's Passion*, Luther described the proper way to contemplate the Passion of Christ and reap the fruits that grow from that. Throughout the rest of the sermon, he put his audience under the grip of the crucified Christ, whom he called an 'earnest mirror.'[15] This Christological image was directly linked, as we saw, to his *theologia crucis* (theology of the cross), about which he had written in the *Heidelberg Disputation* of 1518:

> That person does not deserve to be called a theologian who looks upon the invisible things of God as if they were clearly perceptible in those things which have actually happened ... He deserves to be called a theologian, however, who comprehends the visible and manifest things of God seen through suffering and the cross.[16]

Luther regarded the *theologia crucis* as true theology, which he contrasted with the opposite, the theology of glory (*theologia gloriae*).[17] It is common knowledge among Luther scholars that the cross, far more than being just a subject, was the programmatic principle underlying all of Luther's theology. Walther von Loewenich's words still ring true:

> The theology of the cross is not a chapter in theology, but a specific kind of theology. The cross of Christ is significant here not only for the question concerning redemption and the certainty of salvation, but it is the center that provides perspective for all theological statements.[18]

---

[15] Lienhard, *Luther*, 102.

[16] *LW* 31, 52. Also cited in V.-M. Kärkkäinen, 'Evil, Love and the Left Hand of God: The Contribution of Luther's Theology of the Cross to an Evangelical Theology of Evil', *Evangelical Quarterly* 74 (2002), 215-34 (215).

[17] Kärkkäinen, 'Evil, Love and the Left Hand of God'.

[18] Loewenich, *Luther's Theology of the Cross*, 18. Paul Althaus shares the same view. See his *The Theology of Martin Luther* (trans. R.C. Schultz; Philadelphia: Fortress Press, 1966), 30, where he speaks of Luther's hermeneutical principle: 'The cross of Christ is the standard by which all genuine knowledge is measured, whether of the reality of God, of his grace, of his salvation, of the Christian life, or of the church of Christ.' See also J. Moltmann, *The Crucified God: The Cross of Christ as the Foundation and Criticism of Christian Theology* (trans. M. Kohl; New York: Harper & Row, 1977), 212; J.E. Vercruysse, 'Luther's Theology of the Cross: Its Relevance for Ecumenism', *Centre Pro Unione* 35 (Spring, 1989), 2-11; A.E. McGrath, *Luther's Theology of the Cross: Martin Luther's Theological Breakthrough* (Oxford: Blackwell, 1985), 148-75; Lohse, *Martin Luther's Theology*, 36-39.

The Earnest Mirror: The Revelation of our Sinful Nature

The cross also governed Luther's practice of meditation so as to gain spiritual benefits. In paragraph 4 of the *Meditation*, he held that the total value of Christ's Passion consisted in the fact that we 'view it with a terror-stricken heart and a despairing conscience,'[19] and here he parted from the medieval tradition. Instead, he shared the Pauline emphasis on the cross, not on how much Christ physically suffered, for this was part of medieval spirituality, but on the salvific effects Christ's Passion wrought for us. The efficacy of Christ's Passion was that our sin was absorbed by him in his dereliction and that its effects were negated. Instead of arousing in us pity for the crucified, we ought to contemplate Christ's Passion so as to be devastated by it. We ought to be terrified *coram deo* at the knowledge of our sinful nature, and this terror we obtain only by revelation. The earnest mirror acquaints us with a revelation of God, which is anything but saving, namely, the revelation of divine wrath against sin. Such revelation makes us aware of our condemnation, and we become terrified and crushed by the knowledge. 'This terror must be felt as you witness the stern wrath and the unchanging earnestness with which God looks upon sin and sinners, so much so that he was not willing to release sinners even for his only and dearest Son without his payment of the severest penalty for them.'[20] However full of dread we might be at the knowledge of our sinfulness, we are never as full of dread as is God himself. The knowledge frightened God's 'only and dearest Son' so horribly that in his final cry of misery on the cross he experienced greater anguish than any human person has ever undergone. The severity of God's wrath was reflected most acutely in the cost required to appease it. It cost the loss of God's Son, 'the dearest child', who was punished for us in order to redeem us.[21] If such a great and infinite Son of God had to suffer this punishment in order to save us, Luther explained, how great must be God's wrath and the magnitude of sin. Evidently, Luther had a high doctrine of sin, according to which we are so rooted in evil and so blinded by sin to our own sinful nature that it requires nothing less than the forsakenness of God in his Son's dereliction to expose it. It cost God greater pain to expose us to the horror of our sin than it cost us pain to become aware of it. So a serious consideration of the intrinsic worth of the person, 'God's very Son, the eternal wisdom of the Father, who suffers,' ought to plunge us into radical insecurity before God.[22]

Christ's Passion was both a revelation of sin and an accusation against sinners. We arrive at this knowledge of ourselves, not through mere introspection which, Luther argued, despises the Passion of Christ, but through a consideration of Christ on the cross and, through him, God, in his holiness and mercy. Knowledge of the crucified Christ and knowledge of self coincide, the former leading to the latter.

---

[19] *LW* 42, 8.
[20] *LW* 42, 8-9.
[21] *LW* 42, 8-9.
[22] *LW* 42, 9.

Luther wrote that 'our knowledge of sin flowed from Christ' not from ourselves.[23] Thus, for him, there was no natural knowledge of sin. Only through the 'earnest mirror,' Christ, can our sinfulness be recognized in its radical depravity, for it reveals sin in its starkness and seizes us as wretched sinners. Nevertheless the cross is not primarily the vehicle of self-exposure; rather it is the occasion of the atonement, in the light of which we are acquainted with a true knowledge of who we are.

Looking at the cross makes us conscious of our sins and our need to confess them. Only by the revelation through the earnest mirror can this blindness be lifted and sin be acknowledged by us. 'Unless God inspires our heart,' Luther added, we, by our power or anything we devise, could never attain a true knowledge of our sinfulness.[24] The mirror enlightens us about our sinfulness as a proper fruit of meditating upon Christ's Passion aright. So, Luther wrote, 'the main benefit of Christ's Passion is that man sees into his own true self and that he be terrified and crushed by this.'[25] To look elsewhere for such knowledge, including looking within ourselves for residual sin, is to adopt the theology of glory, the antithesis of true theology. Such meditation would steer us away from the earnest mirror, turning us into enemies of the cross.

Moreover, the terror so aroused is unique to each believer, caused by the realization that the sin revealed by the mirror is theirs, nailing Christ to the cross. Each sinner is the torturer of Christ, each person contributes toward the crucifixion of Christ. No one can rid themselves of sin by blaming the Jews, for we all are the servants of sin. 'Therefore, when you see the nails piercing Christ's hands', Luther explained, 'you can be certain that it is your work. When you behold his crown of thorns, you may rest assured that these are your evil thoughts.'[26] All of us, by our sin, have killed the Son of God. Thus the more we consider this mirror, the more we learn of our sinful natures, and are terrified and crushed by the realization. This he elaborated in paragraph 6 of the *Meditation*:

> For every nail that pierces Christ, more than one hundred thousand should in justice pierce you, yes, they should prick you forever and ever more painfully! When Christ is tortured by nails penetrating his hands and feet, you should eternally suffer the pain they inflict and the pain of even more cruel nails, which will in truth be the lot of those who do not avail themselves of Christ's Passion.[27]

Luther advised that the earnest mirror be taken with utter seriousness. For it 'will not lie or trifle, and whatever it points out will come to pass in full measure.'[28] It does not fail to bring out the reality of who we are *coram deo*. It helps us see what sin truly deserves. Through it, we come to a deeper realization that the eternal

---

[23] *LW* 42, 12.
[24] *LW* 42, 11.
[25] *LW* 42, 10.
[26] *LW* 42, 9.
[27] *LW* 42, 9.
[28] *LW* 42, 9.

sentence, which Christ bore on the cross, should have been passed on us on account of our sin. The mirror helped St. Bernard, as it helps us, to see the severity of divine judgment on sin, which 'God's very own Son' willingly offered to bear for us on account of his compassion for us. This revelation concerning the weight of sin and its just deserts is the true benefit of Christ's Passion. 'The real and true work of Christ's Passion,' he claimed, 'is to make man conformable to Christ,' so that his conscience is tormented by sin, as Christ's body and soul were pitiably tormented.[29] The confession of sin as the proper work of Christ's Passion is nothing other than conformity to Christ. This conformity to 'Christ's image and suffering' is inevitable, whether here on earth or in hell.[30] The terror is most acute at the hour of death, when the Christian experienced everything Christ experienced on the cross.[31] However, proper meditation on Christ's death cannot be accomplished without God's grace. 'Since it is horrible to lie waiting on your deathbed,' he wrote, 'you should pray God to soften your heart and let you now ponder Christ's Passion with profit to you.'[32] Luther underscored the necessity for the person's heart, especially a callous heart, to be touched by the cross of Christ, a work that only God could accomplish. Without God's help, Christ remains a dead letter, to be grasped only by the intellect (*intellectus*), but not reaching the heart (*affectus*) of the people.[33]

The Earnest Mirror: Law–Gospel Distinction

The earnest mirror caused sin to surface in our conscience so that it might cause it to disappear from it. This was made possible only through Christ's atoning efficacy, that it was in his capacity as the bearer of our sin that he exposed us to our sinfulness. He revealed sin not so that sin might forever remain in our conscience, in which case it might foster psychological ill-health, but that sin might be dissipated and borne away by Christ.

> After man has thus become aware of his sin and is terrified in his heart, he must watch that sin does not remain in his conscience, for this would lead to sheer despair. Just as [our knowledge of] sin flowed from Christ and was acknowledged by us, so we must pour this sin back on him and free our conscience of it.[34]

Knowing our sinful nature without knowing Christ as Saviour is likened unto someone knowing his misery without knowing the cure for it, in which case it would certainly lead to utter despair.[35] The sin that the earnest mirror reveals, we in

---

[29] *LW* 42, 10.

[30] *LW* 42, 11. At this point, Luther did not reject the doctrine of purgatory.

[31] *LW* 42, 11.

[32] *LW* 42, 11.

[33] Lienhard, *Luther*, 107. Cf. *LW* 42, 14.

[34] *LW* 42, 12.

[35] *LW* 42, 12. Blaise Pascal made a similar point to that made by Luther. See Pascal's *Pensées*, paragraph 449, as cited in A.E. McGrath (ed.), *The Christian Theology Reader*

turn cast from ourselves onto Christ: 'firmly believe that his wounds and sufferings are [our] sins, to be borne and paid for by him' (cf. Isa. 53:6; 2 Cor. 5:21; 1 Pet. 2:24). Thus Luther advised his readers to relinquish all false attempts at self-justification, and to repudiate widespread false confidence in human works, including penance and pilgrimages, as ways out of the torments of sin.[36] The earnest mirror's revelation of our sinful state will ensure that sin will be done away with by Christ, the bearer of our sin, as its proper outcome. The sins the mirror reveals are ours, not his, for which Christ died. The sins we acknowledge, we cast upon Christ so that we might receive his forgiveness. This was indeed good news, if only we would believe it. Conversely, if sin were to remain in our conscience until we plunged into sheer despair, that, for Luther, surely was not the work of Christ: it was not as 'God conceived of it and wished it.'[37]

The earnest mirror reflects the contradictory activities of the one God, the law as his alien work and the gospel as his proper work. It reflects, first, the alien work in the law, 'its natural and noble work' of 'banishing all joy, delight, and confidence which man could derive from other creatures, even as Christ was forsaken by all, even by God.'[38] The outcome of such work was that the old Adam was strangled, which in turn prepared the sinner for the reception of forgiving grace through the gospel, its proper work. Both result from the same love of God. Constitutive of Luther's theology of paradox is the *simul* of God's dual actions, an action which is alien to God's nature results in an action belonging to his very own. The mirror reflects these two activities. It shows forth humanity's sin in order to lead them to salvation through Christ. The alien work of God gives way to the proper work of God: the revelation of God's wrath against sin leads to the knowledge of God's mercy *pro nobis* (for us). Faith grasps the true knowledge of God, that it is the nature of God to bestow his mercy on those who acknowledge their sins. The proper work is hidden in its alien work, and occurs simultaneously with it. The cross as law strips us of all pre-existent soteriological resources, banishing from us all confidence so that we might cling to Christ the redeemer. This meditation changes 'man's being, and, almost like baptism, gives him a new birth' as its proper outcome.[39] In the light of this, Luther wrote that he who contemplates God's sufferings aright, even briefly or shortly, does himself more profit than to fast for a whole year or hear a hundred masses.

(Oxford: Blackwell, 2nd edn, 2001), 32: 'It is equally as dangerous for someone to know God without knowing their misery as it is for someone to know their misery without knowing the Redeemer who can heal them. One of these insights (*connaissances*) leads to the pride of the philosophers, who have known God but not their misery, the other to the despair of the atheists, who know their misery without a Redeemer.'

[36] Pascal, *Pensées*, paragraph 449. For Luther's criticism of pilgrimages, see *LW* 42, 40 and *LW* 4, 86-87.

[37] *LW* 42, 11.

[38] *LW* 42, 11. Cf. *LW* 14, 355; *WA* 5, 63, 33-39 (Psalms, 1519–21), where the idea of the alien and proper work emerged.

[39] *LW* 42, 11.

What Luther preached here was at odds with the Bielian premise, that we could obtain grace by doing what is in us, a widespread teaching which he opposed throughout his life and career as a theologian and pastor.[40] For him, we obtain grace not by 'doing what is in us,' but by accepting what is done to us, even by God. Forde clarifies this issue: '[Grace] is acquired when we are so completely humbled by God's alien work in law and wrath that we see how completely we are caught in the web of sin and turn to Christ as the only hope.'[41] The gaining of humility is in no way a human performance, but that which is given to us by God. Law so reduces us to the position where we claim absolutely nothing that we cling to Christ.

We have no 'active capacity' to humble ourselves but only a 'passive capacity,' that we are humbled.[42] Thus we obtain grace not by 'doing what is in us,' but by humbly accepting what is being done *to us* within the law–gospel distinction. It is not by our working, so to speak, that we are drawn to God, but by our *not working* that we are drawn by Christ to the gospel. The reflection in the mirror makes us aware of sin so that, having recognized sin, we might seek God's grace and embrace Christ as Saviour. Thus we should neither despair of the paradoxical work of God nor resist it, for the God who works in us the opposite of justification also effects in us salvation. Those who consent to God's paradoxical work, according to which God makes them sad before he makes them glad, really hear the gospel as God wishes them to. However, the work of God does not occur immediately in the believer, and therefore might effect in them a temporary despair. Yet this despair, which cannot be alleviated by good works, might serve as a secret but genuine work of Christ's sufferings. The true meditation on Christ's Passion may be concealed in the Christian life, when some Christians who meditate least truly meditate most, something God often reverses as he sees fit. Once God's alien work has been effected on the cross, it is time for the revelation of the gospel.

Joyous Exchange: Christ was made Sinner, not just Sin

Luther was keenly aware of the despair of believers who saw in the earnest mirror only the wrath of God and their own sin, and could not believe in forgiveness. Therefore, he invited them to cast their sins anew on Christ, those sins that Christ

---

[40] See Thesis 16 of his 'Heidelberg Disputation', in Lull (ed.), *Martin Luther's Basic Theological Writings*, 41, where Luther refuted Bielian's premise. Cf. A.E. McGrath, *The Intellectual Origins of the European Reformation* (Oxford: Blackwell, 1987), 81-83.

[41] G.O. Forde, *On Being a Theologian of the Cross: Reflections on Luther's Heidelberg Disputation, 1518* (Grand Rapids: Eerdmans, 1997), 61.

[42] Forde, *On Being a Theologian of the Cross*, 61. For Bernard's concept of humility, see Loewenich, *Luther's Theology of the Cross*, 132-43. See J. Webster, '"The Grammar of Doing": Luther and Barth on Human Agency', *Barth's Moral Theology: Human Action in Barth's Thought* (Edinburgh: T&T Clark, 1998), 159, where he writes, 'For Luther, even in action one is utterly passive, that upon which another acts; for Barth, even in receiving one is a spontaneous doer, acting in correspondence to the action of the one whose act is received.'

has accepted as his own, for God took the sins that we confess from us and placed them upon Christ. The acknowledgment of sin and the terror of conscience must be seen in the light of union with Christ. United to Christ, we accept what we are before God just as Christ accepts the consequences before God of the sins that we have committed. Here, Luther wrote of a real exchange between Christ and the one who believes in him, based on 2 Corinthians 5:21, where Luther had Paul write, 'God has made him *a sinner* for us, so that through him we would be made just.'[43] What is crucial here is Luther's emphasis not so much on Christ being made 'sin' as being made 'sinner.' For sin in and of itself has no ontic reality except in the person who does it. In this exchange, Christ assumed our sinful nature and we were endowed with his righteousness. The precise meaning of this was clearly elaborated in Luther's commentary on Galatians 3:13 (1535): Christ in his own righteous person as the Son of God knew no sin, but by entering into our place he truly took upon himself our sins and therefore made himself a sinner, 'not only adjectivally, but also substantivally.'[44] In our stead, Christ was 'not acting in his own person now; now he is not the Son of God, born of the virgin, but he is a sinner' who has come to bear the sins of the world 'in his body, in order to make satisfaction for them with his own blood.'[45] Christ's incarnation itself is not his accursedness, nor his poverty nor his humiliation, but is the abiding presupposition of his becoming 'a sinner and a curse.' Christ is first a pure and innocent person, both as God and man, so that he could assume 'upon himself our sinful person and grant us his innocent and victorious person.' For our sake, he assumed 'the mask of the sinner,' and was made a 'sinner' so that we might become the righteousness of God.[46] The fortunate exchange is the point of the *communicatio idiomatum* (communication of properties), that whatever sins we have committed or may commit they are as much Christ's own as if he himself has done them.[47] Our sin must be his, totally his, or we perish eternally. The concept of joyous exchange already appeared in a letter to George Spenlein, in 1516, in which Luther advised his Friar to pour his sin back on Christ in exchange for Christ's righteousness.

---

[43] *LW* 42, 12.

[44] See R. Bertram, 'Luther on the Unique Mediatorship of Christ', in H.G. Anderson, J.F. Stafford, and J.A. Burgess (eds.), *The One Mediator, the Saints and Many* (Minneapolis: Augsburg, 1992), 249-62 (249), where he cites *LW* 26, 288; *WA* 40, I, 448. For a fresh look on Luther's doctrine of justification, see D.A. Brondos, '*Sola Fide* and Luther's "Analytic" Understanding of Justification: A Fresh Look at Some Old Questions', *Pro Ecclesia* 13 (2004), 39-57. For recent debates on justification as deification, see C.E. Braaten and R.W. Jenson (eds.), *Union with Christ: The New Finnish Interpretation of Luther* (Grand Rapids: Eerdmans, 1998). The Finnish Luther Scholar, Tuomo Mannermaa, argues more for an ontological and mystical than an ethical and juridical view of justification as Luther's position. This book contains helpful and critically appreciative responses to Mannermaa's work.

[45] *LW* 26, 277; *WA* 40, I, 432-34.

[46] *LW* 26, 284; *WA* 40, I, 434-444.

[47] *LW* 26, 284; *WA* 40, I, 434-444.

> Therefore my dear Friar, learn Christ and him crucified. Learn to praise him, and despairing of yourself, say, 'Lord Jesus Christ, you are my righteousness, just as I am your sin. You have taken upon yourself what is mine and you have given me what is yours. You have taken yourself what you were not and have given me what I am not.'[48]

Consequently, to 'segregate Christ from sins and sinners and set him forth to us only as an example to be imitated' as the 'sophists' did, in Luther's view, was to turn Christ into a new law. This separation would render Christ 'not only useless to us but also a judge and a tyrant who is angry because of our sins and who damns sinners.'[49] Therefore, to deny that the Son of God was a sinner and a curse, as the sophists did, was to be deprived of the 'most delightful comfort,' that in Christ our sins were borne and borne away.[50] Only in this earnest mirror, Christ, do we encounter the God who is of great benefit to us. To contemplate Christ aright is to contemplate ourselves in him, not outside of or apart from him. In Luther's estimation, the joyous exchange occurs in union with Christ. Being united to Christ, we became the righteousness of God, which Christ imputed to us as a gift, and Christ became a sinner likes us when he assumed our sinful nature. Forgiveness and justification are based purely on Christ's work *pro nobis* (for us) and *extra nobis* (outside us), not on any change effected *in nobis* (in us) by God through Christ.

The reflection that we see in the earnest mirror assures us of this, that the blessing, which is locked in mortal combat with the curse in Christ, has absorbed the effects of the curse and conquered it for us. The secret and the prerequisite of the victory are that it occurs 'in his body and in himself'. Diametrically opposed to one another, both blessing and curse come together in Christ so that they are really his. If the sin were not his, as surely as the righteousness was, the law could easily have avoided blasphemy against him by cursing the one, not the other. However 'he joined God and man in one person. And being joined in us who were accursed, he became a curse for us; and he concealed his blessing in our sin, death, and the curse, which condemned and killed him.'[51] When totally dissimilar qualities meet in Christ, it must be the divine powers – divine righteousness, life, and blessings – which triumph over their opposites – sin, death, and curse. Luther explained:

> Thus the curse, which is divine wrath against the whole world, has the same conflict with the blessing, that is, with the eternal grace and mercy of God in Christ. Therefore the curse clashes with the blessing, and wants to damn it and annihilate it. But it cannot. For the blessing is divine and eternal, and therefore the curse must yield to it. For if the blessing in Christ could be conquered, then God himself would be conquered. But this is impossible. Therefore Christ, who is divine power, Righteousness, blessing, Grace, and Life, conquers and destroys these monsters –

[48] *LW* 48, 12; *WABr* 1, 35, 24-27.
[49] *LW* 26, 278; *WA* 40, I, 434-35.
[50] *LW* 26, 280; *WA* 40, I, 437-38.
[51] *LW* 26, 281; *WA* 40, I, 440-41.

> sin, death, and the curse – without weapons or battle, in his own body and in himself, as Paul enjoys saying.[52]

Christ truly accepted eternal damnation from God, and suffered the divine curse in himself in order to conquer it for us. Christ interposed himself in the law's path, and suffered its alien work in order to free our conscience of it. This, too, is the proper outcome of meditating Christ's Passion aright.

The Simul*: The Cross and Resurrection*

The cross reveals the divine curse, about which we could not do anything except believe that it was borne by Christ's wounds and sufferings, but finally and fully borne away by his resurrection. Justification occurs when God in Christ really took our place, suffered and died a real death 'wrapped in our sins'.[53] That it was the very God himself who became sin and suffered dispels the idea that the divine nature cannot suffer.[54] By this fortunate exchange, Christ, assumed our sinful nature, carried our sin, suffered and died; for us he became a curse so that he might conquer it, and bestow upon us his eternal blessings. The cross beckons us to cast our sins upon Christ so that we might be clothed with his righteousness, his innocent and victorious person in exchange for our sinful one. But because Christ is a divine and eternal person, death cannot hold him. Instead he arose from death on the third day, and now he lives eternally. This means sin, death, and curse no longer remain in Christ, but only righteousness, life, and eternal blessings. To be found in Christ is to behold our sin resting on Christ, but as overcome by his resurrection.

For Luther, the link between law and gospel corresponds to that between Christ's cross and resurrection. Just as the effects of the law are most manifest in Christ's Passion and death, so too our sin and God's wrath by which our consciences are terrified is revealed through the cross. In contrast, Christ's resurrection discloses to us that Christ assumed our sins, died for them, and then triumphed over them. Zachman writes rightly of Luther:

> If the Christ's Passion reveals sin and wrath to our consciences, his resurrection reveals that our sins no longer lie upon us but have been taken up and vanquished by Christ ... The death of Christ drives our sins into our consciences so that we acknowledge that it was for our sins, not his own, that Christ died on the cross. The

---

[52] *LW* 26, 281; *WA* 40, I, 440-41. Also quoted in Bertram, 'Luther on the Unique Mediatorship of Christ', 259-60.

[53] G.O. Forde, 'Luther's Theology of the Cross', *Christian Dogmatics* (2 vols; Philadelphia: Fortress Press, 1984), vol. 1, 55.

[54] Althaus, *Theology of Martin Luther*, 197, where he coined the term 'dei-Passionism' (God suffers) as a description of Luther's position regarding passibility. For a major study of Luther's passibility, see D. Ngien, *The Suffering of God according to Martin Luther's 'Theologia Crucis'* (Bern: Lang, 1995).

> resurrection, however, takes our sins out of our consciences and lays them upon Christ, who is the victor over sin and death.[55]

In justification, we cast our sins anew on Christ in exchange for his righteousness. Christ acquaints us with our sin so that it is done away with by his cross and resurrection. Consequently, not only does sin no longer remain in us but also it no longer remains in Christ. In Luther's words:

> If we behold it resting on Christ and see it overcome by his resurrection, and then boldly believe this, even it is dead and nullified. Sin cannot remain on Christ, since it is swallowed up by his resurrection. Now you see no wounds, no pain in him, and no sign of sin. Thus St. Paul declares, 'Christ died for our sin and rose for our justification' (Rom. 4:25). That is to say, in his suffering Christ makes our sin known and thus destroys it, but through his resurrection he justifies us and delivers us from all sin, if we believe this.[56]

What separates the Reformer from medieval spirituality, Lienhard points out, is his 'fundamental *simul*, which unites the cross and the resurrection. The cross is never given preeminence over the resurrection.'[57] This fundamental unity is already evident in Luther's *Commentary on the Psalms* (1517–21), wherein the suffering and death of Jesus is immediately followed by the resurrection and victory.[58] These two doctrines are distinguished, but for Luther, as for the early Church, they are indissolubly one. The efficacy of Christ's atonement is that he suffered as a consequence of our sin, and defeated it by means of the cross and resurrection, the *simul* of Luther's doctrine of justification. Whereas the cross in its character as law compels us to recognize our sins so that we feel them in our conscience and acknowledge them, the resurrection in its character as gospel enables us to behold, through the joyous exchange, our sins resting on Christ and his victory resting on us. The theology of glory seeks to emancipate the terrified conscience and the feeling of sin by the doing of good works, but fails. On the contrary, in the light of the fortunate exchange, the theology of the cross directs those who feel the effects of their sins and the divine wrath, not to themselves or good works, but to Christ's conquering act on the cross and his victory through his resurrection, which now belong to the believer. Zachman clarifies this: 'Faith gives glory to God by acknowledging the truth of the witness of Christ to the happy exchange, and thus completes the exchange by making it an event in our lives.'[59] The resurrection vindicates the atoning death of Christ by making it efficacious in securing the justification of believers. Thus St. Paul powerfully declared that Christ's sin-bearing death had become triumphantly effective for the forgiveness of sin (cf. Rom. 4:25).

---

[55] R.C. Zachman, *The Assurance of Faith: Conscience in the Theology of Martin Luther and John Calvin* (Minneapolis: Fortress Press, 1993), 35.

[56] *LW* 42, 12-13.

[57] Lienhard, *Luther*, 36.

[58] See *LW* 10, 372; *WA* 3, 63, 1; 432, 84, as cited in Lienhard, *Luther*, 36.

[59] Zachman, *Assurance of Faith*, 64.

The Eternal Heart of God and the Trinity

As soon as we learn of the joyous exchange whereby Christ became a sinner for us and that sin has been swallowed up in victory by Christ's resurrection, we should no longer linger there, but move on in order to appropriate the fourfold *pro nobis* benefits, which, Luther wrote:

> (i) [P]ass beyond that and see his friendly heart and how this heart beats with such love for you that it impels him to bear with pain your conscience and your sin.
>
> (ii) Then your heart will be filled with love for him, and the confidence of your faith will be strengthened.
>
> (iii) Now continue and rise beyond Christ's heart to God's heart and you will see that Christ would not have shown this love for you if God in his eternal love had not wanted this, for Christ's love for you is due to his obedience to God. Thus you will find the divine and kind paternal heart, and, as Christ says, you will be drawn to the Father through him. Then you will understand the words of Christ, 'For God so loved the world that he gave his only Son', etc. (John 3:16).
>
> (iv) We know God aright when we grasp him not in his might or wisdom (for then he proves terrifying), but in his kindness and love. Then faith and confidence are able to exist, and man is truly born anew in God.[60]

The crucified One mirrors the heart of God. The suffering of the cross in history mirrored the unconquerable love of God's compassionate heart. The crucified God of the cross drove us beyond history to God in eternity, revealing the nature of God's eternal love.[61] The Godness of God, Luther asserted elsewhere, is 'nothing but burning love and a glowing oven full of love'.[62] The passionate God of the Bible is in sharp contrast with the infinitely apathetic deities of the Greeks. The depth and certainty of God's love is revealed in the cross. God opens his personal being to us only in the human Jesus, who suffers and dies as the revelation of God's self-giving love. Such knowledge comes solely from the revelation made by the earnest mirror, discernible only by the eyes of faith. Luther wrote that we must entreat God for faith so that we might apprehend his immeasurable love, which Christ reveals to us through contradictions, that is, not in glory and majesty but in the shame and lowliness of the cross.[63]

The story of Jesus Christ is the story of how deeply God himself is implicated in our world. God in Christ has entered the sphere of his counterpart, the sinful

---

[60] *LW* 42, 13.

[61] For a study of Luther's understanding of love, see A. Nygren, *Agape and Eros* (trans. Watson; Philadelphia: Westminster, 1953). For a critique of Nygren's position, see C.H. Lindberg, 'Luther's Concept of God: A Critique of Anders Nygren's Interpretation of Martin Luther' (PhD thesis; Ann Arbor, MI: University Microfilm International, 1965).

[62] See *WA* 36, 425 as cited in Althaus, *Theology of Martin Luther*, 116.

[63] *LW* 42, 13.

humanity, and therefore has entered the area of God-forsakenness, condemnation, contradiction, suffering, and death.[64] In so doing, God reveals his true nature, his true deity as self-giving. Luther's relationship with nominalism sheds light on his ontology. For William of Ockham, a thing is 'essentially' what it 'does,' that is, a thing 'as it is in itself' is known through cognition of its 'acts.'[65] A remark in Luther's *Commentary on the Magnificat* (1521), reflects the similarity between his views and those of Ockham:

> How can one know God better than the works in which He is most Himself? Whoever understands His works correctly cannot fail to know His nature and will, His heart and mind.[66]

Given the correspondence between the divine being and the divine act, the knowledge of what God has done in Christ discloses truly who God is in himself. The event of Christ's self-sacrificial love is indeed the being of God in action. What is true of Jesus Christ is ontologically true of God's eternal being. God's revelation in Christ is therefore the revelation of his essence to us. In Peter's words, 'God's very being, God's essence, is found in this coming into the human sphere. Who God is is the result of what God does, and what God does is to act humanly and lovingly.'[67] The identity of God is inseparable from his actions. Therefore Luther prohibited any theology that sought 'the inner nature of God in some remote sphere above and beyond the structure of God's operations in and upon the world'.[68] His *theologia crucis* requires that we should not bypass this earnest mirror, the incarnate and crucified Christ, for from there we proceed to an apprehension of God's inner being. Althaus identified a movement in Luther's Christology, from 'below to above': 'from Christ as a man to Christ as God and thereby to God (i.e., the triune God).'[69] To grasp God is to grasp him from below. Thus Luther insisted, we 'rise beyond Christ's heart to God's heart.' According to its very nature, God's heart overflows, earnestly seeking to pour out good upon the bad, and to attract objects

---

[64] See *LW* 22, 355, where Luther said that God in Christ has 'entered the belly of death and the devil ... ' in order to conquer them.

[65] See William of Ockham, *Summa Logicae* (2 vols; ed. Boehner; St. Bonaventure, NY: The Franciscan Institute, 19551–54), I.C.XIV.XV, vol. 1, 43-49, as cited in Ngien, *Suffering of God according to Martin Luther's 'Theologia Crucis'*, 99-100.

[66] *LW* 21, 331;*WA* 7, 577, 26. See P. Watson, *Let God Be God: An Interpretation of the Theology of Martin Luther* (Philadelphia: Muhlenberg, 1948), 159-60, for his elaboration of God's love.

[67] T. Peters, *God – the World's Future* (Minneapolis: Fortress Press, 1992). Cf. E. Jüngel, *God as the Mystery of the World: On the Foundation of the Theology of the Crucified God in the Dispute between Theism and Atheism* (trans. D.L. Guder; Grand Rapids: Eerdmans, 1983), 300, 343, 379-80.

[68] See C. Braaten, 'The Problem of God-Language Today', in C. Braaten (ed.), *Our Naming of God: Problems and Prospects of God-Talk Today* (Minneapolis: Fortress Press, 1989), 11–33 (31); and 'Let's Talk about the "Death of God"', *Dialog* 26 (1987), 209-14.

[69] Althaus, *Theology of Martin Luther*, 186.

unworthy in themselves of love. God's 'friendly heart' is known in the efficacious activity of Jesus Christ on the cross. God's eternal heart beats with such intense love for us that 'it impels (the Son) to bear with pain our conscience and our sin.' The love of God creates, through the contradictions of the suffering and lowliness of the cross, a people no longer under divine wrath. God's love, thus, forms the aetiology of Luther's atonement, creating through the redemptive act of the incarnate Christ *sub contraria* (through his opposites), a people of God's mercy as the teleology of his atonement. If God is what he does, then the self-manifestation of his love *sub contrario* in the suffering of the Righteous One means that God is a God of love *pro me* in him – God not only loves me but also loves me in his inner life by virtue of Christ's participation in his inner life. The soteriological aspect of God's suffering for me is genuinely reflective of the ontological being of God as love. The God who is mirrored in Christ is the God who comes in lowliness. The *being* of Jesus Christ in humility, suffering, and dying on the cross is *being* in self-humiliation, and the atonement effected by him is the *act* of Christ's self-humiliation.

Luther instructed us to fix our gaze on the redemptive act performed by God incarnate, and in this act faith apprehends who God is and the way he is *pro me*. By reason of God's essential being as love, 'God is most himself' precisely in the self-sacrifice and self-humiliation in his Son on the cross, achieving for us the atonement. The nature of God's love *pro me* is located in God's efficacious activity in the incarnate and crucified Christ. Gorman's words reflect Luther's thinking:

> For Paul, love is not primarily God's being but God's way of being; not primarily God's essence but God's story. It is the story of self-giving love ('his own Son', Rom. 8, 32), and it corresponds to the self-giving love of Christ. For Paul, Christ's love is both the sign and substance of God's love.[70]

God's way of being 'most himself', for Luther, is by being *pro me*, bearing and suffering the judgment of sin, and eventually dying on the cross. This is how to know God aright, that we should know him in Christ's atoning work where God wills to be found, and where he is most Godlike. Thus to know God aright is to grasp him where he is most divine humanly, that is, not in his power but in his weakness, not in his majesty but in his humility, not in his glory but in the shame of the cross.[71] It is precisely in the contradictions within his revelation that our salvation and faith stand immovably certain. Importantly, what was preached here was reflective of the theology of the cross in Luther's *Heidelberg Disputation* (1518), about which he wrote: 'Now it is not sufficient for anyone, and it does him no good to recognize God in his glory or majesty, unless he recognizes him in the humility and shame of the cross.'[72]

---

[70] M.J. Gorman, *Cruciformity: Paul's Narrative Spirituality of the Cross* (Grand Rapids: Eerdmans, 2001), 154.

[71] *LW* 42, 13.

[72] *LW* 31, 52.

True theology must be concerned with God as he has chosen to reveal himself, not with some preconceived ideas about him. Any attempts to know God by way of intelligent reflection on the nature of humanity's moral sense or the pattern of the created order are repudiated by Luther, and charged with the theology of glory. For instance, in St. John's Gospel, Philip of Bethsaida represents a theologian of glory who seeks God apart from God's self-definition in the crucified Christ (cf. John 14:8-9). But true recognition of God is found in the crucified Christ who drew us to the Father in order that we might be grasped by 'the divine and kind paternal heart'. The love by which Christ loves us is identical with his Father's love, the one and same love. Yet this love did not begin at the cross, but from eternity, when God had resolved to love us in Jesus Christ. This knowledge, too, lies in the revelation of the earnest mirror, the crucified Christ, who led us beyond his own heart into God's eternal heart. The picture of Christ assures us that we are truly the objects of an eternal love, which is God. This fills our hearts not with hatred, but with a reciprocal love for God as its outcome. We are of inestimable worth to God, a priceless reality he eternally finds and loves, a face he beholds from eternity as it now beholds his *via* the 'earnest mirror, Christ.' Our names are already written in his eternal heart, or Christ would not have shown this to us. Whatever the extent of our faith, strong or weak, the assurance that Christ was given *pro me* as God's self-giving love was the outcome of meditating Christ's Passion aright. Whether 'openly' or 'secret[ly]', Luther wrote, we do possess faith and confidence, as if we are truly born anew in God.[73] Our hearts become firm in Christ and in God's love, if we do not take our eyes off the picture of the crucified Christ, even when our faith is dim.

Proper Order: Christ as Sacrament and Example

When our hearts become firm in Christ, so that terror at wrath is being replaced by relief at the knowledge of God's 'friendly heart' *pro nobis*, we must submit to Christ's Passion as a pattern for our entire life. Crucifixion in no way undercuts ethical activity, or else we transform its essence into a mere symbol, turning Christ into letters.[74] Paragraph 15 of this sermon repeats the Augustinian formula of Christ as 'sacrament and example.'[75] After Christ the sacrament has accomplished his active

[73] *LW* 42, 13.

[74] *LW* 42, 13. Cf. G. Tinder, 'Luther's Theology of Christian Suffering and Its Implications for Pastoral Care', *Dialog* 25 (1986), 108 13 (110).

[75] Tinder, 'Luther's Theology of Christian Suffering'. The sacrament (saviour) and example (model) Christology of Augustine finds favour in Luther. These two terms appear in his lectures on the epistles to the Romans (*WA* 56, 321) and the Hebrews (*WA* 57). Cf. Augustine, *De Trinitate*, IV, 3, as quoted in Lohse, *Martin Luther's Theology*, 47-48; D. Ngien, 'Theology of Preaching in Martin Luther', *Themelios* 28 (2003), 28-48 (39-41); D. Lage, *Martin Luther's Christology and Ethics* (Lewiston: Edwin Mellen, 1990), 93-105; N. Nagel, '*Sacramentum et Exemplum* in Luther's Understanding of Christ', in C.S. Meyer (ed.), *Luther for an Ecumenical Age* (St. Louis: Concordia, 1967), 172-99.

work in us while we are passive, we now, in a joyous exchange, must be active in following Christ. Christ is not only the cause of our salvation, but also our model. The proper order must be observed, that Christ's Passion be accepted 'passively' as a sacrament before it be embraced as a pattern to be followed 'actively'.[76] Luther spoke of Christ as the image according to which God leads the Christian through the cross towards glory. The true Christian incorporates 'Christ's life and name' into his own.[77] To embrace Christ as Saviour is to embrace his model as part of our life. Iserloh's comment at this juncture is succinct: 'The crucifixion of Christ is a sacrament. It is an event that does not have its termination in itself but is a sign, that is, it points toward an event in the person affected by it.'[78] Iserloh, elsewhere, wrote well of Luther:

> Thus Luther fights on two fronts – on the one, against a speculative mysticism, which passes over in silence the incarnate Word; on the other, against a late medieval piety based on suffering, which, confined to the psychological and moral domain, seeks to imitate Christ without first having been conformed to him, a piety which wishes to follow Christ as an example before he has become a sacrament.[79]

As an example, the crucifixion behoves us to offer ourselves to meditate on the cross so that Christ's Passion may be met 'not with words or forms, but life and truth.'[80] This is the reality of a life lived under the cross and for the cross, not to be seen as supplementing the act of redemption by means of good works. The cross which God laid on Christ was laid by him on his followers, of whom cruciformity is now required. Luther then listed several negative factors which Christians might encounter, and offered ways to handle each in a Christological way.

> If pain or sickness afflicts you, consider how paltry this is in comparison with the thorny crown and the nails of Christ. If you are obliged to do or to refrain from doing things against your wishes, ponder how Christ was bound and captured and led hither and yon. If you are beset by pride, see how your Lord was mocked and ridiculed along with criminals. If unchastity and lust assail you, remember how ruthlessly Christ's tender flesh was scourged, pierced, and beaten. If hatred, envy, and vindictiveness beset you, recall that Christ, who indeed had more reason to avenge himself, interceded with tears and cries for you and for all your enemies. If

---

[76] *LW* 42, 14.

[77] *LW* 42, 14.

[78] E. Iserloh, *Gnade und Eucharistie in der philosophischen Theologie des Wilhelm von Ockham: Ihre Bedeuntung fur die Ursachen der Reformation* (VIEG 8; Wiesbaden: Steiner, 1956), 110, as cited in Lohse, *Martin Luther's Theology*, 48, n. 10. See also M. Lienhard, 'Luther and the Beginnings of the Reformation', in J. Raitt (ed.), *Christian Spirituality II: High Middle Ages and Reformation* (New York: Crossroad, 1987), 268-99 (277).

[79] E. Iserloh, 'Luther und die Mystik', *Kirche, Mystik, Heiligung und das Naturliche bei Luther* (Göttingen: Asheim, 1967), 61, as cited in Lienhard, *Luther*, 83, n. 60. I follow Lienhard's translation.

[80] *LW* 42, 13-14.

> sadness or adversity, physical or spiritual, distresses you, strengthen your heart and say, 'well, why should I not be willing to bear a little grief, when agonies and fears caused my Lord to sweat blood in the Garden of Gethsemane? He who lies abed while his master struggles in the throes of death is indeed a slothful and disgraceful servant.'[81]

The cross of Christ has a twofold function: an expiatory function and an exemplary function, both of which constitute the one reality of Christ. The exemplary function is derived from the primacy of Christ's expiatory function, but the former has meaning and validity only because of the latter.[82] The essence of the imitation of Christ is found in the epistles of Peter and Paul, where it is written that true Christians, as a response to Christ's sacramental efficacy, move from a conviction of sin to joy in God's overflowing love, from Christ the sacrament to Christ the model. They suffer first because of sin's torments before God, and second from the secret work of God in conforming them to the image of the Christ who suffers for them. To embrace Christ is to embrace his cross. Therefore they must follow the path to glory and life through misery and death. In his *On the Councils* (1539), Luther claimed that following the pattern of Christ's sacrifice on the cross constituted the seventh sign of a true church.[83] Just as God is hidden in Christ's sufferings, so the church is also hidden under the signs of weakness, suffering, and persecution. The pair, Christ as sacrament and example, most closely links faith and discipleship together. As we recognize Christ as our Saviour, we are motivated to respond to our neighbours' need with the same favour with which we are blessed. For the Reformer, orthodoxy without orthopraxy is inconceivable.

Concluding Reflections

*Bernard's for us (*pro nobis*) Christology*

Finally, I shall conclude with a few reflections.

Luther was indebted to St. Bernard, whom he quoted by name throughout his writings, for his Christological focus on the face of God in Jesus. The *pro nobis* aspect of Christ's person is typical of Bernard's Christology. Essential to this is the Bernardine concept of 'Christ's double right to the kingdom of heaven' as found in what was called the *Bernard Legend*.[84] Underlying this concept are Christ's two

---

[81] *LW* 42, 14.

[82] Licnhard, *Luther*, 137.

[83] *LW* 41, 164-65; *WA* 50, 651-52 (*On the Councils*). See R. Kelly, 'The Suffering Church: A Study of Luther's *Theologia Crucis*', *Concordia Theological Quarterly* 50 (1986), 3-17; Kärkkäinen, '"The Christian as Christ to the Neighbor"; C. Moseman, 'Martin Luther on "Becoming a Christ to One's Neighbor"', *Presbyterion* 26 (2000), 93-104.

[84] Cf. J. de Voragine, *Legenda aurea* (Heidelberg: Verlag Lambert Schneider, 4th edn., 1963), ch. 120. The Bernard Legend is found there on 658-72. Voragine also cited in Posset, 'St. Bernard's Influence on Two Reformers', 176, n. 5.

important rights, one inherited by him on account of his being the Son of God and the other earned by the merit of his Passion, which he communicated to all believers. Bernard reportedly acknowledged:

> I know very well that I am unworthy to possess the kingdom of heaven through my own merit. However, my Lord Jesus Christ has won heaven by a twofold right, namely, by inheritance from His Father, and by the merit of His Passion; whereof He is content with the one, and gives me the other. Therefore, I claim heaven as my right, and shall not be confounded.[85]

Bernard's *pro nobis* Christology is more explicitly found in Luther's lectures on the Johannine writings, Sermon on the Mount, and Galatians, where he cited Bernard's words. In 1527, when he lectured on 1 John 1:8, Luther again made use of the Bernardine idea of Christ's double right to heaven.[86] With reference to 1 John 4:10, he accentuated the significance of Bernard's complaint about wasting his time pursuing the monastic life, when compared with the effects of Christ's double right for salvation. This was reflected in his eulogy of the Cistercian abbot:

> I myself have paid attention to no holier monk than St. Bernard, I place him above Gregory, and Benedict: 'Double right, of birth as the Son, of merit which you acquired by the Passion and death, as a gift not to yourself but to me. My life is wasted and does not make an achievement.' There is no better phrase in all of Bernard ... [87]

Bernard's own references to the monastic life and Christ's double right were also quoted in 1531, in Luther's lecture on Galatians 4:31:

> I have lived damnably. But thou, O Lord Jesus Christ, hast a double right to the kingdom of heaven: first, because Thou art the Son of God; secondly, because Thou hast won it by Thy Passion and death. The first Thou dost keep for Thyself by Thy birthright; the latter Thou dost grant to me by the right, not of works but of grace.[88]

The same substance, with the same sentiment, was brought up in 1532, in Luther's *Sermon on the Mount* (Matt. 7:24-27).[89] He cited Bernard, an exemplar of monastic life, as the one who finally recognized the futility of his religious piety, for it did not possess the true knowledge of Christ, the firm foundation upon which a Christian life is based. On his deathbed, the abbot pronounced judgment on his so-called holy life: 'Oh, I have lived damnably and passed my life shamefully!' After

---

[85] Voragine, *Legenda aurea*, 665, as cited in Posset, 'St. Bernard's Influence on Two Reformers', 176; I. Siggins, *Martin Luther's Doctrine of Christ* (New Haven: Yale University Press, 1970), 187, n. 71.

[86] *LW* 30, 230: *WA* 20, 624, 3.

[87] *LW* 30, 296; *WA* 20, 764, 12-19.

[88] *LW* 26, 5; *WA* 40, I, 687, 6-7.

[89] *LW* 21, 283; *WA* 32, 534, 20-26.

quoting Bernard, Luther addressed him directly in heaven and sought an explanation from him: 'How so, dear St. Bernard? Have you not been a pious monk all your life? Are not chastity, obedience, your preaching, fasting, praying precious things?' Luther then had St. Bernard reply: 'No, it is all lost and belongs to the devil.'[90] All these prizes of the monastic life are blown away and destroyed when the rainy and windy seasons come. Luther claimed that had Bernard not altered his course of life toward the end, by forsaking his sand-like monastic ground and clinging to the rock-like ground, that is, to Christ, he would have been damned forever by his own judgment.

Later, Luther referred to the Bernardine passage about the inefficacy of the monastic life and the double right of Christ. The first right Christ as Lord has from eternity belongs exclusively to him; the second right Christ as our redeemer gains through his Passion and death, and 'gives to me as a present.'[91] In 1537, in his exposition of John 1:7, Luther again quoted Bernard's words from memory, albeit freely:

> I have misspent and wasted my life disgracefully; but I take comfort in the knowledge that Jesus Christ, my Lord, has a twofold claim on heaven. In the first place, He can lay claim to it for Himself, because He is true and natural Son of God, governing with the Father from eternity. Hence He is entitled to heaven as an heir from eternity. But this is not the source of my comfort. In the second place, however, He has gained heaven through His holy suffering and death and then presented this to me. In this manner, I, too, fall heir to heaven.[92]

Bernard's Christocentric 'for me-ness' was instrumental in liberating Luther from the captivity of righteousness by works, and finally led him out of the desperation caused by his monastic life, as Luther continued to keep before him Bernard's example.[93] He so highly esteemed Bernard that he called him the only one worthy of the name 'Father' in faith, and of being studied diligently.[94]

Following Bernard, Luther developed his Christology by way of soteriology, understanding the person of Jesus in terms of the redemptive work he performs for us. He was not concerned with the constitution of Christ in the abstract, but rather with the *pro me* aspects of his person. This is evident in Luther's explanation of the second article of the *Small Catechism*, where we observe how quickly he came to soteriology, because this is at the heart of his Christology.

> I believe that Jesus Christ, true God, begotten of the Father from eternity, and also true man, born of the Virgin, is my Lord, who has redeemed me, a lost and

---

[90] *LW* 21, 283; *WA* 32, 534, 20-26.

[91] *LW* 21, 283; *WA* 32, 534, 26-28.

[92] See Bernard of Clairvaux, *Sermones in cantica, Sermon XX*, in *PL* 183, 867, as quoted in *LW* 22, 52; *WA* 46, 580, 24-32, and *LW* 21, 283, n. 49; *LW* 26, 5, n. 2.

[93] Cf. *Wie ich den offt das exempel von S. Bernhardo pflege zu debrauchen. WA* 47, 585, 19-20, 186, as cited in Posset, 'St. Bernard's Influence on Two Reformers', 182.

[94] *LW* 22, 388.

> condemned creature, purchased and won me from all sins, from death, and from the power of the devil, not with gold or silver, but with his holy, precious blood and with his innocent suffering and death, that I may be his own, and live under him in his kingdom, and serve him in everlasting righteousness, innocence, and blessedness, even as he is risen from the dead, lives and reigns to all eternity. This is most certainly true.[95]

The following example further elucidates Luther's soteriological Christology:

> Christ has two natures. What has that to do with me? If he bears the magnificent and consoling name of Christ, it is on account of the ministry and the task he took upon himself; it is that which gives him his name. That he should by nature be both man and God, that is for him. But that he should have dedicated his ministry and poured out his love to become my savior and my redeemer, it is in that I find my consolation and well-being. To believe in Christ does not mean that Christ is a person who is man and God, a fact that helps nobody; it means that this person is Christ, that is to say, that *for us* he came forth from God into the world; it is from this office he takes his name.[96]

The good news, that in Jesus Christ God is for us, not against us, is Bernard's emphasis, as it is Luther's. 'This good news cannot be known in *abstracto*', George explains, 'but only as one grasped it by faith in the depths of experience.'[97] Not until we realize that Christ was given *pro me* do we really discern the significance of Christ's work. Thus Luther declared:

> Read with great emphasis these words, 'me,' 'for me,' and accustom yourself to accept and to apply to yourself this 'me' with certain faith.
>
> The words OUR, US, FOR US, ought to be written in golden letters – the man who does not believe them is not a Christian.[98]

---

[95] See Luther's 'The Small Catechism, 1529', in T. Tappert (ed.), *The Book of Concord: The Confessions of the Evangelical Lutheran Church* (Philadelphia: Fortress Press, 1959), 345. Hereafter is cited as *BC*.

[96] *WA* 16, 217, 33ff, as quoted in Y. Congar, 'Considerations and Reflections on the Christology of Luther', *Dialogue between Christians* (trans. P. Loretz; Westminster: Newman, 1966), 374. See also W. Elert, *The Structure of Lutheranism*, Vol. 1, *The Theology and Philosophy of Life of Lutheranism* (trans. W.A. Hansen; St. Louis: Concordia, 1962), 68; Siggins, *Martin Luther's Doctrine of Christ*, 110; W. Pauck (ed.), *Melanchthon and M. Bucer* (Library of Christian Classics 19; Philadelphia: Westminster, 1969), 21-22, where Melanchthon asserted: 'To know Christ is to know his benefits.'

[97] Timothy George, *Theology of the Reformers* (Nashville: Broadman, 1988), 60.

[98] *LW* 26, 176; *WA* 40, I, 299.

Christ's Humiliation and God's Inner Life

In this conclusion, my second reflection is that, in God's inner life, Christ's humiliation in history mirrored an eternal relation of the Son's obedience to the Father who sent him to suffer and die. That a cruciformity abides already in God's eternal being is implied by Luther's statement, 'Christ would not have shown this love for you if God in his eternal love would not have wanted [willed] this, for Christ's love for you is due to his obedience to God.'[99] This axiom suggests that there already is in God's life a relation between the Father and the Son, which, when the Son becomes incarnate, entails his suffering. The obedience of the Son to the Father is an obedience rendered by God to himself. Because the Father and the Son are one in essence and will, the obedience within the Godhead does not compromise the unity and equality of divine being, thereby avoiding the heresy of subordinationism. Against modalism, the unity within the Godhead is not a simple and undifferentiated unity. For Luther, as for Augustine before him, the Persons are differentiated within the divine life by relations.[100] The distinctions within the Godhead ensure the particular characteristics of each Person. Because the Son comes, suffers, and dies there must be in God's relationships, in his eternal being and life, the form of obedience, which makes incarnation and Calvary possible. The eternal relation of the Son's obedience to the Father constitutes the basis of Christ's self-humiliation in history. Christ's suffering arises from his love for us, suffering that is the response of his obedience to the Father who has sent him into the world. There is in God a sending and an obeying, a giving and a receiving, an active as well as a passive obedient aspect. The Father gave the Son to death, a proper reflection of the Father's eternal relationship to the Son, and the Son willingly accepted and carried out what the Father sent him to do. Thus it is appropriate for the Son to be obedient unto death on the cross, to exhibit his deity in the lowliness of the cross in which God is most divine. Both Father and Son are joined in a concord of love and will in the act of Christ's self-humiliation. In willing obedience and because of the Father's will, Christ assumed our sinful nature, and bore with pain our sin. Luther commented, 'It must be an inexpressible and unbearable earnestness that forces such a great and infinite person to suffer and die to appease' the divine wrath.[101]

Implied here is the experience of anguish shared by both the Father and the Son. The pain of the cross was felt by both the Father and the Son but in different ways:

---

[99] *LW* 42, 13.

[100] See D. Ngien, 'Trinity and Divine Passibility in Martin Luther's "Theologia Crucis"', *Scottish Bulletin of Evangelical Theology* 19 (2001), 31 64; E. Jüngel, *The Doctrine of the Trinity: God's Being Is in Becoming* (Grand Rapids: Eerdmans, 1976), 87, where he quotes favorably Barth's *Church Dogmatics* (ed. G.W. Bromiley and trans. T.F. Torrance; Edinburgh: T&T Clark, 1975), vol. IV/1, 246-47: 'In his (Christ's) Passion and death', says Jüngel, 'he did not therefore somehow "waive his divinity (somewhat like the emperor of Japan in 1945)", but was rather "in such a humiliation supremely God, in this death supremely alive", so that "he has actually maintained and revealed his deity precisely in the Passion of this man as his eternal Son".'

[101] *LW* 42, 9.

the Son suffered and died the death of God-forsakenness whereas the Father suffered the pain of forsaking his Son whom he made 'a sinner' for us. On the cross, God's 'dearest child' was no longer the Son of God, but the greatest sinner, who deserved an eternal punishment. Since the one undivided essence is located in the Son's act of self-humiliation, the redemptive act of Christ's suffering is integral to the one divine essence in the same Godhead. What the Son tasted in his forsakenness by the Father was precisely what the Father tasted in his abandonment of the Son – this is required by the doctrine of the Trinity and incarnation. Such an understanding, though not fully developed here, was already implied in Luther's sermon. There was a *simul* (simultaneity) which united the Son's anguish with that of the Father. The essential unity of the Father and the Son means there was a mutual sharing between them. There was a perichoretic unity of pain flowing from the Son to the Father, when the Son suffered on account of being wrapped in our sinful nature. What the Son experienced on the cross was, then, communicated to the Father because of their unity of essence constituted as love. Both worked together as one God to effect for us an atonement which he foreordained before the foundation of the world.[102] Thus Luther said that we ascended through Christ's heart to God's heart, laying hold of the one and same eternal heart which panted eternally with such passionate love for us, and was given for us in the Son's dereliction on the cross (cf. John 3:16). The pain of the cross has reached God's inner being so that there is no untouched hinterland in his own life. Yet God suffers, not out of a deficiency of being, but out of the richness of his infinite love. Consequently God, for Luther, ceases to be God in the Platonic sense that denies suffering and death to God's heavenly divinity.[103]

The Church's Mission and Vocation

My third reflection is that Christ's Passion has a pertinent implication for the form that the church's mission and vocation in the world must take. For the cross provides the framework not only for our understanding of God's being and his way of being but also of our being and our way of being in the world. Because Christ is the shape and substance of our faith and life, the pattern of the cross is constitutive of our way of being in the world. Just as the shadow of the cross falls on Christ's entire life and ministry, so it falls on his disciples. The 'cruciform' church must exist in and for the world, accepting suffering itself as it cares for the needy, sick, and poor, and seeks the liberation of the oppressed.[104] It must exhibit the life of

---

[102] Cf. *LW* 34, 115; *WA* 39, 1, 49 (*Thesis Concerning Faith and Law*, 1535); *LW* 40, 214; *WA* 18, 203 (*Licentiate Examination*, 1545): 'Christ was not in reality slain from the foundation of the world, except in promise only.'

[103] For Luther, he affirmed divine suffering *in concreto* via his usage of the doctrine of *communicatio idiomatum*, that the human property of suffering is attributed to the divinity in Christ. See D. Ngien, 'Chalcedonian Christology and Beyond: Luther's Understanding of the *Communicatio Idiomatum*', *Heythrop Journal* 45 (2004), 54-68.

[104] Cf. Gorman, *Cruciformity*, 17, where he coins the phrase 'the cruciform God' in lieu of the early fathers' phrase 'the crucified God'. He says: 'For Paul cruciformity

shame and lowliness, mirroring the essence of Christ's own life. The cross, too, calls for a radical abandonment of the worldly understanding of leadership, that a leader is a powerful figure who asserts his power to subdue others. It redefines what true leadership ought to be, giving it its proper context and contents. Derived from Christ's Passion, the church endorses a cruciform leadership, where authority lies not in subduing others but in enduring love for others, in Christ-like humility and sacrificial service. The cruciform leadership consists not in pomposity but in humility and, in obedience to the Father's will, willingly suffers for the cause of others. Christ the example becomes a mirror in which to contemplate how much we are still lacking, lest we become arrogant. Our Old Adam must continually be crucified so that the pattern of the cross becomes a visible part of our own being as it was of Christ. However, mortifications do not necessarily occur in deserts, among religious hermits, away from the society of human beings; they can happen in everyday life, in schools, offices, homes or areas where God places us. We are being constantly reshaped into someone new through our participation in the common life. There we often engage in an internal battle between self-interest and the good of others, but are constantly brought back to repentance and forgiveness as we become aware of the needs of those around us. The Christ-like servant-leader constitutes what a true theologian of the cross is, seeking to serve but not to be served, preferring sufferings to glory as a sign of obedience to God. Wingren's words echo Luther's:

> The person who wills to obey God, for that reason receives more crosses and suffering in his vocation than does a man who, before God, is cold though honest. These sufferings, rather than being self-imposed, are imposed by God; not that God brings them upon him from without, through divine direction of affairs and dispensations. They are brought upon him from within, through God's direction of his heart.[105]

Pastoral Implications

My fourth reflection is that Christ's Passion has enormous implications for pastoral ministries. In the light of the cross, what then shall we preach? If God is found in the human suffering of Jesus, we should not then preach a triumphalist doctrine of health, wealth, and freedom from affliction for those who believe. Triumphalism has nothing to offer, especially at moments when prayers go unanswered or illnesses befall, except lashing the wounded into deeper guilt and pain for their supposed lack of faith. The cross shatters all human speculations about God, and leads us to where he wills to be found, that is, in the efficacious activity of Jesus Christ. It suffices us

---

encompasses and defines all the divine qualities. These include faithfulness, love, power, wisdom, and so forth. Fundamentally for Paul, because the cross reveals God, God is known to be cruciform' (18).

[105] G. Wingren, *Luther on Vocation* (trans. C.C. Rasmussen; Philadelphia: Muhlenberg, 1957), 66.

to perceive in the cross God's deepest pain and his loving scars for us: from there we draw consolation. For Luther, in Althaus's words,

> the knowledge of God's metaphysical attributes is not ultimately decisive for a man who is seeking salvation ... the ultimate decisive factor is knowledge of God's personal nature and activity. '*God is truly known not when we are aware of his power or wisdom which are terrible, but only when we know his goodness and love*.' Luther's deity is ... centered in the fact that it is God's nature to give, to bestow, to sacrifice himself, and to have mercy. Faith can read these divine characteristics in the picture of Christ and places its trust in them.[106]

Furthermore, how do you deal with those who plunge into guilt and despair because of the torments of sin? For Luther, only by revelation do we grasp the nature and plenary extent of our sinful nature. Pastors or spiritual mentors must avoid manipulating people, for example, by fostering guilt and despair in their consciences through psychological introspection or other self-exposure techniques. As regards this, no humanly devised means can heal sick souls. Preachers must inculcate a proper form of meditation and its proper outcome in the life of their congregations. To meditate aright is not to embark on a discursive exercise as in the university, analyzing Christ's Passion intellectually or doctrinally, without having our hearts inwardly touched by the *pro me* of the cross. The theologian-pastor is to assist their people in becoming aware of their sins through Christ's revelation, Christ being the bearer of their sins. Preachers should take their sin-tormented people on a journey from Passion Week to Easter as did Luther, encouraging them to push back the sins they acknowledge onto Christ in order to receive his forgiveness and liberation.

The experience of despair created by sin, although it may be only temporary, can be healed by Christ, and not by any human agency. This despair is God's strange work, through which he crushes the claims of believers to righteousness before him in order that they may cling to Christ the redeemer. The annihilating knowledge of sin *via* the mirror may be useful, causally useful, if it leads us to cleave to the arms of God in Christ.

Luther's pastoral advice on the proper contexts in which preaching Christ as sacrament and as example is done is relevant:

> To those who are afraid and have already been terrified by the burden of their sins, Christ the savior and the gift should be announced, not Christ the example and the lawgiver. But to those who are smug and stubborn the example of Christ should be set forth, lest they use the gospel as a pretext for the freedom of the flesh, and become smug.[107]

---

[106] Althaus, *Theology of Martin Luther*, 191, where he quoted *LW* 42, 13. Italics added.

[107] *LW* 27, 35 (Galatians).

Preaching the cross as sacrament is truly a consolation for those confronted by their sins. Proper preaching must allow Christ to be seen for who he is, namely, a Saviour, who would not stand by idly in the face of unrighteousness, and allow sin to cast us down into sheer despair. Faith lays hold of Christ's righteousness, with which we are clothed in exchange for our sinfulness. Precisely by our unworthiness and sinfulness, which the earnest mirror reveals, we prove ourselves the very people whom God loves, for he finds above all the ungodly, not worthy in themselves to be loved.[108] Through preaching we inculcate the gospel into the life of the congregation, the gospel that Christ's eternal blessings have triumphed over God's wrath, and this we appropriate by faith.

The Question of Assurance and Decision-making Theology

My fifth reflection is that, nevertheless, there is a danger if the question of assurance is purely grounded on *my* decision to cling to Christ.[109] The so-called decision-theology of some ecclesiastical circles could lead to a self-salvation exercise, in which we constantly look inside ourselves (*in nobis*) for assurance. We may be trapped in an egocentricity of doubting whether we have really made the decision or not, in which case the freedom we enjoy in Christ is lost. Had we let the self reign and be the measure of faith, our assurance would have been at stake. This situation cannot be healed by hearing a word we speak to ourselves, that is, our 'yes' to Christ, but the external word that Christ speaks through the preacher, that his wounds and sufferings are because of his love for us. Unlike the Aristotelian deity, Luther's God is the one who speaks with us in human language. He wrote: 'Hear, brother: God, the Creator of heaven and earth, speaks with you through his preachers ... Those words of God are not of Plato or Aristotle, but God himself is speaking.'[110] Just as God hides in his humanity to reveal himself, he too hides himself in human language to meet us in it. So when confronted by real threats, terrible doubts, and unspeakable fears, we look outside ourselves (*extra nobis*) to the external word of grace preached, and place our confidence in the almighty 'yes' of God in Christ. Assurance rests not on the strength of our grip on Christ, but rather on the strength of 'Christ for us,' that is, his grip on us. We stake all on faith's object, Christ, not on the level of our faith. Luther's focus on Christ for us lifts us ex-centrically (out of ourselves), and draws us through Christ into the center of

---

[108] Cf. E.W. Gritsch and R.W. Jenson, *Lutheranism: The Theological Movement and Its Confessional Writings* (Philadelphia: Fortress Press, 1976), 44, where Jenson speaks of being saved by unbelief: 'Just by your very unbelief you prove yourself the very man whom God loves. He chooses above all the ungodly.'

[109] R.H. Olmsted, 'Staking All on Faith's Object: The Art of Christian Assurance according to Martin Luther and Karl Barth', *Pro Ecclesia* 10 (2000), 135-58 (156).

[110] See *WATr* 4, 531, no. 4812, as quoted in Ngien, 'Theology of Preaching in Martin Luther', 32-33.

God's friendly heart. By this, Luther was able to steer away from a kind of theology that is purely subjective and anthropocentric.[111]

In turmoil and trials, Christ must be presented as a sacrament, so that we may have a mirror in which to contemplate how much Christ loves sinners. 'For a single drop of blood, even a part of a drop, is sufficient for all my sins, and how much more so his whole Passion! I do not despair because of my sins, says Saint Augustine, because I remember the wounds of my Lord.'[112] Through contemplation on the wounds of Christ, our hearts shall be assured that we are his. Christ was given *pro me*, and that, surely, is the best news, which we must hold out so that the right fruits of Christ's Passion might belong to those who truly believe.

[111] George, *Theology of the Reformers*, 60.

[112] *WA* 1, 334, 21, as cited in Lienhard, *Luther*, 106-107.

CHAPTER 2

The Art of Dying:
The Glowing Picture of Christ and Its Opposites

Luther's *Sermon on Preparing to Die* (1519) was written two years after the *Ninety-Five Theses* at Wittenberg. The impetus behind this sermon was Spalatin's repeated requests on behalf of Mark Schart, a wealthy landowner and counsellor to Frederick the Wise, who struggled with troubling thoughts about death.[1] Because the request came at the time when Luther was preoccupied with his literary debate with Jerome Emser and his public forum with John Eck at Leipzig on 2 July 1519, his work on the treatise was delayed. Initially he asked that Schart read a little book by Johannes Staupitz entitled *The Imitation of the Willing Death of Christ*, while waiting for his response.[2] In August, in a letter to Spalatin he promised to write the treatise, 'as soon as I can get my breath back again.'[3] Finally, on 1 November, Luther sent printed copies to Spalatin. Within three years of its publication, this treatise appeared in twenty-two editions, with two more to follow in 1523 and 1525. Its authenticity is attested by the copy at the Ducal Library at Wolfenbüttel, which bears the inscription in Luther's handwriting: 'To Mark Schart, my dear friend.'[4]

Luther described various strategies to prepare for death which should strengthen the sufferer's conscience against the temptation to despair in the final hour. Although he appeals to the Church's sacrament of extreme unction and prayers addressed to Mary and the saints, and the holy angels, his theology of exclusive personal faith in Christ already figures largely in this treatise. The beauty of this sermon lies in his remarkable ability to withdraw from the heat of theological controversy into the pastoral context of serene devotion. Here Luther sought to inculcate pastorally the benefits Christ has acquired by the cross and through the resurrection, if we only believe. At the last hour, the saving image of Christ alone should capture our attention. The trinity of evil – death, sin, and hell – will flee

---

[1] *LW* 42, 97.

[2] Johannes Staupitz (1469–1524) was a vicar-general of the Augustinian Order and a close friend of Luther during the Reformer's early years. For Luther's high esteem of Staupitz, see *LW* 54, 72, 97. For a major study of the relationship between Luther and Staupitz, see D.C. Steinmetz, *Luther and Staupitz: An Essay in the Intellectual Origins of the Protestant Reformation* (Duke Monographs in Medieval and Renaissance Studies 4; Durham: Duke University Press, 1980).

[3] *WABr* 1, 508, as cited in *LW* 42, 97, n. 7.

[4] *LW* 48, 130, n. 3.

before the victorious picture of Christ. Only by grasping Christ 'for us' (*pro nobis*) can we find solace at this last hour and face the terror of death with confidence. To Luther, the dogmatic question of how God might be in and for himself is not humanity's concern, but rather what the gospel of Christ bestows upon us. The revealed word is the prophetic word, not ours but his – the voice of the gospel that we must hear above the voice of illness or death. Through this voice, we are persuaded by God to accept death willingly, not to dread it but overcome it by faith in Christ, and the blessings he acquires for us. The true preparation for death is the exercise of faith, through which we grasp the knowledge that death, sin, hell, and the devil are totally vanquished through Christ, the crucified.

A Common-sense Approach to Preparing to Die

Luther was not so heavenly minded that he took total leave of a common-sense or this-worldly appreciation of death. Since death is the termination of all worldly activities and attachments, it is necessary that one should order one's assets properly lest one's death becomes the occasion for quarrels or wrangling among relatives. This pertains to the physical departure from this world and the surrender of our worldly goods. As regards the spiritual departure, Luther advised that we should not bear any grudges, but rather cheerfully and sincerely forgive our enemies, for God's sake. Simultaneously, we should seek earnestly the forgiveness of others whom we have offended by failing to set a good example or failing to love them. This is necessary lest the soul became overburdened by its own sinful deeds on earth. In order to be well prepared for the journey of death, we should sincerely confess our sins, that is, 'at least the greatest sins and those which by diligent search can be recalled by memory.'[5]

Death as the Feast Day of New Birth

We should fix our gaze on God, to whom the path of death leads us. Death, for Luther, is 'the beginning of the narrow gate and of the straight path to life (Matt. 7:14).' Although the gate is narrow, the journey is not long. This view he elaborated by the analogy of physical birth:

> Just as an infant is born with peril and pain from the small abode of its mother's womb into this immense heaven and earth, that is, into this world, so man departs this life through the narrow gate of death. And although the heavens and the earth in which we dwell at present seem large and wide to us, they are nevertheless much narrower and smaller than the mother's womb in comparison with the future heaven.

---

[5] *LW* 42, 100.

> Therefore, the death of the dear saints is called a new birth, and their feast day is known in Latin as *natale*, that is, the day of their birth.[6]

Just as an infant is born through a narrow and dark birth canal to new life, we too are born through the narrow and dark passage of death to new life. To illustrate the journey of death, Luther quoted Jesus' own words in John 16:21: 'When a woman is in travail she has sorrow; but when she has recovered, she no longer remembers the anguish, since a child is born by her into the world.' This road through the dark valley, though painful and frightening beyond words, may be traveled safely when we are assured of its end. Our faith does not demand that the pain of grief and the horror of death be denied. On the contrary, it is the very harsh reality of death that makes the heavenly mansion so desirable, and so gloriously exuberant. Luther wrote, 'So it is that in dying we must bear this anguish and know that a large mansion and joy will follow (John 14:2).'[7] Only in the light of this immeasurable joy of new heavenly life can we celebrate our death as our 'feast day' (*natale*), the day of our birth into the life beyond.

Triumvirate of Evils: Death, Sin, and Hell

In order to benefit properly from the power of the sacraments, we must know the evils which they overcome and whose assaults (*Anfechtung*) we face. Luther named three 'images' of evils from which all other evils proceed. They are the terrifying images of death, the multiform image of sin, and the unbearable image of hell and eternal damnation. Death looms large, and becomes all the more terrifying because of the constant fixation on it by our foolish and weak nature. 'The power and might of death are rooted in the fearfulness of nature.'[8] Moreover, the devil relentlessly mediates the image of death to the believer through the fear-inducing picture of various ways of dying. To Luther, death, this unnatural reality, is always associated with God's wrath. The devil also mediates the image of death by showing forth God's wrath against sinners so as to cast them down into sheer despair. 'In that way, he [the devil] fills our foolish human nature with the dread of death while cultivating a love and concern for life, so that burdened with such thoughts man forgets God, flees and abhors death, and thus, in the end, is and remains disobedient to God.'[9] Luther exhorted us to contemplate death at the proper time. The might of death becomes increasingly powerful, and fear of it becomes more intense because of our lack of timely contemplation. During our lifetime, we should 'invite death into our

---

[6] *LW* 42, 99-100. The feast day dates back to the second century. It was observed originally to commemorate a relative on the anniversary of his death. Later the observance commemorated especially saints and martyrs. See *LW* 42, 100, n. 1.

[7] *LW* 42, 100. Also cited by Althaus, *Theology of Martin Luther*, 408.

[8] See H. Bornkamm, *Luther's World of Thought* (trans. M.H. Bertram; St. Louis: Concordia, 1958), 115-33. In Bornkamm's view, death occupies a significant place in Luther's thinking.

[9] *LW* 42, 101-102.

presence when it is still at a distance and not on the move.' Thus he counseled Christians to banish all thoughts of death at the last hour, but meditate upon life at that moment.[10]

What to do with the second image, sin? The power of sin and its guilt cannot be relieved by introspection. The image of sin looms large when it is coupled with an accusing conscience. The devil magnifies this image in us by reminding us of those who were condemned to hell for lesser sins than ours. This too casts us down into sheer despair, which results in our forgetting God's grace and in disobedience to God in the last hour.[11] Again Luther stressed the proper timing of contemplation of this image in order to reap the right benefits as a result. He admonished that the contemplation of our sins should occur during our lifetime, as was taught in Psalm 51:3, 'My sin is ever before me.' The devil closes our eyes and hides the image of sin during our lives, when we should be thinking of it. He then opens our eyes to the horrible reality in the final hour, when our eyes should be seeing only grace, not sin. He thus turns everything upside down for us, that is, by proposing an untimely contemplation of sin.[12]

Likewise, the third image, hell, is magnified in power by untimely meditation upon it. 'This is increased immeasurably by our ignorance of God's counsel.'[13] Specifically, the devil increases the soul's burden with haunting questions concerning election. He prods the soul into undertaking the one thing forbidden – delving into the mystery of God's hidden will. In this undertaking the devil 'practices his ultimate, greatest, and most cunning art and power,'[14] for he 'sets man above God,' so that we look in the wrong place for assurance of election. This line of inquiry casts doubt on God, and causes us to look for a different God than the one we already embrace. By raising these doubts about election, the devil is determined to replace the soothing balm of God's love with fearful worries about God's wrath. 'The more docilely man follows the devil and accepts these thoughts, the more imperiled his position is.'[15] Hence Luther warned against seeking for God beyond and outside Jesus Christ. This would be to fall into the terror of the hidden God, resulting in hatred and blasphemy of him.[16] He repudiated the presumption of humankind to know all that God knows, but insisted on allowing God to be God. Election 'temptation' (*Anfechtung*) is the assault of hell, as the Psalms lament (cf. Ps. 65:4; 78:67-68; 106:4-5.), and to surmount it is to conquer simultaneously sin, hell, and death.[17] In this regard, Luther advised, we must labor not to open our minds to any of these images or invite the devil's presence into our lives. Should we allow these images to occupy the heart, we would be doomed, and God and his love be

---

[10] *LW* 42, 101-102.
[11] *LW* 42, 102.
[12] *LW* 42, 102.
[13] *LW* 42, 102.
[14] *LW* 42, 102.
[15] *LW* 42, 102.
[16] *LW* 42, 102.
[17] *LW* 42, 102.

completely banished from our mind, in which case we, who would otherwise gladly die, become loath to depart this life. Luther summed up his counsel to those preparing to die: 'You must look at death while you are alive and see sin in the light of grace and hell in the light of heaven, permitting nothing to divert from that view.'[18] Death thus becomes more bearable if we observe this timing and perspective.

Christ, the Glowing Picture

In the throes of these negative images – death, sin, and hell – Jesus Christ becomes the saving image which the believer must contemplate and hold before himself. Luther's advice is this: contemplate Christ, the 'glowing picture,' as the solution to the triumvirate of evil.[19] He first counseled those plagued by fear of impending death to contemplate death not in themselves, nor in their nature, nor in those who died by divine wrath and were overcome by death, in which case they were lost. Instead they should turn their gaze upon Christ who 'overcame death with life.'[20] They are to contemplate death 'only' in those who died in God's grace and who have overcome death, particularly in Christ and in all his beloved saints. The more one fixes one's gaze on these pictures, the more the image of death pales and diminishes in power without resistance. Death begins to appear 'contemptible and dead, slain and overcome in life. For Christ is nothing other than sheer life, as his saints are likewise.'[21] Christ's death is the chief object of meditation, for he is the 'dead bronze serpent' in whose sight the agents and might of death die.[22] Thus we must concern ourselves solely with Christ's death and find life there. Luther rephrased Christ's words: 'In the world – that is, in yourselves – you have unrest, but in me you will find peace (John 16:33).'[23] So, to look at death in any other way will annihilate us with terror and anguish.

Secondly, Luther exhorted us to look at sin, not in sinners, nor in our own conscience, nor in those who live in sin till the end and are damned, but only in the context of grace. 'The picture of grace is nothing else but that of Christ on the cross,' where he removes our sin, bears it, and destroys it, if only we believe this firmly.[24] Christ is the image of life and grace that conquers *pro nobis* the image of death and sin (1 Cor. 15:57).

> Here [in the picture of Christ] sins are never sins, for here they are overcome and swallowed up in Christ. He takes your death upon himself and strangles it so that it may not harm you, if you believe that he does it for you and see your death in him

---

[18] *LW* 42, 102.
[19] *LW* 42, 106.
[20] *LW* 42, 104.
[21] *LW* 42, 104.
[22] *LW* 42, 104. See Nebe, *Luther as Spiritual Adviser*, 222-42.
[23] *LW* 42, 104.
[24] *LW* 42, 105.

> and not in yourself. Likewise, he also takes your sins upon himself and overcomes them with his righteousness out of sheer mercy, and, if you believe that, your sins will never work you harm. In that way Christ, the picture of life and of grace over against the picture of death and sin, is our consolation.[25]

Thirdly, we must not regard hell and eternal pain in relation to predestination – not in ourselves or in itself, nor in those who are damned, but solely in relation to Christ. We are to gaze at the 'heavenly picture' of Christ, who descended into hell (1 Pet. 3:19) as one eternally forsaken by God when he spoke the words of dereliction on the cross, 'Eli, Eli, lama sabachthani!' – 'My God, my God, why hast thou forsaken me?' (Matt. 27:46).[26] In that picture our hell is conquered, and our uncertain election is made sure. 'Never, therefore, let this [picture] be erased from your vision. Seek yourself only in Christ and not in yourself and you will find yourself in him eternally.'[27] The image of Christ is the mirror of the love of God. Thus the dying person can hold on to Jesus Christ when assailed by the terrifying thought of predestination.

Each evil image will flee before the glowing picture of Christ and his saints. These three foes, in Luther's estimation, are already foreshadowed in the Old Testament. Luther provided a Christological interpretation of Judges 7:16-22, alluding to the fact that Gideon attacked the Midianites at night in three different places, by no more than blowing trumpets and smashing glass. His enemies fled and destroyed themselves. Likewise, death, sin, and hell will flee if in the night we but keep our gaze on Christ and his saints, abide in the faith, and strengthen ourselves with God's word as with the sound of trumpets.[28] Isaiah 9:4 introduces the same figure against the three images, saying of Christ, 'For the yoke of his burden, and the staff for his shoulder, the rod of his oppressor, thou hast broken as in the days of the Midianites.' Luther clarified this: 'The sins of your people (which are a heavy "yoke of his burden" for his conscience), and death (which is a "staff" or punishment laid upon his shoulder), and hell (which is a powerful "rod of the oppressor" with which eternal punishment for sin is exacted)' are put to flight and defeated by Christ as it were in the days of Gideon who overcame them by faith, not with a sword.[29] This is precisely what Christ does on the cross, where he vanquishes death by his resurrection, sin by his obedience, and hell by his love. Luther explained:

> There [on the cross] he prepared himself as a threefold picture for us, to be held before the eyes of our faith against the three evil pictures with which the evil spirit and our nature would assail us to rob us of this faith. He is the living and immortal image against death, which he suffered, yet by his resurrection from the dead he vanquished death in his life. He is the image of the grace of God against sin, which he assumed, and yet overcame by his perfect obedience. He is the heavenly image,

[25] *LW* 42, 105.
[26] *LW* 42, 105.
[27] *LW* 42, 106. Also quoted in Bornkamm, *Luther's World of Thought*, 128.
[28] *LW* 42, 106.
[29] *LW* 42, 106.

> the one who was forsaken by God as damned, yet he conquered hell through his omnipotent love, thereby proving that he is the dearest Son, who gives this to us all if we but believe.[30]

Furthermore, Christ not only objectively gained victory over the images of death, sin, and hell, but for our comfort he also subjectively overcame the temptation which these images bring to us. Christ was tempted by the same images just as we are. Like Staupitz before him, Luther used the ridicule hurled by the Jewish leaders on Jesus on the cross as examples of his confrontation with the temptations of death, sin, and hell.[31] In each instance, Christ did not revile but remained silent.[32] Yet Luther eschewed imitation of Christ's silence before these assaults in favor of firmly holding to Christ and believing that sin, death, and hell have been overcome by Christ's actions. Luther differed from Staupitz, who offered the temptations of Christ on the cross as models for those tempted on their deathbeds. To Luther, only Christ's image and his redemptive acts on the cross should reside in us, not our imitation of Christ's suffering.[33] To put it in Augustinian terms, Christ as sacrament (Saviour) must be embraced instead of Christ as model (example).

The Efficacy of Faith and Sacramental Promises

In addition to the three pictures in Christ, Luther advised that we avail ourselves of the 'visible signs' and 'promises' indicated in the sacraments of the Eucharist and extreme unction in the hour of death. At this point, Luther had not repudiated the sacrament of extreme unction, which was administered to the gravely sick, the dying, or the already deceased. By 18 December 1519, however, in his letter to Spalatinus, he rejected all the sacraments except penance, baptism, and the Lord's Supper.[34] The efficacy of the sacraments lies not in us doing them but in the faith accompanying them. As Christ says, 'All things are possible to him who believes' (Mark 9:23). For 'the sacraments are nothing else than signs which help and incite us to faith,' Luther explained, 'without this faith, they serve no purpose.'[35] The sacraments are symbols of faith in God's promises, from whence Christians draw consolation. Therefore, 'We must earnestly, diligently, and highly esteem the holy sacraments, hold them in honor, freely and cheerfully rely on them, and so balance them against

---

[30] *LW* 42, 106.

[31] *LW* 42, 106-107. See also T.C. Peters, *Cherish the Word: Reflections on Luther's Spirituality* (St. Louis: Concordia, 2000), 85-89.

[32] *LW* 42, 108, n. 8, where it is stated that Jesus spoke only once *while on* the cross (Matt. 27:46).

[33] See D.J. Terry, *Martin Luther on the Suffering of the Christian* (2 vols, PhD dissertation; Ann Arbor, MI: University Microfilm International Dissertation, 1990), 1, 211; M.C. O'Connor, *The Art of Dying Well: The Development of the Ars Moriendi* (New York: Columbia University Press, 1942), 190. Both point out that Luther differs *from* Staupitz who considers Christ's suffering as a model to follow in the last hour.

[34] *LW* 42, 100, n. 2, where his letter to Spalatin *WA*s cited. Cf. *WABr* 1, 594-95.

[35] *LW* 42, 100.

sin, death, and hell. We must occupy ourselves much more with the sacraments and their virtues than with our sins.'[36] To grasp the worth of the sacraments, Luther stressed the need to grasp by faith the truth of 'God's word and work' in them. This is how to give the sacraments due honor, that we believe that we truly receive what the sacraments signify and all that God declares and promises in them, so that we can acquiesce with Mary in firm faith, 'Let it be to me according to your words and signs (Luke 1:38).' In contrast, to doubt or ignore God's word and work is to render him dishonor. In the reciprocity of relationship between God and us, there is a giving and receiving. When God speaks and acts through the priest, we, as the recipients of his address and act, believe that his word and work are true and firmly rely on them.

Faith lays hold of God's promises indicated in the sacraments. The fear of one's impending death is dissipated by holding on to the blessings of the sacraments. The sacrament of extreme unction enables the believer to die cheerfully, if it is received by faith. Therefore faith in Christ is the accomplishment of our preparation and readiness for the journey of death. The priest is the instrument of divine power, through which God speaks and works for the believer. In the sacrament of the Eucharist the believer receives all the blessings in connection with Christ. This sacrament is a sign that 'Christ's life has taken your death, his obedience your sin, his love your hell, upon himself and overcome them.'[37] To clarify, by 'sign,' Luther did not have in mind mere symbol, pointing to an absent object. Bornkamm explained of Luther, 'The sign he had in mind is an effective one. Whatever it represents actually happens ... Holy Communion does not only speak of forgiveness of sin; [it] contains and effects it.'[38] The sacraments are not mere indications of God's forgiveness but actually are causes of it. The external words spoken by a priest constitute a truly great comfort for the suffering Christian. Because the sacramental words are truly a 'visible sign of divine intent,' Luther wrote,

> we must cling to them with a staunch faith as to the good staff which the patriarch Jacob used when crossing the Jordan (Gen. 32:10), or as to a lantern by which we must be guided, and carefully walk with open eyes the dark path of death, sin, and hell ... It points to Christ and his image, enabling you to say when faced by the image of death, sin and hell, 'God promised and in his sacraments he gave a sure sign of his grace.'[39]

Those who believe in the visible sign are assured of their election and predestination. Contrary to what Luther called the 'monster of uncertainty' in the Roman Church, he emphasized the certainty of salvation for those who truly believe and trust in the truth of the sacraments. The radical spiritualists in Luther's time abandoned all external evidences of God's grace; they focused on the inner word so much that the assurance of salvation was removed from their consciences. For

---

[36] *LW* 42, 100.

[37] *LW* 42, 108.

[38] Bornkamm, *Luther's World of Thought*, 97.

[39] *LW* 42, 108-109, as cited in George, *Theology of the Reformers*, 94-95.

Luther, there is no other help in death's agonies than a definite and efficacious sign of God's grace. 'This sign and promise of my salvation will not lie to me or deceive. It is God who has promised it, and he cannot lie either in words or in deeds.'[40] God shall bring to pass what he promises for our sake. Therefore Luther admonished his people to learn the nature, purpose, and use of the sacrament because,

> We will find that there is no better way on earth to comfort downcast hearts and bad consciences. In the sacraments we find God's word – which reveals and promises Christ to us with all his blessing and which he himself is – against sin, death, and hell. Nothing is more pleasing and desirable to the ear than to hear that sin, death, and hell are wiped out. That very thing is effected in us through Christ if we see the sacraments properly.[41]

Luther shunned the imitation of Christ's suffering as a means to achieve certainty. For him, the certainty resides in the blessings indicated, given, and promised to us in the sacraments. These blessings are not conferred on the basis of our worthiness or unworthiness, but purely by faith. Luther regarded the question of worthiness and unworthiness as an assault from the devil, which could only be overcome by Christ the sacrament (Saviour). Faith makes us worthy; unbelief makes us unworthy, for it nullifies the sacramental benefits, thereby also turning God into a liar in what he promises. Luther states,

> God gives you nothing because of your worthiness, nor does he build his word and sacraments on your worthiness, but out of sheer grace he establishes you, unworthy one, on the foundation of his word and signs.[42]

Thus he who receives the sacraments aright knows that he has been called into Christ's image, and is the designated recipient of Christ's benefits. To Luther, the sacraments are, as Bornkamm put it, 'tall guideposts along life's highway,' assuring us in life and death of God's unfailing promises and invincible grace.[43]

The Communion of Saints as the Cure of the Soul

The sacrament is also a declaration that the Christian is not forsaken in suffering because he is part of Christendom. Luther intimated, 'If the priest gave me the holy body of Christ, which is a sign and a promise of the communion of all angels and saints that they love me, provide and pray with me, suffer and die with me, bear my sin and overcome hell, it will and must be true that the divine sign does not deceive me.'[44] He linked the communion of saints with the sacrament of the altar. He saw community support as the cure for the human soul. There is a social dimension to

---

[40] *LW* 42, 109.

[41] *LW* 42, 111.

[42] *LW* 42, 111.

[43] Bornkamm, *Luther's World of Thought*, 97.

[44] *LW* 42, 111.

the healing of the *Anfechtung* (assault) of sickness and death. When facing death's agonies, Christians may find support in the fellowship and faith of the Church:

> [I]n the hour of his death no Christian should doubt he is not alone. He can be certain, as the sacraments point out, that a great many eyes are upon him: first, the eyes of God and of Christ himself, for the Christian believes his words and clings to his sacraments; then also, the eyes of the dear angels, of the saints, and of all Christians. There is no doubt, as the Sacrament of the Altar indicates, that all of these in a body run to him as one of their own, help him overcome sin, death, and hell, and bear all things in him. In that hour the work of love and the communion of the saints are seriously and mightily active.[45]

Here we see Luther's great definition of the church as a community of saints (*communio sanctorum*). The saints are not super-Christians who are now in heavenly glory, on whose merits we draw for help in time of need. Rather, all who share their faith in Christ are saints. By this, 'Luther brought down the community of saints out of heaven and down to earth,' as Althaus puts it.[46]

> Whatever it is that you want to do for the saints, turn your attention away from the dead toward the living. The Living saints are your neighbors, the naked, the hungry, the thirsty, and the poor people who have wives and children and suffer shame. Direct your help toward them, begin your work here.[47]

Luther is often viewed as the theologian of justification, the doctrine that forges our identity in Christ; he is typically neglected as a theologian of love, divine and human. Faith and love are themes basic to his theology, regarding which he wrote in his *Advent Postil* (1522),

> All works except for faith have to be directed to the neighbor. For God does not require of us any works with regard to himself, only faith in Christ. That is more than enough for him; that is the right way to give his honor to God as God, who is gracious, merciful, wise and truthful. Therefore, think nothing else than that you do to your neighbor as Christ has done to you. Let all your work and all your life be turned to your neighbor.[48]

The basic idea behind the communion of saints is that of co-dependency, mutual participation, and contribution. We are to be a 'little Christ' to our neighbours, sharing and bearing their burdens, and interceding for them, without thought of

---

[45] *LW* 42, 112, as cited in C. Lindberg, 'The Lutheran Tradition', in R. Numbers and D. Amundsen (eds), *Caring and Curing: Health and Medicine in the Western Traditions* (New York: Macmillan, 1980), 173-203 (179).

[46] Althaus, *Theology of Martin Luther*, 298.

[47] *WA* 10, III, 407, as cited in George, *Theology of the Reformers*, 97.

[48] See *WA* 10, I, 2, 168, 18-26, as cited by Kärkkäinen, '"The Christian as Christ to the Neighbor"', 102; Moseman, 'Martin Luther on "Becoming Christ to One's Neighbor"'; Lindberg, 'The Lutheran Tradition', 179.

return or reward. The communion of saints is most active when the Christian is at their weakest. This is borne out in 2 Kings 6:16-17, where Elisha encouraged his servant, 'Fear not, for those who are with us are more than those who are with them.' Elisha prayed for God to open his servant's eyes, which God did, so that the servant might see nothing but the mighty power of the 'chariots of fire' undergirding his cause.[49] Thus the experience of dying privately, although intensely personal, should never be handled privately without our being crushed by the experience. As each member of the church contends with death, we do not desert him or leave him to die alone. For that reason, we learn to 'shout in the ears' of the dying to assure them of our companionship in the biting loneliness of their death. In fact, God, Christ, angels, saints, and the congregations are there as 'shouters'; their eyes are all upon the dying to embolden them to go face the unavoidable.[50] We should not withdraw or distance ourselves from our neighbour's needs with various excuses or by various defense mechanisms. To be in solidarity with the dying is part of what it means to belong to the community of faith.

Concluding Reflections

This writing highlights Luther's role as pastor and confessor; it is removed from any polemical intent and free of theological jargon. At the same time the sermon is not airy or empty of theological content. On the contrary, the pulpit becomes for Luther an occasion to teach with theological precision, and to inculcate in his congregation a piety formed by theological truth based on Scripture. I shall conclude with five points concerning the interface of theology and piety, which may be gleaned from his sermon.

Hidden God and the Forbidden Quest

Luther considered it hubris on the part of human reason to attempt to grasp God above and beyond his revelation in this world, that is, to seek to discover the hidden God. To engage in such speculation is to attempt what he called 'a theology of glory.'[51] To correct and chastise this tendency, he insisted that we restrict ourselves to the crucified Christ, that is, to God seen from below. From this perspective we succeed in grasping the 'hidden God' as well, for they are one and same God. Later, in his *Bondage of the Will* (1525), Luther criticized Erasmus for failing to observe

---

[49] *LW* 42, 112. See B.R. Hoffmann, *Luther and the Mystic: A Re-examination of Luther's Spiritual Experience and His Relationship to the Mystics* (Minneapolis: Augsburg, 1976), 211-12.

[50] D. Bonhoeffer, *The Communion of the Saints: A Dogmatic Inquiry into the Sociology of the Church* (trans. R.G. Smith; New York: Harper & Row, 1963), 54-56; M.E. Marty, *Health and Medicine in the Lutheran Tradition* (New York: Crossroad, 1983), 162.

[51] *LW* 31, 38; *WA* 1, 354, 17-18 (*Heidelberg Disputations* [1518]).

this distinction between God as revealed and God as hidden, between the word of God and God himself.

> God must be left to himself in his own majesty, for in this regard we have nothing to do with him, nor has he willed that we should have anything to do with him. But we have something to do with him insofar as he is clothed and set forth in his word, through which he offers himself to us and which is the beauty and glory with which the psalmist celebrates him as being clothed.[52]

The true theologian is not one 'who perceives the invisible God through those things which have been made'; rather the true theologian, whom Luther called a 'theologian of the cross,' discerns God's being in his deeds, in the 'visible things of God,' or 'back' of God, in those things which are perceived through the suffering and the cross of Jesus of Nazareth.[53] The God who hides in the incarnate Son is the one with whom we have to do. We must thus begin where Scripture begins – begin with 'the child lying in the lap of his mother Mary and to the sacrificial victim suspended on the cross – there we shall really behold God.'[54] Luther's theology of the cross is primarily concerned with God as he intends to be found. God has designated a place and person, showing where and how he can be discovered. He instructed us to listen to God's word alone if we wish to learn who God is and what his will is towards us. Hence we are to follow the way of the baby in the cradle, at his mother's breasts, through the desert, and finally to his death on the cross. When troubled by the haunting specter of his inscrutable will regarding predestination, we should not trespass on the forbidden area, trying to search out the 'hidden God,' for this God would show us only his absolute wrath, and thus be awe-inspiring and fear-causing, stripping the dying of the comfort they need most at this hour.

In his *Letter to Hans von Rechenberg* (1522), Luther advised that the hidden will of God should not be discussed with children and those whose faith was weak. This subject is 'strong wine' which most Christians could not bear, the exceptions being the spiritually mature. 'For just as strong wine is the death of children, it is a refreshing draught of life for old people.'[55] He insisted that Rechenberg should counsel the assaulted to confine themselves to Christ's humanity, which is 'a ladder' to the Father, and be comforted.[56] The divine hidden will of God which works all in all without distinction is above us. We must observe the Socratic dictum, 'What is above us is none of our business.'[57] About God himself, and what he might do in

---

[52] *LW* 33, 138-39.

[53] *LW* 31, 38; *WA* 1, 354, 17-18.

[54] *LW* 3, 176-77; *WA* 43, 52-3 (*Genesis* [1535–45]).

[55] *LW* 43, 53.

[56] *LW* 43, 54-55. See K. Alfsvag, 'Who Has Known the Mind of the Lord? The Theological Significance of the Doctrine of the Hidden God', *Luther-Bulletin* 12 (2003), 30-45 (38).

[57] *LW* 33, 138-39. For a discussion of Luther's Socratic dictum – 'quae supra nos, nihil ad nos', see E. Jüngel, 'Quae supra nos, nihil ad nos', *Entsprechungen: Gott-WAhrheit-Mensch* (Munchen: Kaiser, 1980), 202-52.

his absolute majesty, we have no knowledge. Faith, however, is acquainted with the clothed God about whom we do know something, because he is the God who has turned towards us with forgiveness and acceptance. Steinmetz writes accurately of Luther's approach to predestination:

> Luther's starting point is God's promise, a promise grasped by living faith. It is the correlation of word (revealed word) and faith in their integrity and reality which is protected by the Pauline doctrine of election. The word is only gracious and faith is only a gift if behind them lies the mystery of predestination.[58]

Christ the revealed Word is the prophetic word whose power prevails over death, whose power consists in a life of faith, and whose voice the believer must attend to in order to overcome the temptations surrounding death and its central element, a fear of God's wrath.

God is known through his acts. His merciful activity reveals the divine subject, the divine character and nature, while the depth of God's being remains hidden. Right access to God is to direct ourselves to where he allows himself to be found, in the human form of Jesus Christ. This is where we find God revealed. Through Jesus the Son we are directed to the Father and guided by the Holy Spirit. As Christians, we discover the heart of God as it is revealed in God's merciful act in his Son. This makes possible the certainty of faith – that is, faith in God's redeeming act, which is known through the revelation of his glory under the antithesis of the cross. Luther emphasized, 'The Scripture urges us above all to attend to love in this passion. The incarnation and the suffering of Christ are offered to us above all to enable us to contemplate the love of God.'[59] Christ is the substance of God's love, and in him God's love has conquered God's own wrath for us. When the believer's conscience faces anxiety concerning his election or the terror of the hidden God, God does not cure him through theological efforts but through contemplation on the flesh and blood of the incarnate, crucified Christ, who came as a baby in the manger and whose life culminates on the cross. Thus the only practically secure response is to cleave to the clothed God, to 'begin from below, from the Incarnate Son,' who has overcome the hidden God for us, if we but believe. What should we do about the unknown will of the hidden God? Nothing – except to cling to the revealed God, who is at the same time the hidden God. The antinomy between the hidden God and the revealed God cannot be resolved by theological edifice, but only by a faith that flees from the inscrutability of the hidden God to the God of mercy in Christ. This has its roots in Staupitz. As indicated in his letter to Spalatinus (1517), Luther sent him Staupitz's tract on predestination, along with other works, and stated that 'of all the books, I have kept only [Staupitz's] *De Arte moriendi* [*The Art of Dying*], the others I have given away.'[60] Throughout his entire career, Luther was indebted to

---

[58] Steinmetz, *Luther and Staupitz*, 112.

[59] *WA* 1, 341, 36, as cited in Lienhard, *Luther*, 107.

[60] *WABr* 1:96, 5-7, as cited in Terry, 'Martin Luther on the Suffering of the Christian', 56.

Stauptiz's pastoral and theological counsel concerning his temptation (*Anfechtung*) about predestination.

> Staupitz used to comfort me with these words: 'why do you torture yourself with these speculations? Look at the wounds of Christ and the blood that was shed for you. From these predestination will shine'. Consequently, one must listen to the Son of God, who was sent into the flesh and appeared to destroy the work of the devil (1 John 3:8), and to make you sure of predestination.[61]

The Cross as a Crisis not 'Eternally' but 'Overcome'

God's suffering is affirmed when God constitutes humanity in himself, bearing our sin and mortality ontically. The greatest marvel occurs when God in Christ receives that which is alien to himself but proper to humanity – the suffering of the opposition or discontinuity between God and humanity. God in Christ suffers the opposition, and eventually defeats it by his suffering, effecting for us reconciliation with God. It must be remembered that by suffering Luther meant in the first place the sort of suffering which God the Son undergoes by becoming a *human sinner, and dying*. Christ is the upwelling of God's grace against sin which he 'assumed, and yet overcame by his perfect obedience.'[62] Important in this context is the perception of God's suffering personally for our sin and dying on the cross, which the Son performed in obedience to the Father's will. The perfect obedience rendered by the Son to the Father underlies Christ's self-humiliation in history. With respect to the issue of whether Christ's suffering is attributable to God in his immanent life, it is helpful to recall that, for Luther, the incarnate One is taken into the immanent life. This he asserted in his *Last Word of David*: 'The humanity in which God's Son is distinctively revealed is complete, it is united with God in one Person, which will sit eternally at the right hand of God.'[63] For the Reformer, God, who became incarnate, continues to be incarnately human. Christ's homecoming to the Father is his exaltation as the whole person constituted as God-man *in concreto*. If God continues to be incarnately human, the question must then be, concerning God's passibility, whether the still incarnately human Son of God continues to bear our sin and mortality. Luther would answer with a *qualified* yes: yes, but the sin and death

---

[61] See *LW* 5, 47; *WA* 43, 461, 11-16 (*Genesis* [1535-45]); Martin Luther, *Luther: Letters of Spiritual Counsel* (ed. T.G. Tappert; Library of Christian Classics 18; Philadelphia: Westminster, 1955), 116, where Luther, on 30 April 1531, exhorted Barbara Lisskirchen, who was troubled by the doctrine of predestination, to contemplate the 'wounds of Jesus.' K. Schwazwaller, *Theologia Crucis: Luther's von Pradestination nach de servo arbitrio, 1525* (München: Kaiser, 1970), 127: 'Precisely for this reason [Luther] holds onto the Gospel: here and here alone God is evidently known as the savior who is wonderful to us because of his boundless mercy and unwavering love towards whom there can only be faithful trust and humble obedience.'

[62] *LW* 42, 107.

[63] *LW* 15, 308: *WA* 54, 62-63.

which the once humiliated Lord now carries are the sin and death as 'overcome' and 'vanquished' in the cross and resurrection. As quoted earlier,

> Christ is the living and immortal image against death, which he suffered, yet by his resurrection from death he vanquished death in his life. He is the grace of God against sin, which he assumed, and yet overcame by his perfect obedience. He is the heavenly image, the one who was forsaken by God as damned, yet conquered hell through his omnipotent love, thereby proving that he is the dearest Son, who gives this to us all if we but believe.'[64]

Since the incarnate One is eternally exalted, the Son of God therefore continues to bear our sin and mortality, but in a *new sense* that springs from their having been been defeated and overcome on the cross and at Easter.[65] This incarnately human Son's return to the Father is a return with our sin and mortality, which he has 'suffered,' 'assumed,' 'vanquished,' and 'overcome.' In this way the cross as a *crisis* which the divine life wills to suffer in the humiliated Lord is *eternally* in God. Yet this is not a *crisis eternally*, but a crisis 'overcome' in his 'exaltation and glorification after resurrection.'[66] In consequence of Christ's victory, he, who 'is' Lord over creatures from eternity, was 'made' Lord in time and as such was and is, therefore, crowned with glory and honor.[67] God's eternal Son and the incarnate Son are one Person, who continually bears our sin and mortality, although in the form of sin and mortality overcome. Christ's suffering in history, suffering 'overcome' by his resurrection, is thus introduced into the eternal nature of God. As Paul declared, 'Thanks and praise be to God, who through Christ gives us the victory over sin and death' (1 Cor. 15:57). Faith grasps the victory Christ has won for us that our sins and death are swallowed up.

Christ's Suffering and the Immanent Life

For the Reformer, the Trinity is known in the Son. The entire essence of God is found in the person of Jesus Christ (Col. 2:9). That the Father and the Son mutually coinhere in one another enables Luther to affirm a marvelous exchange between the Son's suffering and the Father's. Since the Father and the Son are one in essence, as Scripture says, the eternal Son's suffering is therefore also predicated of the Father, except that the Father suffers through the compassion that the Father has for the Son who assumes the destiny of man into the inner life of God. 'The Father loves the Son', declares John the Evangelist (cf. John 3:35). Christ's humiliation shows the

---

[64] *LW* 42, 106-07; cf. *LW* 51, 192; *WA* 10, 3, 49 (5th Sermon at Wittenberg, 1522), where Luther says that Christ continues to bear our sin, that Christ is 'the eternal satisfaction for our sin.'

[65] *LW* 12, 131-32; *WA* 45, 244-45 (Psalm 8).

[66] *LW* 12, 131-32; *WA* 45, 244-45 (Psalm 8).

[67] *LW* 12, 127; 131-132, where Luther distinguishes between Christ as Lord over creatures from eternity, on the one hand, and Christ being made Lord in time, on the other.

eternal love of the Father; both the Father's love and the Son's are identical. It is here that God's trinitarian nature is shown by his love. From the perspective of the Father, he loves the only begotten Son, and therefore suffers the forsakenness of the Son, 'the heavenly image,' in order to communicate his eternal essence of love to the world. The Son's true image as 'God's dearest Son' is demonstrated in his willingness to accept this God-forsakenness, thereby also communicating the essence of God's 'omnipotent love' to us. That Christ entered the terrifying abyss of nothingness is shown by his lamentation in the cry of dereliction on the cross. There, God's omnipotent love suffered, and conquered hell when his very 'dearest Son' willingly accepted this forsakenness. Both the Father and the Son are united in their self-giving love that gives up the Son on the cross. The Father of Jesus Christ suffers, not from any deficiency of being, but from the abundance of love, which is God (John 3:16). Since the one undivided essence is located in the Son's act of self-humiliation, the redemptive act of Christ's suffering is integral to the one divine essence in the same Godhead. By mutual interpenetration (*perichoresis*), the Father is said to suffer along with the Son through their divine unity. The God of Israel, the Father of Jesus Christ, was no apathetic being, whose essence is untouched by the pain and suffering of his beloved Son. This means God's capacity to suffer, in Luther's view, has reached God's inner being, and Luther thus avoids driving a wedge between God *ad extra* and *ad intra*.[68] God not only suffers in the economic Trinity; this suffering extends into the immanent Trinity. There is no untouched hinterland in the inner-trinitarian life of God. Suffering and God-forsakenness, as aspects of God's humble act in history, are thus carried into the divine life of God. God's 'omnipotent love' must therefore be conceived as *suffering love* inasmuch as the cross of the eternal and incarnate human Son exists in the divine life of God.

In our final hours, Luther urges that we ponder on 'the heavenly picture of Christ' who, for our sake, endured the curse and incurred the hell of God-forsakenness. Before this picture, the fear of God-forsakenness dissipates. We should see and seek ourselves only in Christ, God's 'dearest Son,' in whom the Father is well-pleased,

---

[68] Cf. D. Perkins, 'The Problem of Suffering: Atheistic Protest and Trinitarian Response', *St. Luke Journal of Theology* 23 (1979), 14-32. Perkins maintains a radical distinction between God in himself or the immanent Trinity and God for us or the economic Trinity, driving a wedge between God *ad extra* and *ad intra*. See C. Helmer, 'Luther's Theology of Glory', *Neue Zeitschrift für Systematische Theologie und Religionsphilosophie* 42 (2000), 237-45, where Helmer offers afresh a trinitarian 'theology of glory.' For a theologian to be deserving of the name 'a theologian of glory', he must be fascinated by the glory of the triune God. Based on Luther's explanation of the Creed in the *Large Catechism*, she argues that Luther's trinitarian theology of glory consists of two interwoven facets: God is glorified for who God is and for what God does: the former she calls the 'inner-trinitarian glorification', the latter the 'outer-trinitarian glorification.' 'When Luther considers the "visible and manifest things of God" in the trinitarian sense of persons and their works, he can be called a theologian of glory.' An abridgment of her article, by R.A. Krause, appears in *Luther Digest* 12 (2004), 131-33.

and know for certain that we are taken up into God's inner-trinitarian life of love. For to be found in Christ is to be found pleasing to the Father, who gives us all things along with his 'dearest Son.' In Christ we become the people of God's 'omnipotent love,' no longer under divine wrath, if only we believe this. According to Luther, the crux of the atonement is not the question of 'whether there is blood precious enough to God or even to the devil, but whether God can actually give himself in such a way to save us.'[69] Forde further elucidates Luther's view:

> Christ feels himself in his conscience to be cursed by God and really and truly enters into eternal damnation (hell) from God the Father for us. Christ's death is not an active suffering according to some available scheme of recompense. There is no such. His death can therefore only be a passive suffering, a 'passion' in the strict sense of the word. There is nothing to do under wrath, death, and so on but to suffer it and to die. Christ, clothed in our sin, can only suffer himself to be attacked. The event must be a real one, and the outcome hangs in the balance.[70]

The Holy Angels – the Instruments of God's Power

Luther accentuated the need of the Christian to avail himself of every resource, including the ministry of holy angels (Heb. 1:14), which might inspire faith and praise of God in the final hour. He did not consider angelology alien to his teaching, fit only to be demythologized. The Reformer's witness to the angels is praiseworthy: they are the instruments of divine power through which the incarnate Lord acts in our defense. 'His holy angels,' John Stephenson puts it, 'are therefore the sheer realization of the gospel.'[71] In his 1530 Michaelmas sermon, Luther spoke of an infinite advantage to be gained from angels over demons:

> They are much more rational and clever than the evil angels, the cause being that they have a mirror into which they look, that the Devil does not have, which is *Facies patris*, our Lord God's countenance. Therefore a single angel is much cleverer than all the devils rolled into one. Thus they are much mightier than the Devil, for they stand with One Who is called by His name *Omnipotens*, Almighty.[72]

The powerful ministry of the good angels is in line with Luther's appreciation of the atonement – as *Christus Victor* (Christ the victor). Turning to Elisha's vision of the heavenly hosts, Luther concluded his sermon confidently that 'he has more

---

[69] Forde, 'Luther's Theology of the Cross', *Christian Dogmatics*, 2, 55.

[70] G.O. Forde, *Theology is for Proclamation* (Minneapolis: Fortress Press, 1990), 55.

[71] J.R. Stephenson, 'Let Your Holy Angel Be with Me', *Lutheran Theological Review* 9 (1996–97), 32-41 (32). I shall follow Stephenson's translation. Hoffman, *Luther and the Mystics*, 183-86, 211-13, who considered angelology as intrinsic to Luther's thinking.

[72] *WA* 32, 117, 11-16, as cited in Stephenson, 'Let Your Holy Angel Be with Me', 40.

angels than devils.' So in times of trials and doubts, we should cleave to *Christus Victor*, the head of his heavenly hosts in whom:

> Our victory has been won;
>
> The kingdom ours remaineth:
>
> He shall have the glory of being a mighty, wise, and pious God, which takes place when God helps us through His dear angels, so that we lick the Devil. God helps us all to do this. Amen.[73]

The Voice of the Law and the Gospel

By the time we come to die, we should have acquainted ourselves with the three aspects 'for us' (*pro nobis*) of the glowing picture of Christ – life, grace, and heaven over against death, sin, and hell. At the basic level, the negative picture of evil and the positive picture of Christ correspond to law and gospel – the twin but apparently contradictory acts of the one and same God. The law and gospel are instruments for salvation in Christ. The law that condemns us reveals the negative images; the gospel that saves us reveals the positive images. The law condemns, and truly condemns, but so that we might therefore cling to the gospel and be saved. Christ places himself across the law's path and, by his endurance on the cross, defeats its alien works – sin, death, and hell – in order to give us the gospel and its proper works – life, grace, and heaven. Inherent in this sermon is Luther's view of dying understood in the light of the law–gospel distinction, that the voice of the law says, 'In the midst of life, we are in death,' while the voice of the gospel says, 'In the midst of death, we are in life.'[74] The annihilating voice of death may be useful, that is, causally useful, if it drives us to into the arms of Christ, who himself is sheer life, and we have life in him. The voice of the law that incites sin, death, and divine wrath is replaced by the voice of the gospel, which removes these deadly images from us. Thus Luther insisted that we give heed to the voice of the gospel or the revealed word, as a lamp shining in darkness until the day dawns and the morning star rises in our hearts (cf. 2 Pet. 1:19-20).[75] The enlivening voice of God-for-us, which Christ is, fills our hearts with love and praise of God's immeasurable grace – this makes dying much easier, as God said in Isaiah 48:9, 'For the sake of my praise I restrain it (wrath) for you, that I may not cut you off.'[76]

---

[73] *WA* 32, 121, 21-24, as cited in Stephenson, 'Let Your Holy Angel Be with Me', 40.

[74] See *LW* 13, 83; *WA* 40, III, 496, as cited in Althaus, *Theology of Martin Luther*, 408; H. Thielicke, *Death and Life* (trans. E.H. Schroeder; Philadelphia: Fortress Press, 1970), 181-88.

[75] A. Siirala, *The Voice of Illness: A Study in Therapy and Prophecy* (New York: Edwin Mellen, 1981), 141.

[76] *LW* 42, 115, n. 17, where it was said of Luther that he preferred a more literal translation of the original, speaking of God as the one who is willing to forgo being

Above all, the incarnate Christ glows as the ultimate reality, the meaning of which is found not in who he is in himself but in what he performs for us (*pro nobis*), taking us up into himself, towards the life beyond.[77] Luther's burning question is not whether there is an intra-trinitarian life in God's inner being in the sense of how God might be in and for himself but rather what the gospel of Christ bestows upon us. To know God aright is to know Christ in the triumphant act of loving and giving where he makes himself our life, righteousness (grace), and salvation (heaven). We must look at the three pictures in Christ, and the affective signs attached to the sacraments, to drive out the counter-pictures. The salvific significance of the person of Christ consists in this: in Christ, our death is strangled, our sin overcome, and our hell vanquished, if we only believe that these 'great, right, and divine works' are done for us and we persevere in this same faith.[78] From this, we know that Christ is true God, before whom all these images – death, sin, and hell – pale in their assailing power against us (*contra nobis*). And that is indeed our consolation, one that makes the dark passage of death more bearable.

> What more should God do to persuade you to accept death willingly and not to dread but to overcome it? In Christ he offers you the image of life, of grace, and of salvation so that you may not be horrified by the images of sin, death, and hell. Furthermore, he lays your sin, your death, and your hell on his dearest Son, vanquishes them and renders them harmless for you. In addition, he lets the trials of sin, death, and hell that come to you also assail his Son and teaches you how to preserve yourself in the midst of these and make them harmless and bearable. To relieve you of all doubt, he grants you a sure sign, namely, the holy sacraments. He commands his angels, all saints, and all creatures to join him in watching over you, to be concerned about your soul, and to receive it. He commands you to ask him for this and be assured of fulfillment. What more can or should he do?[79]

---

honored by his people. 'I shall curb my mouth in its praise of me, so that you will not perish.' Cf. *WA* 2, 697.

[77] See D. Ngien, 'Ultimate Meaning and Reality in Luther's *Theologia Crucis*: No Other God but the Incarnate, Human God', *Andrews University Seminary Studies* 42 (2004), 383-405.

[78] *LW* 42, 114.

[79] *LW* 42, 114.

CHAPTER 3

Gems for the Sick: Proper Meditation on Evils and Blessings

Written for Elector Frederick the Wise during the prince's serious illness in 1519, Luther's *Fourteen Consolations* (1520) furnished guidance and gems for thought for the seriously sick to dwell upon with profit. Its structure came from a legend of a Franconian shepherd in 1446 who had a vision of the Christ child surrounded by fourteen saints.[1] Gradually these saints acquired names, each being identified as a guardian against a particular disease. Luther arranged his fourteen consolations in the form of an altar screen similar to the altar painting of the fourteen saints by Cranach located in St. Mary's Church in Torgau, the elector's residence. The screen is divided into two panels, with the first devoted to the contemplation of seven evils and the second to the contemplation of seven blessings. In all these consolations the victorious image of Christ looms large, by which we are lifted outside ourselves (*extra nobis*), and are so caught up into Christ that we might see how, with such eagerness, Christ was willing to suffer on the cross to make death contemptible and dead for us (*pro nobis*). Contemplating aright the images of evil and blessings would strengthen the pious heart in the acceptance of suffering as precious relics. Luther affirmed a positive role for suffering, particularly illness, in the life of the Christian. In the sinner it causes despair of self-sufficiency, so that they might cling ultimately to Christ. In Christ, all of life may be embraced. By sheer grace, evils may be transformed into blessings, if only we believe this. The *Fourteen Consolations* is an exercise in the theology of the cross, in which Luther names evils for what they really are and names the corresponding cures for them. The whole treatise is aimed to renew our sight so that we might see through the eyes of faith how greatly we are favoured by God.

Theological Prolegomena: The Word and the Holy Spirit

Luther had as his theological prolegomena the doctrine of the word and Spirit. This departure point must be observed before proceeding to an apprehension of things about God, and the way things are. Accordingly, he insisted that consolations are to be derived not from any creaturely beings or any humanly devised schemes, but from the Holy Scriptures, as Paul had written in Romans 15:4, 'Brethren, whatever was written, was written for our instruction, so that through the patience and comfort of

---

[1] *LW* 42, 119.

the Scriptures we might have hope.' Scripture approaches the subject of comfort in a twofold manner: blessings and evils, radically distinct from one another but not separated.[2] This he drew from the word of the Preacher, 'In the day of evil be mindful of the good, and in the day of the good be mindful of the evil' (Ecclus. 11:25). He accentuates the unity of word and Spirit, working together in accomplishing the proper outcome of any act of meditation.[3] The Holy Spirit assigns value and meaning to a thing on which our mind focuses so that whatever he considers as trivial and of no significance will move us only slightly, be it love as it comes to us or pain when it disappears. The Holy Spirit takes great efforts to divert us away from thinking about trivial things so that we become indifferent to them, and unaffected by them. Yet he does not accomplish this apart from the word, as Luther explains:

> When the Holy Spirit has accomplished this, then all things, whatever they may be, are indifferent. Therefore, the diversion is best effected through the Word, by which our present thought is turned from the thing that moves us at the present moment to something that is either absent or does not move us at the moment. It is thus very true that we shall find consolation only through the Scriptures, which in the days of evil call us to the contemplation of our blessings, either present or to come, and, in the days of blessing, point us to the contemplation of evils.[4]

The consolation offered by the word is a new vision, which enables us by faith to see suffering and death through the perspective of the cross. It turns the common human view of these things upside down, lifting us above our evils and our blessings, making us indifferent to them.

The Seven Images of Evil

The Evil within Us

Luther began with the worst of all evils, 'the evil within us,' our lying nature and vanity, the full revelation of which would torture us more than anything. Basing his argument on Psalm 116:11, 'All men are liars', Luther wrote that all people are devoid of 'truth and reality,' and to be in such a state is to be without God and in hell. If one were to feel this evil, he would feel hell as if it were in himself. It is of a divine scheme, thus of God's grace, that the full extent of our innermost evils is hidden from us or we perish by the total revelation of them. 'God hides them and wants us to see them only by faith, when he points them out by the evil that is felt.'[5] We could never fully experience the depth of the evil within us without being completely crushed by it. So the evil we actually suffer is indeed a lighter one than that which we should suffer and our freedom from pain is greater than the pain we

---

[2] *LW* 42, 124.

[3] For a discussion of the connection between the word and the Spirit, see Althaus, *Theology of Martin Luther*, ch. 6.

[4] *LW* 42, 124.

[5] *LW* 42, 126.

should feel. We should be thankful for the many hours that we experience without pain when they are compared with the pain that we should experience as a result of evil. God's fatherly chastening of the Christian is a lesser evil, for physical pain is nothing compared to the revelation of our true innermost evil nature. Physical sufferings are a 'monitor' of our internal evils, for these 'scourgings' are God's instruments, which he uses to drive out the evils from within us.[6] Thus we are to view this external suffering simply as the disciplining of a child by its parent, embracing it as 'mere child's play' in comparison to the horror and terror of the true evil that is within us.[7] We should be grateful precisely because the goodness of God has kept the magnitude of evil hidden so deeply that we become insensitive to it.

> Just see what a great good it is not to know the whole of our evil. Be mindful of this good, and the evil that you feel will torment you less. On the other hand, in the day of good be mindful of the evil. That is to say, while you do not feel the true evils, be grateful that you do not, but keep the true evils in mind. The evil that you feel will then be less of a burden. It is therefore clear that in this life a man's freedom from pain is always greater than his pain. This is because his whole evil is not present, but because the goodness of God keeps it hidden so that he neither thinks of it nor feels it.[8]

The true evil within, though hidden from us, does nonetheless reveal itself in the troubled conscience, especially when faith is weak, and when confronted with the reality that nothing we do on earth is complete and perfect. These experiences of evil are real but, by familiarity with them, they are blunted. Jane Strohl puts it bluntly, 'Our insensitivity is our salvation.'[9] This, according to Luther, is another sign of God's providential care. Luther argued that the Elector Frederick, whom he had specifically in mind, should not be overwhelmed by the evils with which we are all familiar. Of high rank, the Elector was inevitably surrounded by an infinite number of trials and should learn to despise such evils through familiarity with them, so that his feelings and thought about them become dulled.[10] Yet they 'do not cease being evils just because they are less sharply felt by us.'[11] These evils within us cannot be measured objectively 'on the basis of the facts, but (subjectively) on the basis of our own thoughts and feelings.'[12]

Although God hides from us the full knowledge of our inner evil, he sometimes offers a taste of this to some, of whom it is spoken, 'He brings down to hell and brings back again' (1 Sam. 2:6). The full revelation of the evil within is God's work, nevertheless his alien work of humbling as in the law in order to achieve his

---

[6] *LW* 42, 125.

[7] *LW* 42, 126.

[8] *LW* 42, 126.

[9] J.E. Strohl, 'Luther's "*Fourteen Consolations*"', *Lutheran Quarterly* 3 (1989), 169-82 (172).

[10] *LW* 42, 127, n. 9.

[11] *LW* 42, 127.

[12] *LW* 42, 127.

proper work of exalting as in the gospel. As an example, Luther cited David (Ps. 6), to whom the full extent of his evil nature was revealed. Consequently, David attacked himself furiously, regarded whatever suffering life might bring as nothing, and voluntarily embraced earthly suffering as mere child's play in exchange for the full revelation of his true sinful nature. However, God only allows the Christian to feel scarcely a thousandth of his internal evils, for which we should be grateful.[13]

> Therefore, the first image becomes a consolation when a man says to himself, 'Not yet, O man, do you feel your evil. Be glad and grateful that you do not have to feel it.' When compared with the greatest evil, the small evil thus becomes light. It is this that others mean when they say, 'I have deserved something far worse, even hell itself' – a thing so easy to say, but horrible to endure.[14]

The Evil before Us

The second image, that of 'the evil before us,' speaks of the tragedies, infirmities, and indignities that may yet befall us. The present sufferings will pale into insignificance if we concentrate upon future possible evils. Future evils are so plentiful and so great that they give rise to one of the most disintegrating emotions, namely, fear.[15] This evil increases in power and intensity because we are uncertain of its form and the force it might assume. An individual may suffer any or all of the evils others have suffered. Thus, in regarding the present affliction we should be thankful that we have been spared all the other possible evils. 'From this we see how dearly we should love God whenever some evil afflicts us, for by that one evil our most loving Father would want us to see how many evils would threaten and attack us if he himself did not stand in the way.'[16] In support of his argument, Luther quoted Luke 22:31, where God sets a limit to the extent that evil should fall upon Peter, and also Job 38:11, where God restricts the activity of the waves of the sea.

Yet even if one should remain untouched by any of the evils listed, none could escape the inevitable evil, the greatest of all – death.

> Because death is such a great evil, we see many who would rather live with all the evils mentioned above than to die once and have them ended. Disdaining the other evils, this is the one to which the Scriptures ascribe fear ... There is no one who would not choose to submit to all other evils if thereby he could avoid the evil of death. Even the saints dreaded it, and Christ submitted to it with trembling fear and

[13] *LW* 42, 127.
[14] *LW* 42, 128.
[15] *LW* 42, 128.
[16] *LW* 42, 128.

> bloody sweat (Luke 22:42-44). Therefore, in no other area has divine mercy been more concerned about comforting faint hearts than in the matter of this evil ...[17]

There is no greater evil than death, and thus, by comparison, the present evils endured by the righteous are reduced in power. Yet there is an evil greater than death, namely, falling from grace. To Luther, the greatest reason why Christians dread the evils to come is the possibility that these evils might cause them to fall into sin. Thus they face an even more dreadful threat of the possibility of falling from grace (1 Cor. 10:12). 'What true Christian will not want death and even sickness when he sees that as long as he lives and is healthy, he is in sin and always likely to fall, yes, daily does fall into more sins, thus constantly thwarting the loving will of his loving Father?'[18] Taking his cue from Cyprian's *De Mortalitate*, Luther exhorted the Christian to 'embrace death as a quick means of escape from these evils.'[19] The lesser evil of death is to be preferred to the greater evil of falling into sin. This is proper to God's ordained order, that the evil of sin be annihilated by death so that we are preserved from the greater evil, that is, the eventual fall from grace. The fear of death is thereby dispelled by comparison with something worse, the fall into sin. The misery of death is transformed from an evil into a blessing. Death puts to death the evil of sin, and thus becomes 'the minister of life and righteousness.'[20] Accordingly, those who choose sin over death do not love God much but love evil much.

The Evil behind Us

The third evil Luther described is 'the evil behind us,' the evil that is past. For Augustine, it is in this evil that 'the sweet mercy of God the Father shines forth more brightly.'[21] Like him, we too feel God's hands more intimately upon us when we remember our past life.[22] The basic argument behind this image is this: if our lives and actions were under God's guidance and grace in the past, during the times of disobedience, how much more would our present life be under his, even when his presence is not felt? Just as God helped us in the past, he too will come to our rescue in the present with great mercies. In support of this, Luther quoted Proverbs 16:9, 1 Peter 5:7, Psalms 119:52 and Isaiah 54:7. Implied in this image is the test of faith, where God allows his dearest children to undergo a single malady, as if he hides his care, while in reality shielding them from so many evils far worse than any they actually encounter. The sufferer's present affliction is less of a burden when he weighs his single evil against the magnitude of God's providential care in the past.

---

[17] *LW* 42, 129.
[18] *LW* 42, 130.
[19] *LW* 42, 130.
[20] *LW* 42, 130.
[21] *LW* 42, 130.
[22] See Augustine's *Confessions*, xxix, 39, as cited in *LW* 42, 130.

When troubled by present evils, Luther advised that we ponder the providential works of God in the past, to which our whole life witnesses.

There is an inherent power in memory, that which creates life and hope in all its beauty, so that in our adversities our faith shall be strengthened by the remembrance of our deliverance from evil in the past (Ps. 143:5). This is the crux of Luther's theology of the cross (*theologia crucis*), that God is indeed hidden in the opposite of human reason or experiences, that God is most present in places least expected or observed.

> These and other exhortations are all intended to teach us that since God was with us when we did not think so, or he did not seem to be with us, we should not doubt that he is always with us, even when it seems that he is absent from us. He who upheld us in many times of need, even without our request, will not forsake us in a smaller affliction, even though he seems to do so.[23]

The Evil beneath Us

The fourth evil is 'the evil beneath us,' or the 'infernal evil,' which includes death and hell.[24] When the Christian considers the manifold terrible deaths by which other sinners are punished, he should be content that he suffers less than he rightfully deserves. Their many tortuous ways of dying form an image by which Christ reveals to us the extent and severity of the sinners' just deserts.[25] Death itself is the punishment of sin, and God's justice is rendered to all without distinction (Luke 13:1-5).[26] Hell, in contrast, is not experienced by the Christian, although they fully deserve it. For it has been conquered by Christ's actions on the cross, if only the Christian believes this. Thus the hearts of Christians shall be filled with gratitude to God for every evil of this life, as each is only a fraction of what we have deserved (cf. Job 6:3). This restraint on God's part is a sign of God's inestimable mercy towards those who rightfully deserve everlasting damnation. Instead of focusing on the evils that befall them, Christians should be thankful that God has not allowed manifold evils to assault them.

> I ask you, what are all the sufferings life can bring compared with the eternal punishment which they indeed suffer justly because of one sin, while we go free and unpunished for our many sins which God has covered? (Ps. 32:1). That we give no thought to these benefits of God or esteem them only lightly is a sign of our ingratitude and a hardening of our unbelieving and unfeeling hearts.[27]

---

[23] *LW* 42, 131.
[24] *LW* 42, 133.
[25] *LW* 42, 133.
[26] *LW* 42, 133.
[27] *LW* 42, 134.

The Evil on our Left Hand

The fifth image is 'the evil on our left hand,' referring to the many agents of evil, that is, adversaries and wicked people.[28] Here is another allusion to the Elector who, because of his office, was easily exposed to the agents of evil on his left hand. Again, Luther exhorted him to marvel at the extent to which God limits their powers.

> You see how deep is the abyss of evils that is here opened up, and how it is an opportunity for pity and compassion and for overlooking our own paltry ills, if the love of God abides in us ... What else does God intend with these lamentable specimens [e.g. disfigurement] of our flesh and common humanity but to open the eyes of our mind so that we might see even more horrible forms in which the sinner's soul shows forth its disease and decay, even though he himself may live in purple and gold among roses and lilies like a child of paradise? ... Even in regard to bodily ills, these people are worse off than we are. How can they, I ask you, find sweet and pure joys, even if they have obtained everything their heart desires, as long as their conscience can find no peace? Can there be an evil more dreadful than the unrest of a gnawing conscience?[29]

The horrors of physical pain and disfigurement mirror the horrors of spiritual illness and decay, a greater evil endured by the ungodly – this knowledge is obtained by divine revelation. The true suffering of our enemies is the unrest of a conscience at enmity with God. 'Their plight is worse than ours, because in both the bodily and spiritual sense they are outside our fellowship.'[30] The suffering the Christian endures is nothing compared to the situation of their enemies, 'for they are in sin and unbelief, under the wrath of God and under the domain of the devil, wretched slaves to ungodliness and sin.'[31] The benefit for the Christian is that he can see by faith the grace of God in his ills, while his adversaries remain outside the realm of sweet grace and the pure joys of God. Knowing that he is in the middle of the abundant riches of God's blessings, the Christian bears his ills 'while in the faith, in the kingdom of Christ, and in the service of God.'[32] When compared with the evil of spiritual decay that the ungodly suffer, the evils suffered by the godly seem like pleasures, not pain. It is this awareness of the eternal suffering because of sin that drove Christ to forget himself, empty himself of all goods and suffer eternal damnation in order to defeat the enemies – sin, death, and hell. Enkindled with zeal and love, as was Christ, Moses (Exod. 32:32) and the Apostle Paul (Rom. 9:3) not only forgot their own evils but also desired to die for their enemies so as to bring them freedom. This is in keeping with Augustine's distinction between Christ as sacrament and Christ as

---

[28] *LW* 42, 135.

[29] *LW* 42, 136.

[30] *LW* 42, 135, n. 14, where it is stated that the word 'fellowship' corresponds to 'the communion of saints.'

[31] *LW* 42, 135.

[32] *LW* 42, 135.

example, which Luther accepted, the former necessarily leading to the latter.[33] Inspired by God's love and Christ's kenotic example (Phil. 2:4-7), we too reach out to the wicked not as agents of evil on their left hand but as agents of good on their right hand, seeking their interests rather than bemoaning our own injuries. In so doing, Christ's work and burden becomes ours, through the joyous exchange.

The Evil on our Right Hand

The sixth image is 'the evil on our right hand,' that is, the evils experienced by the saints, both living and dead.[34] There are innumerable examples of saints who suffer more bitterly both in spirit and body than we do. Luther held up John the Baptist as an example, whose excruciating humiliation and undeserved death shamed those who boast too much of their sufferings or who try to avoid them at all cost. The saints who have gone before spur us on to imitate their example and endure the same evils as they did. We meditate upon this image so that we might receive inspiration from the saints in bearing suffering, not in order that we might escape it. Luther exhorted the sufferer to see his suffering as a chastisement, something to be cherished as a sign of God's love for his beloved (Heb. 12:4-11). He was critical of those (whom he called 'the theologians of glory,' in his *Heidelberg Disputation*) who honour the saints in the hope that they would be freed from all sorrows and ills.[35] He also chastised those sinners who objected that they could not be expected to imitate the saints because of their different manner of suffering: the righteous suffered for their innocence, whereas sinners suffer for their sins. 'That,' wrote Luther, 'is a very stupid statement,' for both achieve purgation as the proper outcome.

> If you are a sinner, good! The thief was also a sinner, but by his patience he merited the glory of righteousness and holiness. Go and do likewise. Whenever you suffer, it is either because of your sins or your righteousness. Both kinds of suffering sanctify and save if you will but love them.[36]

The two causes of suffering merge into one, and the sinner is transformed into the saint by the act of confession, for the one who suffers and confesses that he suffers deservedly for his sins is made as righteous as the thief on the cross. Luther wrote:

> Since confession is truth, it justifies and sanctifies. Thus in the moment of your confession, you are no longer suffering for your sins, but for your innocence. The righteous man always suffers innocently. You are made righteous by the confession of your deserved suffering and sins. Thus your suffering may be compared with the

---

[33] Augustinian concepts of Christ as sacrament and as example appear also in his sermon *A Meditation on Christ's Passion*, *LW* 42, 13-14. See Lohse, *Martin Luther's Theology*, 48; Lage, *Martin Luther's Christology and Ethics*, 93-105.

[34] *LW* 42, 137-38.

[35] *LW* 31, 52. See Loewenich, *Luther's Theology of the Cross*, 18-22; McGrath, *Luther's Theology of the Cross*, 148-75; Lohse, *Martin Luther's Theology*, 36-39.

[36] *LW* 42, 140.

> sufferings of the saints as truly and worthily as your confession of sins may be compared with the confession of the saints.[37]

The righteous always suffers innocently by the act of true confession. It is in this context that the Christian's suffering is similar to that of the saints, for both admit that they deserve suffering. There is thus merit in suffering, that this acknowledgment of just deserts produces in a justified sinner a proper righteousness.

The Evil above Us

Finally, Luther completed the first panel of his altar screen with the image, 'the evil above us' – the suffering and death of Jesus Christ for our sins.[38] In this evil, Luther extolled the power of the word to accomplish far more than mere diversion of our thoughts from our injuries.

> Thus the bride says, 'His lips are lilies, letting sweet-smelling myrrh fall in drops' (Song of Sol. 5:13). What resemblance is there between lilies and lips, since lips are red and lilies white? It is said in the mystical sense, as if to say that Christ's words are clear and pure, without even a vestige of bloodred bitterness or malice, but only sweetness and mildness. Yet into them he drops precious and chosen myrrh (that is, the most bitter death). These purest and sweetest lips have the power to make the bitterest death sweet and fair and bright and dear, for death (like precious myrrh) removes all of sin's corruptions at once.[39]

The efficacy of Christ's passion consists in this: there is nothing it cannot 'sweeten,' not even the bitterest death. Christ's death is a 'precious myrrh,' which has the power to transform the bitterest of life's experiences into the sweetest blessings, for in his death 'all of sin's corruptions' are conquered. Luther repeated what was already taught in the second image, that death, by putting an end to the evil of sin, finally delivers us from the power of sin. By the supreme power of the crucified Christ, all evils are transformed. How does this occur?

> Surely, it comes to pass when you hear that Jesus Christ, God's Son, has by his most holy touch consecrated and hallowed all sufferings, even death itself, has blessed the curse, and has glorified shame and enriched poverty so that death is now a door to life, the curse a fount of blessing, and shame the mother of glory. How, then, can you be so hardhearted and ungrateful as not to long for and love all manner of sufferings now that these have been touched and bathed by Christ's pure and holy flesh and blood and thus have become holy, harmless, wholesome, blessed, and full of joy for you?[40]

---

[37] *LW* 42, 140.
[38] *LW* 42, 141.
[39] *LW* 42, 141.
[40] *LW* 42, 141-142, as cited in Terry, 'Martin Luther on the Suffering of the Christian', vol. 1, 188.

Christ's 'innocent flesh and blood sanctified every form of death, all suffering and loss, every curse and shame.' Christ 'pants and thirsts' to 'sanctify sufferings and death and make them things to be loved.'[41] However, the physical death of the Christian is likened to that of all people, except that transubstantiation occurs in the believer. The outward accidents of death remain the same for all mortals, while the inner substance is deeply changed for the justified saints.[42]

> [T]he outward mode of our dying is not unlike that of others, except the thing itself is different, since for us death is dead. In like manner, all our sufferings are like the sufferings of others, but only in appearance. In reality, our sufferings are the beginning of our freedom as our death is the beginning of life. It is this which Christ says in John 8:51, 'Whoever will keep my word shall never see death.' How shall he not see it? Because in his death he enters upon life, so that because of the life that he sees he is not able to see death ... This is assured not for the unbelievers, but for all who believe in Christ.[43]

Elector Frederick was known for his fondness for relics, in virtue of which Luther exhorted him to embrace his own sufferings as 'sweetest relics.' Luther asked: '[W]hy will you not much more rather love, embrace, and kiss the pain and evils of this world, the disgrace and shame which he not only hallowed by his touch but sprinkled and blessed with his most holy blood, yes, even embraced with a willing heart and with supreme, constraining love?' For 'far greater merits, rewards, and blessings [are gained] in these sufferings than in those relics. In them victory over death, hell, and all sins is offered to you, but in those relics nothing at all.'[44] Anybody who meditated on Christ's passion aright would not use the 'signing of the cross' to ward off evils and sufferings. Such action was 'contrary to the cross and death of Christ.'[45] To appreciate the meaning of Christ's passion was not to shun evils and death, but 'to love them, desire them, and seek them out.'[46] For Christ transforms the believer's existence, turning life's evils upside-down so that in him all of life may be embraced, not as a source of grief but of 'delight.'[47] Consequently, this last image lifts us 'above and outside ourselves' in order that we might see 'the heart of Christ,' and be drawn into him, who for our sake suffered the evils mentioned before, those 'beneath and near us' – sin, death, and hell, but defeated them by the resurrection.[48] 'In his resurrection we see that nothing evil befell him,

---

[41] *LW* 42, 142. See Tinder, 'Luther's Theology of Christian Suffering', 111-12.

[42] See Strohl, 'Luther's "*Fourteen Consolations*"', 176.

[43] *LW* 42, 142. Cf. E. Jüngel, *Death: The Riddle and the Mystery* (trans. I. and U. Nicol; Edinburgh: St Andrew Press, 1975), 95-99.

[44] *LW* 42, 142-43. See n. 23, where it is stated that the Elector was noted for his extensive collection of relics, nearly 19,013 items listed in a catalog published in 1520.

[45] *LW* 42, 144.

[46] *LW* 42, 144-45.

[47] *LW* 42, 144.

[48] *LW* 42, 143. Cf. Nebe, *Luther as Spiritual Adviser*, 233.

in fact, only the greatest good.'[49] Christ's resurrection reveals to us this – how with such fervency and joy Christ tastes the bitter myrrh to offer us the sweetness of the lily. Thus Luther claimed that Paul wrote in Hebrews 12:3, 'Consider him who endured such hostility from sinners against himself, so that you may not be weary or fainthearted.'

The Seven Images of Blessings

The Blessing within Us

The first image is that of 'the internal blessings,' which the believer possesses within himself. These include physical beauty, bodily strength, mental power, and spiritual blessings.[50] In view of this excessive abundance of blessings, Luther argued that we should be willing to accept that our life be intermingled with a small amount of bitterness. Too much pleasure would render life 'intolerable' because the constant and unvarying sweetness conferred by such a life would make us unable to enjoy the goods without 'a tempering of evil.'[51] In order to preserve us from spiritual 'decay,' God wills that each Christian be 'salted' with 'the relics of the cross.'[52] Evil is the seasoning necessary to preserve the savor of blessing. Luther asked, 'Why then do we not gladly accept this tempering sent by God, which, if he were not to send it, our own life, weakened by pleasures and blessings, would demand of itself?'[53] Just as the first evil image is not fully revealed, the depth of these internal blessings is also mercifully hidden from us because we simply could not bear their revelation without being weakened by it. There are infinite and incomparable blessings hidden within, but we experience them only in 'little drops and tiny rills,' that is, only to the extent that God makes this knowledge known to us.[54] In addition, a Christian possesses far greater blessings, namely, faith in Christ, and all benefits. 'To have faith is to have the word and truth of God, and to have the word of God is to have God himself, the maker of all.'[55] To perceive God fully and all his manifold blessings is forbidden by God, for that would cause one's soul in a moment to leave the body and live in ineffable ecstasy. The fullness of this revelation is also hidden, but is occasionally felt by some contemplative souls, among whom Luther cited Augustine whose conscience rejoiced in trusting God and clinging to God's word.[56]

---

[49] *LW* 42, 143.
[50] *LW* 42, 144-47.
[51] *LW* 42, 145.
[52] *LW* 42, 145-46.
[53] *LW* 42, 146.
[54] *LW* 42, 147.
[55] *LW* 42, 147.
[56] Cf. Augustine, *Confessions* IX, 10, as cited in *LW* 42, 146.

The Blessing before Us

In his second image concerning the altar screen, Luther described 'the blessing before us,' the future blessings in which the believer finds comfort. This is not so with the unbeliever, who in fact is paralyzed by the uncertainty of their destiny. The believer could take comfort in the hope that 'the evils will come to an end, and that its opposite, the blessing, will increase.'[57] However, the believer's chief concern is not with the evils behind him but with the blessings before him, that his own particular blessings might increase, namely, 'the truth that is in Christ,' in which he advances during his daily walk with Christ.[58] He looks to the enjoyment of the greatest blessings in the future, but only through sufferings and death. Luther again took up the transforming power of death, that it effects a permanent end to all evils – the ills, sins, and vices of this life. Death in itself has no intrinsic worth. Yet God deems death 'the greatest blessing' precisely for the work it performs, that death, the very 'fruit' of sin, meets sin and abolishes it, the very root of death.

> Thus the zeal of God arms this very death against the sin which had caused death so that you may see the truth spoken by the poet, 'The artist perishes by his own art.' So also, sin is destroyed by its own fruit and is slain by the death to which it gave birth, as a viper is devoured by its own offspring. It is a glorious spectacle to see how sin is destroyed, not by the work of another, but by its own, and how it is stabbed with its own accord, as Goliath is beheaded by his own sword (1 Sam. 17:51).[59]

Christ is the end of our existence, neither sin nor death. Thus the meaning and value of our death are derived from faith in Christ. Christ, by his death and resurrection, has turned the worst evil upside down. For the believer death becomes a blessed curse on account of 'a divine work that Christ wrought.' 'It is a great thing that death, which to others is the greatest of evils, is made the greatest gain for us. If it was not this that Christ obtained for us, what then did he do that was worth such a cost, yes, actually the cost of his life?'[60] Knowing that our worst loss shall become the greatest gain diminishes any pain endured as a result of present evils. 'For the believer death is thus dead and behind its cloak and mask it holds no terrors. Like a slain serpent, death still has its former terrifying appearance, but now this is only a mask, for it is now a dead and harmless evil.' For this reason, death in the Scriptures '*is called* a sleep' for the believer (cf. Matt. 9:24; 1 Thess. 4:13) because death's power has been reduced to a mere shadow and has no power over them.[61] Our death dies like the living serpents of the story in Numbers 21:8-9 when our eyes of faith are upon the death of Christ, the brass serpent. The curse of death, which entered the

---

[57] *LW* 42, 148-49.
[58] *LW* 42, 149.
[59] *LW* 42, 151.
[60] *LW* 42, 149.
[61] *LW* 42, 150.

world as punishment for sin, was intended by God after the fall from paradise as a cure for sin, and thus is a blessing for the Christian.

> And that God had appointed death to be the destroyer of death can be gathered from the fact that he imposed death on Adam immediately after his sin as a cure for sin (Gen. 3:19). God did this before he drove him out of paradise to show us that death works us no evil but rather every blessing, since it was imposed in paradise as a penance and satisfaction. It is true that through the envy of the devil death entered the world, but it is evidence of God's surpassing goodness that, after death entered, it is not permitted to harm us, but is taken captive from the very beginning and appointed to be the punishment and death of sin.[62]

For all mortals, death was the curse for sin. But for the Christian, it was the agent of God's mercy. For death is the termination of sin and the beginning of life and righteousness. Thus those who love life and righteousness must embrace death, 'his servant and workshop.'[63]

The Blessing behind Us

In the third image, that of 'the blessing behind us,' Luther contrasted it with its opposite, the evils of the past. He claimed that God's sovereign goodness has overcome evil. Had we been left to our own free will, our destiny would have been at stake. Basing his argument on Psalm 139, Augustine's key text, Luther wrote that the benefits of God had been given us from our mother's womb, irrespective of any merit that we might have. Everything that we are and have, we owe them to God's ordering and governing. It is God 'who works all things in [us]' (1 Cor. 12:6), without our working or help, thus also without our boasting. Luther took joy in being created and cared for by God from all eternity. He disagreed with those who drove a wedge between God's creative and sustaining grace, acting as if God, having created us, then became impassibly uninvolved in our lives, and made us responsible for our own salvation. With Augustine, Luther maintained that God's creative grace and his governing grace are distinguished, but are inseparably one. He cited Augustine's *Enarrationes in Psalmos* 39 (40): 'Let him who made you care for you. Why should he who cared for you before you existed not care for you now that you are what he willed you to be?'[64] Thus he counseled the sufferers to cast their cares upon Christ, 'the faithful Creator in well doing' (1 Pet. 4:19). Divine compassion and comfort are also extended to those who are unaware of them, such as infants.[65] To see God in a proper light is to see him as the One who seizes us by his most gracious will as the object of his providential care. Our faith and confidence then are

---

[62] *LW* 42, 151. For Luther's argument of life beyond death, see J.R. Wilch, 'Belief in Life beyond Death in Genesis', *Lutheran Theological Review* 3 (1991), 57-66.

[63] *LW* 42, 151.

[64] See Augustine, *Enarrationes in Psalmos* 39 (40), as cited in *LW* 42, 153.

[65] *LW* 42, 153.

certain, since we truly have a caring God from whom all his fortunes proceed lavishly and unceasingly, and whose firm word, encapsulated in 1 Peter, 'He cares for you', is a sweet sound to our ears, especially in difficult times.

The Blessing beneath Us

The fourth image is 'the blessing beneath us,' in those who are dead and damned. It is the goodness of God that enables the believer to discern the redeemable even in the greatest evil, namely, the damned. As had Gregory the Great before him, Luther held that the examples of the damned are useful to us as admonitions and pedagogical tools.[66] The more the believer sees the extent of the suffering of the damned, the more they ought to rejoice in the most wonderful mercy of God (Isa. 5:13-15). 'Great as the evils of death and hell are that we see in the damned, so great certainly are the gains that we see in ourselves, and the greater our blessings, the worse are their evils.'[67] Interestingly, the way to receive blessings is through meditation on their opposites, that is, by putting ourselves in the miserable place of the damned, feeling the horror and terror of their torments, so that, as a result, we are so moved that we praise God's goodness for preserving us from such evils.[68] The troubled Elector Frederick was advised to consider the opposite of his blessings, and be encouraged to thank God for shielding him from the greatest evils, even hell. The prospect of God's justice raging against the damned comforts the Christian in that, not only does he rejoice that God in mercy spares him the extremity of suffering, which enables him to face present evils with a lighter heart, but also he rejoices in this revelation of God's righteousness, which avenges those evils inflicted upon him by his foes.

Earlier Luther had advised believers to feel pity for the wicked, who suffer more harm from their own evil doing than that suffered by their victims. However, he now warned against misplaced mercy, which might easily degenerate into mere sentimentalism, and so disregard divine justice. For Luther, God's justice demands that he sends the wicked into hell. 'The justice of God is God himself and God is the highest good.'[69] Therefore, both divine justice and mercy must be loved and praised. God's justice in condemning the wicked to hell should be glorified as highly as his mercy in sending the righteous to heaven. In support of his argument, Luther cited 2 Samuel 19:6, where David was reproached by Joab for mourning too greatly for his ungodly and murderous son Absalom. Divine justice is no respecter of persons. It executes wrathful judgment on all without distinction. Thus Luther exhorted the believer not to grieve too much over the punishment of unbelievers or his own punishment for sin, for in both acts the justice of God is revealed. By consenting

---

[66] See Gregory the Great, *Books of Dialogs (Dialogorum libri)* IV, as cited in *LW* 42, 156, n. 37.

[67] *LW* 42, 156.

[68] *LW* 42, 156.

[69] *LW* 42, 156.

with joy to divine punishment of sin in us, or others, we show ourselves loving God, and proclaiming his supreme goodness.

> What wonder, then, if by way of your present evil God punishes your enemy, that is, the sin in your body? You ought rather to rejoice in this work of God's supreme justice, which even without your prayer slays and destroys your fiercest foe, namely, the sin that is within you. But if you should feel pity for it, you will be found to be a friend of sin and enemy of the justice at work in you. Guard against this strongly, lest it also be said of you that you love those who hate you and hate those who love you ... Thus you see that the greatest blessings may be found in the greatest of evils, and that we can rejoice in the greatest evils not because of the evils themselves, but because of the supreme goodness of God's justice which avenges us.[70]

The Blessing on our Left Hand

The fifth image is 'the blessings on our left hand,' the enemies we have in this life. To Luther, the evils we endure at the hands of our adversaries work ultimately for our good.[71] The enemies are so blessed by the possession of temporal goods that the righteous might be moved to envy them (Ps. 73:2-3). The proper outcome of this blessing lies in the comparison, that if God so lavishes and wastes his blessings on the wicked, how much more will he do the same to the righteous. The worldly goods which the wicked so lavishly enjoy serve as a sign to the righteous in their present sufferings of the far greater blessings, which are so often hidden and still to come.[72] The visible blessings of the ungodly provide an incentive to the godly to hope for the invisible blessings and to disdain present evils. But present evils endured may be transformed into something redemptive, for they present us with opportunities to implement our faith, exercise virtue and receive God's holy comfort.[73] Luther retained the catholic sense of merit, that the endurance of trials is a means of amassing merit.[74] The adversities, the incitement to evil, the provocations, and offences of this world, which supposedly work us harm, work us profit. They constitute for Luther the meritorious means of grace, by which the obedient advances in his righteousness, not alien but proper righteousness.[75] God makes us holy, and procures victories for us through various struggles. Thus, if God gives us such great victories through contemplation of the sins of others, ought we not to believe firmly

---

[70] *LW* 42, 157.

[71] *LW* 42, 158.

[72] *LW* 42, 158.

[73] *LW* 42, 158.

[74] *LW* 42, 159.

[75] For Luther's understanding of two kinds of righteousness, see Lull (ed.), *Martin Luther's Basic Theological Writings*, 155-64; R. Kolb, 'Luther on the Two Kinds of Righteousness', in T. Wengert (ed.), *Harvesting Martin Luther's Reflection on Theology, Ethics and the Church* (Grand Rapids: Eerdmans, 2004), 38-55.

that he will work much greater victories for us in our present troubles, even though our flesh and blood judge it to be otherwise! All Scripture, the writings of all the Fathers, and deeds of the saints concur that 'those who inflict the greatest harm on believers are their greatest benefactors, as long as they [believers] bear their sufferings in the right spirit.'[76] All things are transformed for the obedient by the providence of God's goodness. This is already taught in Augustine's *Harmony on the Gospels*, where he asserts that evil is so wondrously tempered by the goodness of God that even Herod can do more good with his hatred than his favour.[77]

The Blessing on our Right Hand

The sixth image is 'the blessing on our right hand,' that is, the church of the saints. The blessing on our right is held in common with all. Bonhoeffer observed that Luther revived Augustine's idea that it is the holy church that bears the sins and shame of its members, but later, in the same sentence, he added that it is Christ who bears them.[78]

> Who could then despair in his sins? Who would not rejoice in his sorrows? He no longer bears his sin and punishment – and if he does bear them he does not bear them alone – but is supported by so many holy children of God, yes, by Christ himself. So great a thing is the communion of saints in the church of Christ.[79]

The bitterness of suffering is thereby mitigated by the merits of the communion of the saints. The believer never travels the road of suffering and death alone, separated from Christ and his church. The faith, chastity, fastings, and prayers of the saints are means of grace to wounded Christians. Every blessing of the saint is communicated to all Christians *via* the sacrament of the altar, where Christians become 'one bread, one cup.' The whole church by virtue of 'one body,' which we are in Christ, felt the pain Christians experienced.[80] In addition to the blessing behind us, that of God's continuous care for us, we are constantly supported by the blessing on our right hand, that of the communion of the saints. Yet this knowledge that in the church community we have nothing but blessing and consolation is obtained only by revelation.

> Therefore, when we feel pain, when we suffer, when we die, let us turn to this, firmly believing and certain that it is not we alone, but Christ and the church who are in pain and are suffering and dying with us. Christ does not want us to be alone on the road of death, from which all mortals shrink. Indeed, we set out upon the road of

---

[76] *LW* 42, 160.

[77] *LW* 42, 160, n. 40, where Augustine's *Harmony on the Gospels* 6 was cited.

[78] D. Bonhoeffer, *Sanctorum Communio: A Theological Study of the Sociology of the Church*, *Dietrich Bonhoeffer Works* (ed. C.J. Green; Minneapolis: Fortress Press, 1998), vol. 1, 189-90.

[79] Bonhoeffer, *Sanctorum Communio*, vol. 1, 189-90.

[80] *LW* 42, 162-63.

> suffering and death accompanied by the entire church ... All that remains for us now is to pray that our eyes, that is, the eyes of our faith, may be opened that we may see the church around us.[81]

At the close of this section, Luther repeated the biblical story of 2 Kings 6:16-17, where Elisha assured his fearful servant of the heavenly host around them: 'Fear not, for those who are with us are more numerous than those with them.' Just as Elisha prays that his servant might see the chariots of fire around them, so Luther prayed that God would open Elector Frederick's eyes to see the church around him in his suffering, bearing it with him, and upholding his cause.[82]

The Blessing above Us

The final image Luther offered is that of the risen Christ. To him, the resurrection of Jesus Christ is the greatest blessing in which the believer can find his supreme joy and lasting possessions.[83] All that Christ accomplished through his death and resurrection is proof of 'that furnace of love and fire of God' for us.[84] Jesus Christ slayed death by his death and restored life by his resurrection so that in him there is not the slightest sign of evil but only good. His death destroyed sin and his resurrection raised up righteousness; his death conquered hell and his resurrection bestowed glory on the Christian. These incalculable blessings are communicated to the believer who is united to Christ. By the principle of joyous exchange, all that is Christ's belongs rightly to the believer. As in the story of Genesis 45:16-18, Jacob was not convinced that his son Joseph was still alive until he saw the wagons that Joseph had sent for him, so Christ is the priceless 'wagon,' sent by God as 'our righteousness, sanctification, redemption and wisdom' (1 Cor. 1:30), in which we ride.

> I am a sinner, but I am borne by his righteousness which is given to me. I am unclean, but his holiness is my sanctification, in which I ride gently. I am an ignorant fool, but his wisdom carries me forward. I deserve condemnation, but I am set free by his redemption, which is a safe wagon for me.[85]

By faith, the merits of Christ are indeed ours as if we had won them. So true is this that we are emboldened to face the judgment of God with anticipation. For, in Christ, we become the glorious sons of God, inheriting all the Father's blessings. The law that makes us sinners is conquered; the sin that makes us guilty of death is destroyed. Both acts are done not by our righteousness and life but by 'Jesus Christ, rising from death, condemning sin and death, imparting [imputing] his righteousness

---

[81] *LW* 42, 163.
[82] *LW* 42, 163.
[83] *LW* 42, 163.
[84] *LW* 42, 164.
[85] *LW* 42, 164.

to us, bestowing his merits on us, and holding his hand over us.'[86] All evils have yielded to righteousness and life, and no longer terrify us as they did before. The outcome of this 'most sublime image' is that we are elevated above the experience of both evils and blessings – this is made possible on account of the inestimable merits wrought by the labor of Christ.

There is a striking congruence of language when Luther spoke of the effect of the seventh image of evil and the seventh image of blessing. Just as the last image of evil elevates us 'above and outside ourselves' so that we might be caught up into Christ, who for our sake conquers the evils of sin, death and hell, so this last image of blessing elevates us 'above' our evils and blessings so that we might be drawn into Christ, and be established in his justifying grace, and his 'strange blessings.'

> If we have learned from the preceding images, those beneath and near us, to bear our evils with patience, then surely this last image, in which we are lifted above and outside ourselves, caught up into Christ and placed above all evils, should teach us that we ought not only to tolerate these evils, but love them, desire them, and seek them out.[87]

> This, then, is the most sublime image, for in it we are lifted up not only above our evils, but even above our blessings, and we are set down in the midst of strange blessings gathered by the labors of another, whereas formerly we lay among evils that were also brought about by the sin of another and enlarged by our own (Rom. 5:17). We are set down, I say, in Christ's righteousness, with which he himself is righteous, because we cling to that righteousness where he himself is acceptable to God, intercedes for us as our mediator, and gives himself wholly to us as our high priest and protector.[88]

Therefore, just as it is impossible for Christ in his righteous person not to please God, so it is impossible for the believer who is clothed with Christ's righteousness not to please God. His identity is so forged in Christ that Christ himself becomes his identity: this occurs by way of imputation. Not his, but Christ's identity is that which settles and safeguards the believer's legal, vertical standing before God. To be in Christ is to know that his sins are completely swallowed up in victory by the inexhaustible righteousness of Christ, that he is totally acquitted, and hence is found well-pleasing to God just as the righteous Son of God is. This resurrection image alone, Luther concludes, suffices to fill our hearts with such comfort in sufferings that we may 'glory in our tribulations, scarcely feeling them for the joy that we have in Christ (Rom. 5:2-3).'[89]

---

[86] *LW* 42, 165.

[87] *LW* 42, 144.

[88] *LW* 42, 165. For a major study of the righteousness of God in Luther, see G. Rupp, *The Righteousness of God: Luther Studies* (London: Hodder and Stoughton, 1953). See also Lohse, *Martin Luther's Theology*, 260-61; Althaus, *Theology of Martin Luther*, 224-50.

[89] *LW* 42, 165.

Concluding Reflections

There are several theological themes that constitute a rich harvest from this treatise. My reflections will focus on seven of them, while using other writings of Luther either to clarify or to elaborate his viewpoint.

Suffering and Sanctification

In *On the Councils and the Church* (1539), Luther mentioned seven signs by which the Christian could discern the presence of the true/hidden church.[90] The first and most important sign is the preaching of the word, the gospel. The second is baptism, as taught, believed, and administered in accordance with Christ's command. The third is the sacrament of the altar, as taught, believed, and administered also in accordance with Christ's command. The fourth is the office of the keys administered publicly so that sin may be confessed and forgiven. The fifth is the consecration and call of people to the public offices of the word, sacraments, and keys. The sixth sign is public prayer, praise, and thanksgiving to God in public worship. The possession of the sacred cross is the seventh sign of a true church. The true church is not sanctified by a sliver of wood, but by actual participation in the crucifixion of Christ. Luther was very sceptical of institutional success. He frequently warned about the dangers of the peace and prosperity of the church, which would eventually result in the loss of the gospel. This was brought out in his commentary on Galatians 5:11, where Luther quoted in favor of Bernard's view that the church is better off when persecuted, and worse off experiencing external success and prosperity. He went so far to say that, where there is a lack of persecution and the cross, 'this is a sure sign that the pure teaching of the word has been taken away.'[91] In his church postil of 1522, Luther criticized the clergy for their prosperity and charged them with betraying the cross of Christ: 'They have set [the cross] in silver, making it easy to bear without hurting.'[92] The glory of power and wealth is not the true glory of the church; rather, like Paul, the church should glory in the cross of Christ. Luther understood the cross of Christ as 'the afflictions of all the faithful' or as 'the afflictions which the church suffers on Christ's account.' '[I]gnominious and merciless persecution' proceeds not from our condition as *totus peccator* [the total sinner] but from our communion and identification with the crucified Christ.[93] Christ's cross and the Christian's cross must be distinguished from each other, but

---

[90] *LW* 41, 143-78. For a study of Luther's doctrine of the church, see E.F.A. Klug, 'Luther on the Church', *Concordia Theological Quarterly* 47 (1983), 193-207; M.A. Noll, 'Martin Luther and the Concept of a "True" Church', *Evangelical Quarterly* 50 (1978), 79-85; S. Peura, 'The Church as Spiritual Communion in Luther', *Lutheran World Federation* 42 (1997), 93-132.

[91] *LW* 27, 43; *WA* 40, II, 1, 53-54. For an exclusive study of the seventh mark of the Church in Luther, see Kelly, 'The Suffering Church'.

[92] *LW* 52, 233-34; *WA* 10, I, 1, 660.

[93] *LW* 27, 43; *WA* 40, II, 1, 53-54. See also C.R. Trueman, *Reformation: Yesterday, Today and Tomorrow* (Bridgend: Bryntirion, 2000), 51-55.

not separated. Believing in the cross of Christ presupposes carrying the cross. As Hermann Sasse put it, 'A "yes" to the cross of Christ is also a "yes" to my cross.'[94] A theologian of glory seeks to avoid suffering, for it, to him or her, is 'evil.' In contrast, a theologian of the cross embraces suffering as 'good,' thereby naming it as it really is, that is, good because Christ undergoes suffering first hand.[95] Christ then lays his suffering on his followers so that they might wear his yoke and share his burden. Thus suffering is a gift of grace, and is pleasing to God.[96] Christ and suffering are so inextricably linked that Luther could assert that those who avoid persecution thereby surrender Christ.[97] What makes a true church is her willingness to live in God's passion, willingly suffering the opposition of the devil and the world and, in so doing, bearing witness to the truth (Christ). The true church does not confront the cross as a spectator, but is drawn into this event so that she is confronted with the demand of a life under the cross.

Luther's *Fourteen Consolations* is not an exercise of the theology of glory, in which suffering and weakness are avoided as evils. For Luther, the cross not only defines the nature of God himself but also the nature of Christianity. Cruciformity is thus required of true faith. Christianity must not be presented as the answer to the immediate demands of comfort-seeking consumerism. Christian life, preaching, singing, worship, and liturgy are to be defined, not by the consumer culture but by a king whose crown came through making himself of no reputation and dying a terrible death on the cross. The cross is found in the context of vocation. Just as we embrace Christ as our Saviour, we also embrace him as our example, which we are to follow in our suffering. We suffer not so that we can be saved by it or earn some merits through it to secure a standing before God. We suffer after Christ so that we might be conformed to him. Nevertheless it should not be the kind of suffering which is self-inflicted, as fanatics who seek suffering for its own sake. It should be the kind of suffering laid upon us by the devil or the world. The cause of our suffering should be the same as that for which the saints have suffered, not because of public scandals or vices. 'Rather they and we suffer because we hold to the word of God, preach it, hear it, learn it and practice it.'[98] To the sufferer, Luther advised that they should pay their 'greatest attention' to the inestimable blessings – 'the mighty promises of God and confidence in God,' in order that their cross and pain may be turned to good.[99] He is unlike the heathens who do not have these blessings.

---

[94] H. Sasse, *We Confess Jesus Christ* (trans. N. Nagel; St. Louis: Concordia, 1984), 52.

[95] *LW* 31, 43. See T. Peters, *Radical Evil in Soul and Society* (Grand Rapids. Eerdmans, 1994), where he revisits the dark side of human nature. He uses illustrations from everyday life as well as the social sciences to examine the kinds of evil – both personal and societal. Following Luther, the author names the evils as they truly are in essence, for which he is worthy to be called a theologian of the cross.

[96] *LW* 52, 392; *WA* 51, 194.

[97] *LW* 21, 45; *WA* 32, 335.

[98] *LW* 51, 200; *WA* 32, 28, 22-25 (Sermon on the Cross and Suffering).

[99] *LW* 51, 201; *WA* 32, 28, 22-25 (Sermon on the Cross and Suffering).

It is 'highly necessary' that he, as the saints have done, clings to the divine promise, with which he comforts himself with the assurance that God will aid him to bear his cross with patience. This in turn rules out stoic indifference to evil.

The cross also enters the realm of sanctification. It mortifies the flesh of those who have already died and come alive as righteous before God (*coram deo*). Luther appropriated the sanctifying benefits that come from a true possession of the sacred cross:

> Even if it were a genuine holy possession [i.e., the papists' possessions from dead saints or slivers of wood from the cross], it would nonetheless not sanctify anyone. But when you are condemned, cursed, reviled, slandered, and plagued because of Christ, you are sanctified. It mortifies the old Adam and teaches him patience, humility, gentleness, praise and thanks, and good cheer in suffering. That is what it means to be sanctified by the Holy Spirit and to be renewed to a new life in Christ; in that way we learn to believe in God, to trust him, to love him, and to place our hope in him, as Romans 5:1-5 says, 'Suffering produces hope,' etc.[100]

Some have claimed that Luther's great emphasis on justification by faith alone unfortunately led to moral laxity among Christians. For instance, John Oyer states that Luther's 'declarations on the necessity of works, and the nature of those that ought to be performed, are not numerous.' In favour of the view of the sixteenth-century Anabaptists, he declares, 'Essentially Lutheran faith was erroneous because it was unfruitful. Those who adhered to its tenets continued to live in sin. There was no effort to unify faith and the new life in Christ, and this could only mean that the faith was false.'[101] However, this is far from truth. Programmatically, Luther maintained a distinction between justification and sanctification, the former leading to the latter. Sanctification, as Egil Grislis notes, is a distinct moment experienced in the middle of justification.[102] And it must not be relegated to a separate or higher realm in which believers work towards various degrees of perfection. Luther underscored not only the importance of the grace of justification which secures our righteous standing before God but also the effective operation of the Holy Spirit in our new life in Christ. His view was clearly stated in *On the Councils and the Church* in a brief formula: 'Christ did not earn only *gratia*, "grace", for us, but also *donum*, "the gifts of the Holy Spirit", so that we might have not only forgiveness of, but also cessation of sin.'[103] Although the justifying act is instantaneous and complete, there are degrees of sanctity and growth as Christians, by the effective

---

[100] *LW* 41, 165. Cf. D.P. Scaer, 'Santification in Lutheran Theology', *Concordia Theological Quarterly* 49 (1985), 181-97.

[101] J.S. Oyer, *Lutheran Reformers against Anabaptists* (The Hague: Martinus Nijhoff, 1964), 219 and 222. For an able defense of Luther's position that does not drive a wedge between justification and sanctification, see H. Loewen, *Luther and the Radicals* (Waterloo: Wilfrid Laurier University Press, 1974).

[102] E. Grislis, 'Luther on Sanctification: Humility and Courage', *Consensus* 9 (1983), 3-16 (3).

[103] *LW* 41, 114.

bestowing of the Holy Spirit, advance in their proper righteousness. To Luther, true faith is not an idle faith, but an active one that drives one into action. Although sin does not preside in our new life in Christ, it still resides. It is only at death when all of sin's corruptions will be terminated. St. Paul exhorted the saints to put to death the sin Christ has slain (Col. 3). Hence the process of sanctification continues in the Christian life until death.[104] Against the Antinomians, Luther affirmed:

> Now he who does not abstain from sin, but persists in his evil life, must have a different Christ, that of the Antinomians; the real Christ is not there, even if all the angels would cry, "Christ! Christ!" He must be damned with this, his new Christ ... [T]he Antinomians fail to see that they are preaching Christ without and against the Holy Spirit because they propose to let the people continue in their old ways and still pronounce them saved. And yet logic, too, implies that a Christian should either have the Holy Spirit and lead a new life, or know that he has no Christ.[105]

The Doctrine of Equality

In accordance with his perfect justice, God deals with his people as does a sovereign. This renders the doctrine of equality, that all are given equal measures of blessings, an absurdity. Blessings differ with individuals. As God wishes it, he grants more to some, while withholding from others. To one he gives a greater peace of mind, to another he does not. In accordance with the execution of God's justice, not all are given equal wealth, equal health, equal power, equal opportunities or equal gifts before the world (*coram mundus*), but all, in accordance with the image of God in us, are vested with equal value and dignity before God (*coram deo*). Be they great or small blessings, they come from the bountiful hand of God which we should receive with gratitude and cheerfulness. Such joyful reception dispels envy or jealousy, those germs that so often infect church life and so quickly destroy church harmony.

Although we do not possess God's blessings in equal measure without distinction, faithfulness is required of all of us. We look at life through the principle of stewardship, that we are not the absolute owners of anything but responsible stewards for everything, be they small or large gifts, as they have been given to us. This principle, which is inherent in Luther's treatise, is liberating, for it enables us to be what we are made to be, and accept what has been given to us by God. It also affirms the value of individuality, together with its responsibilities. There is a striving after excellence which belongs to a proper ambition, but there is a striving after greatness which is insanely self-serving and overtly condescending. This is contrary to the cross of Christ, where God reveals himself in weakness, not in power. And the insatiable passion to be what we cannot be, and what God never intends us to be, is also against the principle of stewardship. We are called to be

---

[104] 'Two Kinds of Righteousness', in Lull (ed.), *Martin Luther's Basic Theological Writings*, 157-58.

[105] *LW* 41, 114-15.

good stewards of what we have. We are to use our own gifts, exercise our own responsibilities, discover and develop what God has entrusted to us, and not to be jealous of others. Before God's wise apportionment of his gifts, we can rejoice in the greater gifts or greater opportunities of others, making their blessings ours by celebrating them, since all are part of the same family of God, fulfilling what God requires of us without distinction. Thus the measure of stewardship is faithfulness, not success; obedience, not popularity; humble service, not being better than others; reaching the end, not the top; suffering, not glory. These radical reversals are derived from Luther's theology of the cross and are programmatically opposed to worldly standards.

For Luther, God acts with purpose, like a loving mother who at times gives her beloved children foolish little toys by means of which she might lead their hearts to long for better things.[106] In a similar way, God withholds blessings from some because those people have not attained their full maturity. This lack of maturity God hallows as a redemptive means to better ends. God's people should thus take comfort even in their weaknesses or infirmities, and not be embittered by the lack of some spiritual blessings, for faith reveals divine purpose in the lack. We rejoice in the fact that we are not given the full revelation of God's manifold blessings, for we might not bear them without wasting or squandering them. To support his point, Luther frequently quoted the sayings, 'Every pleasure too long continued turns into loathing' and also 'Even pleasure itself turns into suffering.'[107] In the same way, too great a mental power might lead one to an intellectual smugness, effecting in the possessor the opposite of godliness. To preserve us from such spiritual degeneracy, God mercifully hides his greater mental blessings from us until we are made ready to receive them. Here abides a principle of God's fatherly governance, that he calculates the amount of revelation according to the epistemic heart of the receivers. That is, he will go overboard in revealing more to the humble heart, while withholding much from the haughty heart. This too is a sign of God's providential care, which sanctifies and preserves us from unnecessary downfalls.

The Extent of Revelation in Pastoral Care and Cure

In accordance with his ordained order, God also hides from us the full extent and severity of our failings, that by which we would be crushed to pieces. This is a sign of his grace and has a vital bearing on the way in which we deal with people who are riddled with faults or failures. Part of what it means to be in the community of faith is to be bearers of the sins, vices, sufferings and shames of God's people. Pastorally, how do we restore a wayward sinner without condoning their sins? Some suggest an absolutely honest approach, that is, being vociferous about their failures all at once or disclosing more than that which they could bear, with the result that sheer despair or bitterness are the outcome. Such an approach is frequently brutal, resulting in

---

[106] *LW* 42, 147.
[107] *LW* 42, 145.

self-righteous condemnation of the wrongdoer. Others tend towards an approach of absolute mercy, that is, for fear of offending the wrongdoer they withhold from them much of the truth regarding their faults or lie about them, as a result of which spiritual decay or loathing are the outcome. Such an approach is frequently turned into a loose condoning of sin, and may be guilty of loving what others hate and hating what others love. Some have proposed a middle road, steering between absolute honesty and absolute mercy, but leaning towards the latter. This may be practically helpful, since an effective pastor does not see all the bad and deny the good. Nor do they see all the good and deny the bad. They see both, but aim at the good, and what good may come out of bad as God wishes it to be. This is what a true theologian does, that is, to see evil for what it really is, without excusing it or condoning it, while simultaneously acknowledging the good as good.

For effective pastoral care, a pastor thus observes a fundamental difference between failure and hypocrisy, the former referring to those who truly try to live the Christian life but fail, the latter referring to those who pretend to be other than what they really are. To those who fail, we hold out the sweet voice of the gospel, in which consolation may be found. The central Reformation doctrine of justification by grace alone is to be asserted not as the goal of life but as its presupposition. In line with this, those who fail should look not at their own deeds or lacks, but outside themselves at God's promises found in Christ:

> The gospel commands us to look, not at our own deeds or perfection but at God himself as he promises, and at Christ, the Mediator ... And this is the reason why our theology [i.e., God's unconditional gift of salvation] is certain: it snatches us away from ourselves and places us outside ourselves, so that we do not depend on our own strength, conscience, experience, person, or works but depend on that which is outside ourselves, that is, on the promise and truth of God, which cannot deceive.[108]

To the self-righteous hypocrite, we hold out the stern voice of the law, in which all acts of self-justification and self-pretense are exposed, and condemned. The law shows forth God's wrath, accuses, judges, and condemns all that is not in Christ (Rom. 4:15).[109] This, too, is the work, the alien work, of the same loving God, who brings down the hypocrite in order to raise them up into God's boundless mercy as his proper work. The pastor's duty is not to assist their parishioners in the exercise of discovery of sin through self-introspection, which might lead them away from God. Rather, the pastor is to lead them to the place of discerning the signs of God's immeasurable grace, in the wake of which they come to a deeper apprehension of the evil within themselves. Yet this cannot be accomplished without God's revelation. Thus Luther insists in his *Meditation on Christ's Passion* on contemplation of 'the earnest mirror, Christ' who exposes the sins of the wayward in order that he might

---

[108] *LW* 26, 387; *WA* 40, I, 589-90.
[109] *LW* 31, 54.

bear them and carry them away by his cross and resurrection.[110] The cross forces the self-righteous to ask the question, 'Am I a sinner?,' while simultaneously fostering hope in the one who answers in the affirmative. The cross peels the mask off the evil that often poses as banality in modern culture. On the cross, just as sin is named for what it actually is, so it is conquered as it really is. This is what a true theologian does – to name sin as it really is, and name the cure for sin, which is Christ himself. An effective preacher holds out Christ not only as the revealer of sins but also as the remedy for them.

However, pastoral care and church ministries would not bear fruit unless believers feed on God's word, by means of which faith is strengthened and the callousness of our hearts mitigated. The word of God, in the power of the Holy Spirit, makes possible the actualization of the communion of saints. The body of Christ, God's new creation, feeds on God's word. As a result, it is impelled to assume the noble and kenotic task of Christ, risking vulnerability in bearing the burden of sins and the shame of its members. The true church is constituted by Christ's self-emptying love, where her members no longer face each other in a demanding and unforgiving but in a loving and forgiving way. This genuine transformation of hearts occurs through the efficacy of God's word. Bonhoeffer expands the practical outworking of Luther's *Sanctorium Communion* (Communion of the Saints) as follows:

> The church-community is thus able to bear the sins that none of its members can bear alone; it is able to bear more than all of its members combined. As such, it is a spiritual reality that is more than the sum of all the individuals. Not all the individuals, but the church-community as a whole in Christ is the 'body of Christ'; it is Christ existing as church-community. It bears the sins by receiving forgiveness through the word and seeing its sins wiped out on the cross. It is by the word alone, but in doing so it has the Spirit. It is bearer of the word, its steward and its instrument. It has authority, provided it has faith in the authority of the word; it can take the sins of individuals upon itself, if it builds itself on the word of the cross, and knows itself reconciled and justified in the cross of Jesus. It has itself died and risen with Christ, and is now the *nova creatura* (new creation) in Christ. It is not merely a means to an end but also an end in itself. It is the present Christ himself, and this is why 'being in Christ' and 'being in the church-community' is the same thing; it is why Christ himself bears the sins of individuals, which are laid upon the church-community.[111]

Real Death Defined: The Feeling of its Terror and Fear

Encapsulated in his explanation of Thesis 24 of his *Heidelberg Disputation* is Luther's definition of death: 'To be born anew, one must consequently first die and then be raised up with the Son of Man. *To die, I say, means to feel death at hand.*'[112]

---

[110] *LW* 42, 9. See also Lienhard, *Luther*, 101-109.

[111] Bonhoeffer, *Sanctorum Communio*, 190.

[112] *LW* 31, 55 (emphasis mine).

At surface level, it looks as if Luther has toned down the language of death, reducing it to a mere '*feeling*' of it, rather than the '*reality*' of it all.[113] But for Luther, as for Paul, the real 'sting' of death is the way it assaults or terrifies us in soul and spirit. Thus, for him, the sinner's feeling of the terror of death is the real death. Physical expiration, as painful as it is for loved ones, is a much lesser matter. In the seventh image of evil, Luther, quoting John 8:51, 'Whoever will keep my word shall never see death,' explained, 'Because in his death he enters upon life, so that because *of the life that he sees he is not able to see death.*'[114] The agony of death is nothing but spiritual, that which goes on within the soul while a man is still alive physically. In *Lectures on Genesis* 22:11, Luther argued that Abraham '*actually*' dies seven times because he senses a mental pain over the demand to sacrifice his son Issac.[115]

> Natural death, which is the separation of the soul from the body, is simple death. But to feel death, that is, the terror and fear of death – this indeed is real death. Without fear death is not death; it is a sleep. As Christ says (John 11:26): 'He who believes in me will not see death.' For when fear has been removed, the death of the soul has been removed.[116]

The same occurs in his funeral sermon for the Elector, Duke John of Saxony, where Luther regarded the agony and suffering the Duke felt in making his confession before the Diet of Augsburg as a real death:

> We should therefore take comfort in the fact that Christ died and our beloved prince is caught up and fallen asleep in Christ's death and that he suffered a far more bitter death at Augsburg than now, a death that we are still obliged to suffer daily and incessantly from the tyrants and sectarians, and, indeed, also from our own conscience and the devil. This is the real death. The other physical death, when we pass away in bed, is only a childish death (*kindersterben*) or animal death.[117]

Another related passage is Romans 5:3, where Luther, in commenting on being baptized into Christ's death, asserted that death, in Paul's deliberation, really applies only to the death of sin and its fruit, death itself.

> The good death is the death of sin and the death of death, by which the soul is released and separated from sin and the body, is separated from corruption and through grace and glory is joined to the living God. This is death in the most proper sense of the word, for in all other forms of death something remains that is mixed with life, but not in this kind of death, where there is purest life alone, because it is eternal life. For to this kind of death alone belong in an absolute and perfect way the conditions of death, eternal nothingness, and nothing will ever return from this

---

[113] Forde, *On Being a Theologian of the Cross*, 100.

[114] *LW* 42, 142.

[115] Forde, *On Being a Theologian of the Cross*, 100.

[116] *LW* 4, 115 (emphasis mine).

[117] *LW* 51, 237-38; *WA* 43, 218, as cited in Plass (comp.), *What Luther Says*, 367, no. 1079.

> death because it truly dies an eternal death. This is the way sin dies; and likewise the sinner, when he is justified, because sin will not return again for all eternity, as the Apostle says, 'Christ will never die again,' and so forth (v. 9).[118]

God in Christ has rescued us from eternal death, that which separates us from God, and gained for us a home with God. Death, if understood properly, is a gateway to new birth, and the righteousness that avails before God. Death ends the worst of evils – sin. Sin and all of its corruptions are slain by its own fruit, death. Accordingly, the old Adam no longer twitches, but finally dies. Death evinces its deepest comfort, thereby preparing the justified sinner to be the recipient of life everlasting. 'It is not *our death*, since we have a home with the Father; but it is *the death of our sin*, the end of our imperfections.'[119] This is a good death because unlike other forms of death, where remains mixed with life still abide, nothing remains except purest, eternal life, awaiting the godly immediately beyond death. Death is the greatest blessing and greatest gain. Where, then, are death's terror and fear? For those whose lives are hid with Christ in God (Col. 3:3), there remains nothing to endure but

> a little death, yes, a sweet death, since a Christian dies after the flesh, that is, passes from unbelief to belief, from the remnants of sin to eternal righteousness, from all misery, sadness, and affliction to all the eternal joys. For all the life, all the goods, all the joys and pleasures of this world cannot make a person so happy as the ability to die with a good conscience, in the certain belief in, and comfort of, life eternal.[120]

Death as Sleep: Theological Understanding versus Topographical Understanding

As early as 1520 when the *Fourteen Consolations* appeared and as late as 1545 when he wrote *Lectures on Genesis*, Luther did not have in mind the soul–sleep theory, that the soul enjoys a disembodied existence in some underworld until the Last Day. In these places, his emphasis was not on death '*is*' sleep but death '*is called*' sleep, meaning that the terrors of death were overcome for the believer.[121] Thus, dying and going to sleep are identical. Luther admittedly accepted the dualistic definition of death as the separation of the soul from the body: 'Thus the spirit comes from the same seed as the body does and yet it can be separated from the body, but afterwards they shall again be reunited.'[122] In its disembodied existence, the soul 'sleeps' in the

---

[118] *LW* 25, 310.

[119] Bornkamm, *Luther's World of Thought*, 130 (emphasis his).

[120] *Sommerpostille* (1536), *WA* 22, 101, 10-15, as cited in Bornkamm, *Luther's World of Thought*, 130.

[121] *LW* 42, 151 (emphasis mine); *LW* 4, 314. See P.J. Secker, 'Martin Luther's Views of the State of the Dead', *Concordia Theological Monthly* 38 (1967), 422-35, for a discussion of whether the dead are literally 'asleep' until the resurrection.

[122] *WA* 39, II, 386, as cited in Althaus, *Theology of Martin Luther*, 414.

bosom of Christ as the condition between death and the resurrection. Luther is critical of the traditional doctrine of 'the intermediate state,' which speculated on the topographical condition of departed souls.[123] He moved away from topographical towards theological discussions, in which he answered the question of the condition of the souls of the dead only by reference to the word of God or of Christ. All who die in Christ have their 'place' in God and 'rest' in the 'bosom of Christ.'[124] This too is borne out in Jesus' own words, 'Whoever believes in me will never die' (John 10:26). 'So all of the fathers who lived before the birth of Christ have gone to Abraham's bosom, that is, they died firmly believing this word of God (Gen. 22:18) and they have all fallen asleep, are preserved and protected in this word and sleep in it until the Last Day as though this word were a bosom.'[125] Luther knew that all earthly measurements and concepts of time collapse at death. For this reason, the intermediate state, the distinctive period between death and the Last Day does not find full acceptance in his thinking. Time understood by us here on earth does not apply to time understood by God beyond death. In God's eyes, everything occurs at once; there is no before and after. 'Here you must put time out of your mind and know that in that world there is neither time nor a measurement of time, but everything is one eternal moment.'[126] For those who have died, the Last Day comes 'immediately' at the moment of death. 'Each of us has his own Last Day when he dies.'[127] This constitutes Luther's theological, not topographical, understanding of the state of the departed. What is noticeably absent from Luther's writings is any speculation on 'how' the one who dies in faith is with Christ: the 'that' of his being with Christ preoccupies Luther.

Resurrection and Justification as Consolation

Luther's inclusion of Christ's resurrection in his doctrine of justification by faith is significant. The intrinsic linkage between resurrection and justification is stated in his seventh image of blessing: 'Jesus Christ, rising from the dead, condemning sin and death, imputing his righteousness to us, bestowing his merits on us, and holding his hands over us.'[128] In his sermon on resurrection (1544), Luther emphasized that the resurrection must not simply be viewed as that which happens

---

[123] *LW* 4, 314ff.; *WA* 43, 361.

[124] *LW* 4, 313; *WA* 43, 361.

[125] *WA* 10, III, 191, as cited in Althaus, *Theology of the Martin Luther*, 412.

[126] *WA* 10, III, 194, as cited in Althaus, *Theology of the Martin Luther*, 416.

[127] *WA* 10, III, 194, as cited in Althaus, *Theology of the Martin Luther*, 416.

[128] *LW* 42, 165. For an exposition of Luther's understanding of the resurrection, see D. Scaer, 'Luther's Concept of the Resurrection in His Commentary on I Corinthians 15', *Concordia Theological Quarterly* 47 (1993), 109-24; A.C. Thiselton, 'Luther and Barth in I Corinthians 15: Six Theses for Theology in Relation to Recent Interpretation', in W.P. Stephens (ed.), *The Bible, the Reformation and the Church: Essays in Honour of James Atkinson* (Sheffield: Sheffield Academic Press, 1995), 258-89; G. Sauter, 'Luther on the Resurrection', in Wengert (ed.), *Harvesting Martin Luther's Reflections*, 99-118.

in history, but that which happens for me (*pro me*).[129] Just as the cross happens for me, so the resurrection happens for me. Consequently Christ's resurrection, in a joyous exchange, is ours by faith. The Easter message is given not just to inform us of the history and event *per se*, but is given to us, since Christ dies and rises for our good. 'The resurrection of Christ should serve us as well as his suffering, since both happened for our sake.'[130] In this resurrection image are found the eternal and heavenly blessings, which we now receive solely by faith, but which will be visible and tangible on the Last Day:

> Thus we see another picture at Easter, that no sin, no curse, no disgrace, no death, but only life, grace, blessedness, and righteousness are in Christ. With such a picture we should lift up our hearts. For it is put before us and presented in such a way, that we should receive nothing else than this, that God has himself awakened us today along with Christ. For as little as you see sin, death, and the curse in Christ, so you should also believe that God, for Christ's sake, will see these in you, when you receive his resurrection for yourself and receive its consolation. Such grace faith brings to us. When that day will come, however, one will no longer believe, but will see, touch, and feel.[131]

The manner in which Luther offered resurrection as a source of consolation is intriguing. The offering of consolation is causally connected with the confession of Christ made by the deceased. This is apparent in a letter to Matthias Knützsen and his wife, Magdalena (1531), where Luther assured them that their son, who has Christ as the object of his faith, is safe in Christ.

> So also you, when you have grieved and cried in measure, comfort yourselves again, indeed thank God with joy, that your son has had such a good end. For he has fallen asleep in Christ, so that there can be no doubt that he must be sweetly and softly sleeping in the eternal rest of Christ. For everyone marveled at the great grace expressed in his prayer and the confession of Christ, in which he remained firm until the end.[132]

However, for Luther, peaceful 'rest' in God is not consolation enough. Perfect consolation is found in the awakening to come. This is indicated by the very word 'sleep,' referring to those who lie down, but are not bereft of all hope of rising

---

[129] *WA* 10, I, 2, 214, 12-16, as cited in G.S. Krispin, 'A Study in Luther's Pastoral Theology', *Logia* 10 (2001), 13-19 (15). The same article also appears as 'The Consolation of the Resurrection in Luther', *Lutheran Theological Review* 2 (1989–90), 37-51 (44).

[130] *WA* 52, *Hauspostille*, 1544, '*Erst Predigt am heyligen Ostertag*', 253, 14-28, as cited in Krispin, 'Study in Luther's Pastoral Theology', 16.

[131] *WA* 52, 250, 37-251, 6.

[132] *WABr* 6, no. 1876, 212-13, 12-19, as cited in Krispin, 'Study in Luther's Pastoral Theology', 13.

again.[133] With this hope, Luther assured the bereaved parents of the certainty of seeing their dearly missed son again:

> The Lord and highest comforter, Jesus Christ, who has loved your son more than you, who had earnestly called him to himself through his word and now has requested him to himself away from you, comfort and strengthen you with grace until that day, on which you will again see your son in eternal life.[134]

The whole weight of the Christian faith is wrapped up in this confession of Christ, specifically the risen Christ, who has overcome death and the grave. The risen Christ is the basis of consolation given to us. In Christ, death and the grave have been vanquished, and all of their horrors are but empty threats for the believer. Appealing to Paul in 1 Corinthians 15, Luther consoled his dying mother:

> In the same way St. Paul also glories and mocks the terrors of death: death is swallowed up in victory: death, where is your victory? Hell, where is your sting? You can terrify and agitate like a wooden death-mask, but you do not have the power to murder. For your victory, sting, and power are swallowed up in Christ's victory; you may bare your teeth, but you cannot devour me. For God has given us the victory over you in Jesus Christ our Lord, to whom be praise and thanks, Amen.[135]

Luther also drew consolation from the resurrection after the painful loss of his fourteen-year-old daughter Magdalena on 20 September 1542. At the moment when the coffin was sealed, Luther cried out, 'Hammer away! On doomsday she'll rise again.'[136] In language reminiscent of his explanation of the fourth of his *Ninety-Five Theses* (1517), 'If a person's whole life is one of repentance and a cross of Christ ... then it is evident that the cross continues until death and thereby to entrance into the kingdom,' Luther, in baptismal language, spoke of Magdalena's death as an entrance into the kingdom of Christ.[137] In a letter to Justin Jonas two days later, Luther, still grieving, declared his hope:

> I believe that the rumour has informed you, that my very precious daughter Magdalena has been born anew to the eternal kingdom of Christ, and although I and my wife should only say joyous thanks for such a happy departure and blessed end, through which she has escaped the power of the flesh, the world, the Turk and the

133 *LW* 28, 109-110.

134 *WABr* 6, no: 1876, 213, 22-27, as cited in Krispin, 'Study in Luther's Pastoral Theology', 18.

135 *WABr* VI, no. 1631, 105, 60-67, as cited in Nebe, *Luther as Spiritual Advisor*, 235; Krispin, 'Consolation of the Resurrection', 40.

136 *WATr* 5, 193-94, as cited in George, *Theology of the Reformers*, 105.

137 *LW* 31, 89: *WA* 1, 534.

> devil, the strength of natural love is so great, that we are unable to do so without the sobbing and groaning of the heart, indeed, without great mortification.[138]

The Christ who consoles the bereaved in their loss, and consoles Luther in his own bereavement, is the same who finally consoles Luther in his last hour. He, too, partook of the consolation of Christ's resurrection. Luther gently rebuked his anxious wife Kathy:

> Leave me alone with your worry. I have a better comforter than you and all the angels. He lies in the manger and at the breast of a virgin, but at the same time sits at the right hand of God the almighty Father. Therefore be at peace! Amen.[139]

Luther's doctrine of the justification through Christ's cross and resurrection is the abiding presupposition of his existence, the very basis of his consolation. Undoubtedly, he entered his grave standing firm upon the same faith with which he consoled himself and others. On 18 February 1546, early in the morning, he screamed out, 'Oh, dear God! My pain is so great! Oh dear Dr. Jonas, I am certain that I will remain here in Eisleben where I was born and baptized.'[140] Those attending Luther at his deathbed comforted him with the constant repetition of the words, 'For God so loved the world that he gave his only begotten Son ... ' Jonas, having observed that Luther was near his last breath, intervened: 'Do you want to die standing firm on Christ and the doctrine you have taught?' To which Luther replied in a loud voice, 'Yes,' and the Reformer passed into glory. This explains why the Reformer stressed that it suffices to meditate on this victorious image alone – the king of glory, for in it lies only good, nevertheless 'the greatest good.'[141] The power of Luther's doctrine of justification here and now consequently calls for the final liberation of the world from sin and misery. For the Reformer, the end of sin requires a quantitative change – divine intervention that will put an end to sin, which eventually overcomes the fearful wrath of God (*dies irae*), the 'Day of the Wrath' of the Middle Ages.[142] Proclamation must include Christ's resurrection and the goods it delivers, namely, the present consolation and the certainty of an eternal hope. From the throne, the resurrected Christ continues to be active through his Spirit, who inculcates in the believer's heart that he is the recipient of the treasure of salvation. Resurrection accentuates the claim that God cannot negate himself, and thus cannot abandon the justified to death. In Luther's own words:

---

[138] *WABr* 10, 149, 20-150, 25, as cited in Krispin, 'Study in Luther's Pastoral Theology', 14.

[139] *WABr* 11, no. 4201, 186-87, as cited in Krispin, 'Consolation of Resurrection', 43.

[140] Luther's near-death account is cited in J.M. Kittelson, *Luther the Reformer: The Story of the Man and his Career* (Minneapolis: Augsburg, 1986), 297.

[141] *LW* 42, 143.

[142] See Althaus, *Theology of Martin Luther*, 419-21.

> Therefore see, my beloved, what the resurrection of Christ wants to create and produce in us, namely that we should not be afraid, but should recognize and glory in Christ as our brother, to console ourselves as heirs of the kingdom, which he has put before us ... God grants us his Holy Spirit through Christ, that we should truly comfort ourselves with such a resurrection and increase such faith, confidence, and hope from day to day, finally to be saved thereby. Amen.[143]

God as Hidden and Revealed

Although the Reformer's emphasis is on God as revealed, he never abandoned the doctrine of God as hidden and the paradoxical concept of the God who smites in order to enliven. In considering the image of the damned, Luther held out the image of the hidden God (*deus absconditus*), who might deliver creatures to temptation (*Anfechtung*) and evil, and who is capable of damning the sinner.[144] Integral to Luther's theology is a revelation of anything but salvation, that is, God's impassible and inscrutable wrath, before which we are terrified. Yet the reflection upon this God must not be done apart from Christ, the revealed God (*deus revelatus*). For Luther, the negative aspects of the hidden God and of the law are not the same. The hidden God truly condemns the sinner to hell as the sinner's ultimate end (*telos*), whereas the law sends the sinner to hell as its alien work in order that he might be raised up as the proper work of the gospel. The distinction between God as hidden and as revealed parallels the distinction between the law and the gospel, however, only insofar as the hidden God condemns so that we might cleave to God as he is revealed in mercy. The annihilating knowledge of the hidden God is useful, causally useful, if it causes the sinner to flee from its inscrutable terror into the immeasurable grace of God as revealed in Christ. The gospel occurs within this distinction, that God as hidden incites in us terror and despair of self-justification under the law, at which point God works faith in us. Not until we reach the point of utter helplessness are we prepared to receive God's grace. Friedrich Mildenberger discovers in Luther the proper time and place at which God creates faith, thereby taking faith completely out of human control:

> [W]e receive God's salvation in Christ only when we are past the point of being able to do anything. At this point, the point at which we are unable to do anything for ourselves, the Holy Spirit works faith. This kind of faith, therefore, comes only at a specific time and place. The time and place at which we experience temptation is the time and place at which God wills to create the faith which is God's own work in us.[145]

---

[143] *WA* 52, 259, 11-23, as cited in Krispin, 'Consolation of Resurrection', 45, n. 26.

[144] *LW* 42, 157.

[145] F. Mildenberger, *Theology of Lutheran Confessions* (trans. E. Lueker; Philadelphia: Fortress Press, 1986), 41.

The distinction between God as hidden and God as revealed constitutes for Luther a paradox, by virtue of which even in God's hiddenness in the incarnate Christ he remains the divinely unsearchable and impassible majesty in whose presence we would be annihilated if we did not take refuge in the love of God who has appeared in Christ. Under temptation before God as hidden, says Gerrish, 'faith really does take into itself something of the meaning of God's hiddenness even though it is not directed against that hiddenness: rather, it is a movement away from the hidden God.'[146] The forbidding image of God as hidden 'waits on the edge of faith and, for this reason, determines (in some measure) the content of faith, which has the character of a turning away from the hidden God' to God as revealed, the God with whom we have to do.[147] The haunting specter of a terrifying yet hidden God is confirmed but more crucially conquered in the gospel, 'for those who believe' (Rom. 1:16-17). As Forde puts it, 'The fact is that the terror of the absolute God reigns until the proclamation that creates faith announces its end and liberates the believer from it.'[148] It is only in Christ by whom God is revealed that the contradiction between the hiddenness and revelation of God becomes clear and is finally resolved by faith.[149] With this in mind, Luther advised the troubled Elector Frederick to consider the image of God as hidden, that is, by putting himself in the miserable place of the damned, to feel their terror so that he might be effectively persuaded to praise God's wonderful mercy in preserving him from such evils. For those who believe, when they are afflicted with spiritual temptations, there is nothing to do except to cleave to the revelation of God through Christ. This is the beauty of Luther's treatise, that what is perceived as evil ends up as a blessing, that sufferings of all kinds may be transformed into blessings, when seen in a proper light.

---

[146] B. Gerrish, '"To the Unknown God": Luther and Calvin on the Hiddenness of God', *Journal of Religion* 53 (1973), 263-92 (291).

[147] Gerrish, '"To the Unknown God"'.

[148] Forde, *Theology is for Proclamation*, 29-30.

[149] For further discussion of the hidden and revealed God, see D. Steinmetz, *Luther in Context* (Grand Rapids: Baker, 2nd edn, 2002), 23-31; Lienhard, *Luther*, 260-66; E. Grislis, 'Luther's View of the Hidden God', *McCormick Quarterly* 21 (1967–68), 81-94; Ngien, *Suffering of God according to Martin Luther's 'Theologia Crucis'*, 121-33.

CHAPTER 4

Sacramental Piety: 'Do unto Me according to Thy Words'

Luther's sermon on the *Worthy Reception of the Sacrament* (1521) was preached not long after he was pronounced a full-fledged heretic.[1] It was borne out of a pastoral concern for a proper understanding of the Lord's Supper. Luther steered away from polemical controversy on the Eucharist to focus on the practical way of approaching the sacrament of the altar.[2] The question that confronted Luther was not the theological meaning of Christ's words 'This is my body,' which he inscribed with chalk at the Marburg Colloquy, and which generated division among the Reformers themselves. The objective presence of Christ's body and blood in the bread and wine, a doctrine so central to Luther's theology, was not discussed here. Hence the doctrine of the communication of properties (*communicatio idiomatum*), that which separates Luther from Zwingli and others, did not surface.[3] Driven solely by pastoral concerns for God's people, Luther made mention of the prevalent lay abuse of the sacrament, the root of which was to be found in the improper reception of it, as some partook purely out of obedience to the Church, or habit, or belief in the attainment of righteousness by works. He led God's people away from such abuse into what he regarded as a worthy or proper reception of the sacrament. For him, a sacrament is to be recognized by both its content, the same content that the gospel has – the

---

[1] *LW* 42, 169-77. The papal bull *Exsurge, Domine* was issued on 15 June 1520. For a detailed account of the bull, see J. Mackinnon, *Luther and the Reformation* (London: Longmans, Green, 1928), vol. 2, 192-221. Regarding the difficulty of publishing the bull in Germany, see E.G. Schwiebert, *Luther and His Times* (St. Louis: Concordia, 1950), 484-85.

[2] For a historical study of Luther's Eucharistic controversy, see M. Brecht, *Martin Luther: Shaping and Defining the Reformation 1521–1532* (trans. J.L. Schaaf; Minneapolis: Fortress Press, 1990), 293-334. For a systematic analysis of Luther's contention for the real bodily presence, see H. Sasse, *This Is My Body* (Minneapolis: Augsburg, 1959).

[3] For a discussion of Luther's usage of the doctrine of *communicatio idiomatum*, see my 'Chalcedonian Christology and Beyond'. Luther retained the traditional interpretation, that the properties of Christ's two natures are communicated to the *concretum* of his person. But he went beyond it, affirming a real communication between the two natures. The logic of his usage of this doctrine enabled Luther to move beyond the Chalcedonian understanding of Christology, and also set him apart from the Reformed tradition.

forgiveness of sin – and its external form in which God is present and active. Rather than viewing the sacrament as a work which we must do in order to achieve our righteous standing before God (*coram deo*), Luther saw it purely as a gift of God, to be received by faith. Worthy reception consisted in recognizing one's sinfulness and desiring divine forgiveness. The mass is a sign of God's testament in which God pledges us his grace and bestows upon us – his appointed heirs – the inheritance that he has promised through the efficacious act of a dying man, himself. The promise is effective, since it emanates from God and points to him, and, in this sense, is to be grasped purely by a personal act of faith, not by any human accretions – works, powers, or merits. Faith receives the precious gift – the forgiveness of sin, the exchange of Christ's righteousness for our sinfulness. Luther's view of the justifying word as God's action permeates this sermon. Although it was devoid of polemics and Aristotelian metaphysics, it was not devoid of the major constituents of Luther's theology of the Lord's Supper. It is an illustration of how Luther's sacramental theology informs the piety and shapes the religious life of the congregation. Luther's writings on the same subject will form the basis of my exposition, and help elucidate what has been taught in this concise, but compact sermon.

Sacrament as a Searching Event

Not only is the sacrament a sacred event where the communicants receive with joy the divine word of promise, it is also a searching event which invites all to examine themselves so as to avoid receiving the sacrament unworthily. Luther had in mind the 'commandment' mentioned in 1 Corinthians 11:28-29, which forbade the sacrament to those who openly lived in rebellion against God.[4] The unruly should not receive it because of their contempt for its forgiving power. The Church's command that all should receive the sacrament does not apply to those who willfully harbor evil within themselves. 'It is better to obey God's command than that of the Church (Acts 5:29). It is better to refrain from receiving the sacrament than to receive it and thereby sin against God's commandment, which forbids the holy sacrament to such sinners.'[5] The Church's command or the communicants' habitual practice are not legitimate criteria for a proper reception of the sacrament because there may be a lack of good will and longing in the hearts of those who freely come, or they may be driven to partake of it primarily by horror or dread. Along with Augustine, Luther held that 'the sacrament seeks a hungry, thirsty, and desirous soul which yearns for it.'[6] Those who yearn for the sacrament do not wait for a command, nor are they moved by precept or habit, but, impelled by their need, they fix their minds only on the sacrament, which their hearts desire. This means that only a minority receives it worthily, since many come only in obedience to the Church or

[4] *LW* 42, 171.

[5] *LW* 42, 171.

[6] Augustine, *Preaching on Psalm 21* (*Enarratio in psalmos xxi*), as cited in *LW* 42, 171, n. 3.

out of habit. Luther substantiated his argument by way of an analogy drawn from nature:

> There must be hunger and thirst for this food and drink; otherwise harm is sure to follow. The same is true in nature. When your body is sated and filled, and yet you partake of a plentiful and rich meal, this is bound to end in sickness and death. But if your body is hungry and thirsty, such a meal will make you cheerful, healthy, and strong.[7]

The Hunger for God Precedes the Church's Precept

Luther faulted the pope for failing in his duty to instill spiritual hunger and thirst in those who would receive the sacrament, while commanding indiscriminate reception of the sacrament.[8] So approaching the sacrament purely as a sign of obedience to the Church turns the pope's command into an evil and harmful one. Such a command should be discarded until our hunger constrains us to draw near to the sacrament. Conversely this hunger so constrains us to come that there is no need of any commandment, even the pope's. 'After all, the sacrament – even God himself – can bestow nothing on you against your will. Since God's gifts are so great, they demand a great hunger and desire, but they avoid and flee from a forced and unwilling heart.'[9] Here we observe in Luther an Augustinian version of divine–human interaction in sanctification. For Augustine, a proper doctrine of sanctification involves a concurrence of God's provision and the believer's participation. This Augustine asserted, 'Without God we cannot; without us God will not.' 'It is he who makes us will what is good ... it is he who makes us act by supplying efficacious power to our will.'[10] Sanctification, then, results from God's initiative of grace to which is joined the diligence of the believer. Although the initiative in sanctification lies with God, the believer's diligence in willing and working is also necessary.

The Creation of Spiritual Hunger by Means of the Law

But how could such hunger and thirst be generated? Certainly not by human compulsion or any humanly devised means, but by a revelation of who we really are before God (*coram deo*). This, too, is God's work. Nevertheless, it is an alien work (*alienum opus*) which he performs by putting us under the law so that we might thereby see our wretched condition and feel the need to be liberated from it as God's

---

[7] *LW* 42, 172.
[8] *LW* 42, 172.
[9] *LW* 42, 172.
[10] See Augustine, *On Grace and Free Will* 17.32.

proper work (*proprium opus*).[11] God first performs an alien work by the law in order to achieve his proper work by the gospel. God wants to kill us by the law in such a way that we may be humbled and acknowledge our need for God's mercy and Christ's blessing. Thus the annihilating knowledge of God revealed in the law is causally useful, if and when it causes us to cleave to the arms of Christ. God's proper work is only established and revealed through his alien work. God's assuring 'yes' is hidden in his severe 'no,' and only through faith can the believer perceive this. The contrasting ways in which God deals with us are integral to Luther's theology of the cross. Vercryusse explained:

> It is through his visible and apparent *opus alienum* (alien work), consisting of sorrow and tribulation, and also of judgement, wrath, death, and evil ... in brief, consisting of the cross, that God brings a man to his real, invisible, true work, the rejoicing and pacifying justification, yet not revealed, but hidden *sub contrario* (under the opposites), within the storm of his *opus alienum*. This is, however, only understood by the believer ... [whose] life ... consists in faith, that is, in the cross and sufferings.[12]

Both ways of working are practiced by 'the same God who works everything in everyone' (1 Cor. 12:6).[13] God works in these contradictory activities: the alien work and the proper work, the former leading to the latter. In the alien work, God judges us and inspires us with the terrors of death, pain, and hell so that we might experience his grace as his proper work. He does this not in order that we might be condemned forever, but that we might long for godliness and thus be prepared for a proper reception of the sacrament. 'This [hunger] happens,' Luther elaborated, 'when you recognize that you are weak in faith, cold in love, faint in hope. You will find that you are disposed toward hatred and impatience, impurity, greed, and whatever other vice there is.'[14] God reveals our sins in order to create in us an awareness of our need for forgiveness. The revelation of sins by means of God's commandment and the believer's willing resolve to get rid of them and longing for godliness constitute for Luther the beginning of a hunger and thirst that are pleasing to God. 'Then a man no longer heeds the Church's command but is happy that he can partake of the sacrament because of his own urging and need, without any command or demand.'[15] To Luther, the pope and all the priests, by their emphasis 'only' on the command of the Church, have robbed the people of joy and freedom, thus causing harm to Christendom. Instead, Church leaders should implant in the people the importance of recognizing their spiritual needs, and leave their own commands aside,

[11] For a major study of law and gospel, see T. McDonough, *The Law and the Gospel: A Study of Martin Luther's Confessional Writings* (Oxford: Oxford University Press, 1963).

[12] J.E. Vercruysse, 'Luther's Theology of the Cross at the Time of the *Heidelberg Disputation*', *Gregorianum* 57 (1976), 523-48 (530).

[13] See *LW* 33, 175-79: *WA* 18, 709, 28-30, where Luther discusses how God's omnipotence can be said to work evil, without attributing evil acts to God.

[14] *LW* 42, 172.

[15] *LW* 42, 173.

thus giving everybody the freedom to come joyfully to the Eucharist. And the greater the intensity of this desire is in us, the better fitted are we to receive the sacrament as a remedy. Thus believers should seek the sacrament precisely for their betterment when they find themselves driven by the flesh, enticed by the world, and assailed by Satan. In the same vein, in another sermon preached on the same subject (1528), Luther declared,

> The need (which drives us to the sacrament) is that sin, the devil, and death are always present. The benefit is that we receive forgiveness of sins and the Holy Spirit. Here, not poison, but a remedy and salvation is given, in so far as you acknowledge that you need it. Don't say: I am not fit today, I will wait a while. This is a trick of the devil. What will you do if you are not fit when death comes? Who will make you fit then? Say rather: Neither preacher, prince, pope, nor emperor compels me, but my great need and, beyond this, the benefit.[16]

The Constitution of a Sacrament

Paragraph 7 of the *Worthy Acceptance of the Sacrament* clearly defines the three features which make up a sacrament: the word of promise of divine forgiveness, a material sign, and institution by Christ. In Luther's words: 'I am referring to the *words* Christ spoke when he *instituted the mass*: "Take, *eat*, this is *my body* which is given for you. Take, *drink*, all of you; for it is the *cup* of the *new and eternal testament* in *my blood*, poured out *for you and for all for the forgiveness of sins*" (Matt. 26:26-28).'[17] These words are studied fully in his *Babylonian Captivity of the Church* (1520), written about a year before this sermon.[18] A sacrament consists of the word of promise accompanied by a material sign instituted by Christ and a material sign accompanied by the word of promise. A sign or a symbol by itself does not constitute a sacrament, unless it is combined with 'the word, which is a heavenly, holy word which no one can sufficiently extol, for it contains and conveys all the fullness of God.'[19] In his *Large Catechism* (1529), Luther quoted Augustine with approval: 'From the word it derives its nature as a sacrament, as St. Augustine taught, "*Accedat verbum ad elementum et fit sacramentum*" [When the word is attached to the element, it is a sacrament]. This means that, when the word is added to the element or the natural substance, it becomes a sacrament, that is, a holy, divine thing and sign.'[20] So where the word of promise is missing, as in marriage or confirmation, there is no sacrament, even when the characteristic of a sign is present. Luther explained, 'in every sacrament there is a word of divine promise, to be

[16] *LW* 51, 192-93; cf. *LW* 42, 177.

[17] *LW* 42, 173.

[18] *LW* 36, 5-8.

[19] 'The Large Catechism, 1529', in *BC*, 438.

[20] Augustine, *Tractate* 80, on John 3, as cited in Luther's 'The Large Catechism', in *BC*, 438.

believed by whoever receives the sign, and that the sign alone cannot be a sacrament ... but figures or allegories are not sacraments, in the sense in which we use the term.'[21] The sacraments are only a distinct type of the word, and their content is the same as that of the gospel: the message of forgiveness. In contrast, where the material sign is wanting, as in prayer, hearing and meditating on the word and the cross, and penance, to which God has attached a promise, sacramental status is missing. Sacraments may be recognized by God-ordained, external signs in which God is present and active. Therefore, strictly speaking, Luther accepted only baptism and the Lord's Supper as sacraments, because they possess both a sign and the word of promise, namely, the forgiveness of sins.[22]

The Lord's Supper is an outward form in which the word comes to us. This form takes on a guarantee, a pledge, and a seal of God's promise as its unique nature and peculiar significance.[23] The forgiveness of sins is the real gift of the sacrament, and Christ's body and blood are a 'sure pledge and sign' which assures us of it.[24] The very purpose of the sacrament is to nourish faith, and help it in its struggles with sins and all kinds of vices. Luther expanded on this elsewhere:

> Now we come to its power and benefit, the purpose for which the sacrament was really instituted, for it is most necessary that we know what we should seek and obtain there. This is plainly evident from the words just quoted, 'This is my body and blood, given and poured out *for you* for the forgiveness of sins.' In other words, we go to the sacrament because we receive there a great treasure, through and in which we obtain the forgiveness of sins. Why? Because the words are there through which this is imparted! Christ bids me eat and drink in order that the sacrament may be mine and may be a source of blessing to me as a sure pledge and sign – indeed, as the very gift he has provided for me against my sins, death, and all evils.[25]

The Trinitarian Form of the Eucharist

So when we are driven by spiritual hunger and prepared to come to the Eucharist, we do so not trusting in our own worthiness but trusting solely on the efficacious power of 'His word and work.'[26] Faith lays hold of 'the intent and content' of the words of Christ, namely, that Christ's body and blood are given *for us* as our priceless treasure and gift, and that we are appointed by him as heirs of God's grace and favor for eternal life.[27]

---

[21] *LW* 36, 92.

[22] *LW* 36, 124. Cf. Bornkamm, *Luther's World of Thought*, 100-101.

[23] *WA* 2, 694, 692, 686. *WA* 7, 323; *LW* 32, 15. *WA* 10, III, 142, as cited in Althaus, *Theology of Martin Luther*, 346.

[24] 'The Large Catechism', in *BC*, 449.

[25] 'The Large Catechism', in *BC*, 449.

[26] *LW* 42, 175.

[27] *LW* 42, 175.

Just as the gospel is prior to the church, so faith is prior to the sacrament. This treasure is communicated to the believer in no other way than through Christ's own words, 'given and poured out for you', the 'sweet' and 'blessed' sacramental words spoken by the priest in Christ's stead to all who stand around him. We embrace these words of Christ, placing our trust in them and not doubting that we are indeed his guests at the table. God has given us the Holy Spirit who applies to us this treasure of salvation, gives faith to our hearts, and brings us to Christ to receive God's richest blessings, which we could not obtain by ourselves. Luther's trinitarian formulation of the Lord's Supper, which receives elaboration later in both his catechisms and the *Confession*, is already latent in this sermon:

> Faith creates godliness and drives out all sin, grants strength in sickness, enlightens in all blindness, heals all evil inclinations, guards against sin, and performs every good deed. Indeed, the fruit of such faith is that never can there remain any frailty; for in faith the Holy Spirit is given, and thereby a man loves God because of the abundant goodness received from him, becomes cheerful and glad to do all that is good without compulsion of law and command.[28]

In his gospel sermon preached on a Pentecost Sunday in 1522, Luther spoke of the work of the Holy Spirit in relation to the word and the community of the word. Luther expressly stated,

> It is a faithful saying that Christ has accomplished everything, has removed sin and overcome every enemy, so that through him we are lords over all things. But the treasure lies yet in one pile; it is not yet distributed nor invested. Consequently, if we are to possess it, the *Holy Spirit must come and teach our hearts to believe and say*: I, too, am one of those who are to have this treasure.[29]

The interplay of the Holy Spirit and the word is also stated in his *Large Catechism*, that the God who came to us in Christ is the same God who comes as the Holy Spirit. Just as apart from Christ we know nothing but a terrifying, inscrutable, and impassible deity so, apart from the Holy Spirit, Christ's work and word remain hidden, and his blessings in richest measure would have been in vain or lost. The Holy Spirit's work is to mediate Christ's work to us, to do his work, and remind us of his efficacious words. God's fatherly heart is mirrored in the Son and revealed

---

[28] *LW* 42, 175.

[29] See 'Gospel Sermon, Pentecost Sunday', in J.N. Lenker (ed.), *Luther's Church Postil: Pentecost or Missionary Sermons* (6 vols; Minneapolis: Lutherans in All Lands, 1907), vol. 12, 279, no. 16. For Luther's view of the Holy Spirit, see E. Herms, *Luthers Auslegung des Dritten Artikels* (Tübingen: Mohr, 1987); A. Carlson, 'Luther and the Doctrine of the Holy Spirit', *Lutheran Quarterly* 11 (1959), 135-46; Won, 'Work of the Holy Spirit'; V.-M. Kärkkäinen, 'The Holy Spirit and Justification: The Ecumenical Significance of Luther's Doctrine of Salvation', *Pneuma: The Journal of the Society for Pentecostal Studies* 24 (2002), 26-39.

through the Holy Spirit. God works in full unity with himself as the one and same God of the gospel, but in a threefold self-giving.

Luther expressed this more fully in his *Confession*, which is trinitarian in structure and substance:

> There are three persons and one God who has given himself to us all wholly and completely, with all that he is and has. The Father gives himself to us, with heaven and earth and all the creatures, in order that they may serve us and benefit us. But this gift becomes obscured and useless through Adam's fall. Therefore the Son himself subsequently gave himself and bestowed all his works, sufferings, wisdom, and righteousness, and reconciled us to the Father, in order that, restored to life and righteousness, we might also know and have the Father and his gifts.
>
> But because this grace would benefit no one if it remained so profoundly hidden and could not come to us, the Holy Spirit comes and gives himself also, wholly and completely. He teaches us to understand this deed of Christ which has been manifested to us, helps us receive and preserve it, use it to our advantage and impart it to others, increase and extend it. He does it both inwardly and outwardly – inwardly by means of faith and other spiritual gifts, outwardly through the gospel, baptism, and *the sacrament of the altar*, through which as through three means or methods he comes to us and inculcates the sufferings of Christ for the benefit of our salvation.[30]

As trinitarian, the whole *Confession* speaks not of three different gifts from God, but rather of God's threefold giving of himself as the one act in the economy of our salvation. The God with whom we have to do is the triune God of the Nicene Creed, an ever-present and active God, not an aloof and impassible one.[31] God continues to work causatively through the created forms, that is, the sacrament of the altar, to effect his saving will, and to recreate us through the visible words in the image of the One whose innocence we receive with joy in exchange for our sinfulness. Speaking of the peculiar function of Holy Spirit, Luther asserted,

> The Creation is past and redemption is accomplished, but the Holy Spirit carries his work unceasingly until the last day. For this purpose he has appointed a community on earth, through which he speaks and does all his work. For he has not yet gathered together all his Christian people, nor has he completed the granting of forgiveness. Therefore we believe in him who daily brings us into this community through the word, and imparts, increases, and strengthens faith through the same word and the forgiveness of sins.[32]

---

[30] *LW* 37, 366.

[31] See T.F. Torrance, *The Trinitarian Faith: The Evangelical Theology of the Ancient Catholic Church* (Edinburgh: T&T Clark, 1988), 115.

[32] 'The Large Catechism', 419, in *BC*, 419. Cf. 'The Small Catechism', in *BC*, 345, as cited in J.E. Strohl, 'Luther's Spiritual Journey', in D.K. McKim (ed.) *The Cambridge Companion to Martin Luther* (Cambridge: Cambridge University Press, 2003), 149-64

The Efficacy of God's Word

In his *Small Catechism* (1529), Luther emphasized the fact that the words of Christ's institution of the Eucharist are the principal point of the sacrament. Just as the water of baptism is effective only through God's word, so it is not the eating and drinking of the eucharistic elements that are effective but the words 'for you' and 'for the forgiveness of sins.'[33] Both baptism and the sacrament of the altar proclaim the promise of grace and the forgiveness of sins. In both instances, the majesty of the word of God reigns.[34] The power and worth of the sacrament lie primarily in the words of Christ which we take to heart. The sacraments therefore are not efficacious in themselves, that is, in being celebrated, but in being believed – this too is to be attributed to God's initiative and grace. God's grace then is active by creating in us, through the law, his alien work, hunger for a proper reception of the sacrament. God's prior act in the sacraments precedes faith, calls to faith and establishes it so that we possess it. Central to Luther's teaching is the dogmatic assertion that justification comes not from the sacrament itself but from the faith that it arouses in us. Faith grasps the benefits Christ has acquired for us, which are communicated to us through the sweet, blessed and majestic words of Christ in the mass. For the gift of Christ's body and blood is a sign which assures us of the promise of God's forgiveness, the very content of the sacrament and the gospel. As Augustine had taught so Luther defined the sign of the sacraments as more than merely symbols of a heavenly reality. He claimed that God had determined to use certain elements of the created order as the vehicles through which he exercised his recreative power to save and restore sinners to himself, effecting in us the joyous exchange of Christ's righteousness for our sinfulness.[35] The created form of the Eucharist is for Luther an instrument of divine power. Therefore the Eucharist does not merely *signify* forgiveness of sins and eternal life but actually *effects* them, if only we believe. 'The sacrament is nothing without the word. It has no other content and no other effect than the word of promise does.'[36]

So the ground of the efficacy of the sacrament is the causative word of God, which conveys the grace of Christ. The Lord's Supper is not a propitiatory sacrifice offered to God, and thus is not effective '*ex opera operato*' – 'on account of the work

---

(156). V.-M. Kärkkäinen, *Pneumatology: The Holy Spirit in Ecumenical, International, and Contextual Perspective* (Grand Rapids: Baker, 2002), 82-84; Lohse, *Martin Luther's Theology*, 234-35, where he boldly states that 'with this constant reference to Christ the Holy Spirit assumed an extraordinarily important place in Luther's Theology.' Kärkkäinen comments on Lohse's statement, 'The accuracy of this statement also has a wider context, namely, that for Luther there was not a single doctrine in all theology in which the activity of the Spirit was not fundamental. The Spirit's work and activity cannot be limited to the spheres of faith and church alone' (82-83).

[33] 'The Small Catechism', in *BC*, 349 and 352.

[34] *LW* 40, 23; *WA* 12, 182.

[35] R. Kolb, *Teaching God's Children His Teaching: A Guide for the Study of Luther's Catechism* (Hutchinson: Crown, 1992), ch. 6, 1.

[36] Althaus, *Theology of Martin Luther*, 346.

that is done.' It is grounded objectively in the word of God, irrespective of the merits or demerits of the presiding priest. So it is not effective '*ex opera operantis*' – 'on account of the work of the one who works.'[37] The sacramental causality lies not in the worthiness of the administrant, but solely in the majesty of God's word. In his *On the Councils and the Church* (1539), Luther asserted with audacity that 'even if Judas, Caiaphas, Pilate, the pope, or the devil himself baptized truly, they [God's people] would still receive the true, holy baptism [the sacrament of altar is included].'[38]

In a similar way, as the assurances of God's promises, sacraments are completely independent of the recipient's disposition. For example, gold jewelry, even when worn by a harlot, still retains its purity. Worthy reception of the sacrament is not based on anything we do or bring, including our good works, prayers or fasting, but on the truth and strength of God's words. Luther hailed the words of Christ's institution, and wished that the presiding minister would utter them not 'softly' as was the usual practice but 'shout them (so) loudly' that everyone present would hear them clearly, hold them near and dear to themselves, and fix their minds on them above all else.[39] Both the priest, by his elevation of the elements, and the bell-ringer, when he rings the sanctus bell, work together to give way to the words of Christ, with which the communicants satisfy their spiritual hunger and rely on the truth of the divine promise.

Thus, according to Luther, those who taught that to be a worthy recipient of the sacrament communicants should be 'perfectly pure' had deviated from 'a proper path.'[40] 'Fear and desire cannot exist side by side. Thus they [those who taught the wrong path] hindered us with the very means by which they thought to advance us.'[41] The sacrament was instituted to purify us and help us against sin and ought to attract us with joy and longing. Those who wait to receive the sacrament until they have already perfected themselves no longer have need of any sacramental help. That, for Luther, is like someone being invited to a splendid banquet who had gorged and swilled before going to the feast, in which case all the fine dishes would be served to him in vain. This is an insult to the host. However, those who are weak and frail but desire forgiveness and godliness are worthy of the meal, and are the ones whom the Lord does not cast away. 'God neither wants to nor will he grant this grace to those who were forced, pressed, and driven to the sacrament by commandment and law, but only to hearts that long and pine and thirst for it, to hearts that come voluntarily.' 'Nor does [the Lord] issue a command or compel anyone to go to the sacrament, but rather he kindly invites and encourages all who are sinners and find

[37] See A.E. McGrath, *Christian Theology: An Introduction* (Oxford: Blackwell, 3rd edn, 2001), 515; T.G. Tappert, 'Meaning and Practice in the Reformation', in Martin E. Lehmann (ed.), *Meaning and Practice of the Lord's Supper* (Philadelphia: Muhlenberg, 1961), 88-102 (92); Sasse, *This is My Body*, 83-84.

[38] *LW* 41, 218; *WA* 51, 521, as cited in George, *Theology of the Reformers*, 93.

[39] *LW* 42, 173-74.

[40] *LW* 42, 175.

[41] *LW* 42, 175.

themselves burdened and who yearn for help. The sublime sacrament must be regarded by us not as a poison, but as a medicine for the soul.'[42]

Keenly aware of the ignorance and possible abuse of the Eucharist in popular piety, Luther cautioned against misusing the fruits of the mass for the attainment of bodily and temporal benefits, in which case nothing remains of the power and use of God's promise. The entire essence of the mass consists 'in the remission of sin and reception of grace and help so that the human heart, clinging to these words [of Christ] by faith, should gain strength in everything good against sin, death, and hell. His word and work were not intended to help us in a temporal way, but in a spiritual and eternal way.'[43] The reception of the sacrament must not be converted into an occasion for the attainment of righteousness by works; nor can it be used as a temporal way to achieve certain personal ends such as security and happiness. Such actions are an insult to the God who intends the sacraments for spiritual purposes, the opposite of temporal attainments.

The Concept of Testament: Promise and Faith

Inherent in Luther's view of the sacrament is the idea of a 'new and eternal testament,' which appears in this sermon. He derived this concept from the Pauline epistles (cf. Gal. 3 and 4; and Heb. 9). He was deeply aware of the frailty of fallen human nature, and realized that it required constant and concrete reassurance concerning God's love. He conceived of Christ's death as a token of both the trustworthiness and the enormous price of God's grace. He developed this by means of the concept of a 'testament,' which is understood in a sense of a 'last will and testament' in which Christ is the very content. Thus he wrote at length in *The Babylonian Captivity of the Church*:

> A testament, as everyone knows, is a promise made by one about to die, in which he designates his bequest and appoints his heirs. A testament, therefore, involves, first, the death of the testator, and second, the promise of an inheritance and the naming of the heir ... Christ testifies concerning his death when he says: 'This is my body, which is given, this is my blood, which is poured out' (Luke 22:19-20). He names and designates the bequest when he says 'for the forgiveness of sins' (Matt. 26:28). But he appoints the heirs when he says 'for you (Luke 22:19-20; 1

---

[42] *LW* 42, 176-77. Cf. *LW* 51, 192, where he again regarded the sacrament not as a poison but as a medicine for the soul.

[43] *LW* 42, 173. In a *Treatise on the New Testament, That is, the Holy Mass* (1520), Luther enumerated several temporal benefits connected to the sacrament in the popular mind, and charged that the sacrament had degenerated into a kind of 'witchcraft.' Cf. *LW* 35, 75-111, esp. 92, n. 17, as cited in *LW* 42, 174, n. 7.

Cor. 11:24) and for many' (Matt. 26:28; Mark 14: 24), that is, for those who accept and believe the promise of the testator.[44]

In the words of institution, Christ makes his will or last testament in which he affirms the promises of grace and forgiveness, identifies those to whom the promises are made, and confirms these promises by his own death since he is the testator who makes them. 'For there is a testament, the death of a testator must of necessity occur' (Heb. 9:16). This is a direct implicate of the ordained power (*potentia ordinata*), which William of Ockham says is guided by necessity, not by absolute necessity but by consequential necessity. To elaborate: God does not act out of the necessity of compulsion (*necessitas coactionis*), which is inapplicable for a being like God, for it violates the divine freedom. Instead he acts out of the necessity of consequence (*necessitas consequentiae*), in that if God wills something, that event or thing will of necessity occur, not as a violation of his freedom but rather as a consequence of his will.[45] God has promised to die. But God cannot die unless he becomes man. The Incarnation is soteriologically necessary, as Luther said in *The Bondage of the Will* (1525), 'Here, God Incarnate says, "I would and thou wouldst not"; God Incarnate, I repeat, was sent for this purpose, to will, say, do, suffer and offer to all, all that is necessary for salvation.'[46] According to God's ordained order, and by a conditional necessity, God therefore had to become man in his Son so that he might die and validate his promise. Christ, the testator, must die, making certain that the promised love is realized in the death of the one who promises. By remaining true to himself, 'God does not confine Himself to giving us His Son in the Incarnation, but He also delivers Him into death for us' to fulfill what he has promised.[47] The Incarnation and the death of Christ are both ingredients in God's testament which bequeaths forgiveness of sins. The Lord's Supper is 'a promise of the forgiveness of sins made to us by God, and such a promise as has been confirmed

[44] *LW* 36, 38. Cf. Lienhard, 'Luther and the Beginnings of the Reformation', 282; H. Junghans, 'Luther on the Reform of Worship', in Wengert (ed.), *Harvesting Martin Luther's Reflections on Theology, Ethics, and the Church*, 207-25 (212-13).

[45] See McGrath, *Luther's Theology of the Cross*, 56, where he elaborates: 'The significance of the distinction between the two powers (absolute and ordained power) lies in the conception of necessity involved: how can God be said to act reliably, without simultaneously asserting that he acts of necessity? The dialectic between two powers of God allowed the reliability of God's action to be upheld, without implying that God acts of necessity. God is understood to have imposed upon himself, by a free and uncoerced primordial decision, a certain self-limitation, in that he is faithful to the order which he himself has established. In that God is faithful to this ordained order, he may be said to be reliable; in that this order is itself the contingent consequence of a free decision of God, God cannot be said to act of absolute necessity, but merely by a conditional necessity.'

[46] See Luther, *The Bondage of the Will* (trans. J.I. Packer and O.R. Johnson; London: Clarke, 1957), 176.

[47] *LW* 22, 354 (John, 1537). For a study of Luther's understanding of testament, see K. Hagen, *A Theology of Testament in the Young Luther: The Lectures on Hebrews* (Leiden: Brill, 1974).

by the death of the Son of God.'[48] The sacramental sign and promise of God attached to it will not lie or deceive us, because it is God who has promised it and therefore must act reliably, without implying that he acts under compulsion.

God meets us in his word, and we receive his word in faith. Luther laid particular emphasis on faith as the human correlative to the promise of the gospel. God deals with us precisely within the context of this correlation between the divine promise and human response. 'For it is not a sacrament unless it is expressly given with the divine promise which demands faith, since apart from the word which promises and faith which receives we are not able to enter into any kind of relationship with God.'[49] Luther's view of the sacrament as a sign of the promise offered in the word establishes an essential unity between the sacrament and faith. 'For the sacramental form of the word, like the word itself, is present for faith; it depends on faith and contributes nothing to a man's salvation without faith.'[50] Towards the close of this sermon, he affirmed the all-important nature of faith: 'If you believe, the sacrament gives you everything you need.'[51] God gave us the sacraments so that faith could 'have something to which it may cling and on which it may stand.'[52] Although God's promise and human faith are distinguished, they are necessarily one. They form such a seamless garment that without the promise there is nothing to be believed, and without faith nothing would remain of the divine promise, since it is established and fulfilled through faith. The entire power of the Lord's Supper lies not in any magical forms or any accretions we bring to the sacramental service, but rather 'consists in the words of Christ, in which he testifies that forgiveness of sins is bestowed on all those who believe that His body is given and His blood poured out for them.'[53] Chemnitz's words echo Luther's: 'For we must not believe that the testator willed anything other than what he expressed in his words.'[54] No one is permitted to tamper with a person's last will and testament, especially Christ's, that of the very Son of God. The Eucharist thus is 'nothing else than the divine promise or testament of Christ, sealed with the sacrament of Christ's body and blood.'[55] It radically proclaims as a present, experienced reality that the promises of grace and forgiveness are now effective for those with faith. Luther himself made such a point:

> You see, therefore, that what we call the mass is a promise of the forgiveness of sins made to us by God, and such a promise as has been confirmed by the death of

---

[48] *LW* 36, 38.

[49] *LW* 36, 38.

[50] Althaus, *Theology of Martin Luther*, 348.

[51] *LW* 42, 177.

[52] 'The Large Catechism', in *BC*, 440, 443-44. Cf. Althaus, *Theology of Martin Luther*, 351; M. Gray, *The Protestant Reformation: Beliefs and Practices* (Brighton: Sussex Academic Press, 2003), 45-46.

[53] *LW* 36, 42.

[54] M. Chemnitz, *The Lord's Supper* (trans. J.A.G. Preus; St. Louis: Concordia, 1979), 19.

[55] *LW* 36, 43; 47, 42.

> the Son of God. For the only difference between a promise and a testament is that the testament involves the death of the one who makes it. A testator is a promiser who is about to die, while a promiser (if I put it thus) is a testator who is not about to die. This testament of Christ is foreshadowed in all the promises of God from the beginning of the world; indeed, whatever value those ancient promises possessed was altogether derived from this new promise that was to come in Christ ... Now God made a testament; therefore, it was necessary that he should. But God could not die unless he became man. Thus the incarnation and the death of Christ are comprehended most concisely in this one word, 'testament.'[56]

With his emphasis on the sacrament as testament or promise, Luther was particularly opposed to the view that the Lord's Supper confers grace because we participate in it rather than because God gives himself to us through the word. To Luther, we are unable to 'give anything to God that was not previously his own.'[57] The key to Luther's theology of the atonement, says Forde, lies in the radical 'reversal': 'not that something is given to God, but that God gives something to us.'[58] Light is thrown on this point by its parallel in Luther's understanding of the Eucharist, not as a sacrifice but as a sacrament (gift). He wrote,

> We do not presume to give God something in the sacrament, when it is he who in it gives us all things ... We see, then, that the best and greatest part of all sacraments and of the mass is the word of promises of God, without which the sacraments are dead and are nothing at all ... I accept for myself alone the blessing therein offered by God – and here there is no *officium* but *beneficium*, no work or service, but reception and benefit.[59]

The testament comes as a free gift from Christ, the testator who demonstrates his love by bestowing it through the last will he makes in the words of institution. The promise is effective, since it proceeds from God and points to God. God is the origin and end of the testament he makes with us. In it, God makes a bequest and offers it to his designated heirs without their input, or any contributions of their own to earn it. What is in view is the monergism of God's grace, not the synergism of divine and human efforts. Access to the promise is to be gained by faith alone, without any works or powers or merits of our own. 'It is the nature of the promise simply to be trusted.'[60] Therefore, the testament of Christ's body and blood 'can be dealt with in no other way than by faith alone.'[61] 'Without this faith, whatever else is brought to

---

[56] *LW* 36, 38.

[57] *LW* 14, 106.

[58] Forde, 'Luther's Theology of the Cross', in *Christian Dogmatics*, vol. 2, 50.

[59] *LW* 35, 89. Cf. *LW* 22, 9: 'Whatever we are, we received from Him and not from ourselves. He alone has everything from Himself.' This understanding appears first in Anselm of Canterbury, *Monologium*, ch. 6, which is the medieval scholastic doctrine of the 'aseity' of God. See *LW* 22, 9, n. 5.

[60] Kolb, *Teaching God's Children His Teaching*, ch. 6, 8.

[61] *LW* 36, 42.

us by way of prayers, preparations, works, signs, or gestures are incitements to impiety rather than exercises of piety.'[62] Luther elaborated this point:

> When one deals with words and promises, one needs faith even between men here on earth ... Now, as we can plainly see, God deals with us in no other way by his holy word and sacraments, which are like signs or seals of his words. The very first thing necessary, then, is faith in these words and signs, for when God speaks and gives signs, man must fully and wholeheartedly believe that what he says and signifies is true.[63]

God constitutes us as hearers of his speech, and when he speaks we are impious if we do not believe his words. Faith as such cannot possibly be a work we do to earn God's promises, but is 'the Lord and life of all works.'[64] To Luther it is a 'sacrilege' to turn faith into a work, thereby turning the testator, the dispenser of his own goods, into the recipient of ours. He elaborated:

> Who in the world is so foolish as to regard a promise received by him, or a testament given to him, as a good work, which he renders to the testator by his acceptance of it? What heir will imagine that he is doing his departed father a kindness by accepting the terms of the will and the inheritance it bequeaths to him? What godless audacity is it, therefore, when we who are to receive the testament of God come as those who would perform a good work for him! This ignorance of the testament, this captivity of so great a sacrament – are they not too sad for tears? When we ought to be grateful for benefits received, we come arrogantly to give that which we ought to take. With unheard-of perversity we mock the mercy of the giver by giving as a work the thing we receive as a gift, so that the testator, instead of being a dispenser of his own goods, becomes the recipient of ours.[65]

The strength and power of the testament lie in its promise, which elicits the faith that resides in it. By his will, Christ wrote our names into the testament so that upon his death the promises of grace and forgiveness became effectual, and the whole inheritance belongs rightly to us, his appointed heirs.

So when it came to instructing his students regarding the benefits of the Lord's Supper, Luther's principal picture of God's deed here is that of a last will and testament.[66] God promises and bestows through the efficacious act of the dying man, himself, treasures upon the heirs who can do nothing to earn them. The Lord's Supper thus is the re-enactment of that will, and the reading of that testament, through which the precious promises of forgiveness and eternal life are now effective, if only we believe. 'Hence to seek the efficacy of the sacrament apart from

---

62 *LW* 36, 42.

63 *LW* 32, 15.

64 *LW* 36, 47. For more on the relation between faith and works, see *A Treatise on Good Works* (1520), in *LW* 44, 15-114.

65 *LW* 36, 47-48.

66 Kolb, *Teaching God's Children His Teaching*, ch. 6, 13.

the promise and without faith,' Luther intimated, 'is to labor in vain and to find condemnation.'[67] So efficacious, sweet, blessed and reliable are the words of Christ's institution, understood as the new and eternal testament in which God affirms his promises and confirms them by the death of his Son, that we, as his appointed heirs, thereby are persuaded to receive the sacrament. By virtue of the power of Christ's last will re-enacted in the mass, Luther exhorted communicants to make their way to God and say,

> Lord, it is true that I am not worthy for you to come under my roof, but I need and desire your help and grace to make me godly. I now come to you, trusting only in the wonderful words I just heard, with which you invite me to your table and promise me, the unworthy one, forgiveness of all my sins through your body and blood if I eat and drink them in this sacrament. Amen. Dear Lord, I do not doubt the truth of your words. Trusting them, I eat and I drink with you. Do unto me according to your words. Amen.[68]

Concluding Reflections

The worth of this sermon lies in the link between Luther's sacramental theology and the religious shape of the congregation, the former informing the latter. I shall conclude my reflections on this sermon with three interrelated themes: God hides in the created elements of bread and wine in order to bestow upon us his infinite grace, by which we are driven to him in repentance and faith; the majesty of God's word reigns in the sacrament of the altar; and it incites a sacramental piety, not dependent on any human accretions, and quite apart from the subjective condition of the Christian life.

Theological Premise and Biblical Vision

Luther's theological premise, his faith in the Creator who brings new life through the re-creative word, informs this sermon. This premise came from his own study of Genesis and Psalms in particular. In his *Lectures on Genesis* (1545), Luther, explaining the verse 'And God said: Let there be light and there was light,' spoke of the word as the instrument which God employs to accomplish his work of creation.[69] The phrase 'God said' means not only the utterance of God, but also the

---

[67] *LW* 36, 67.

[68] *LW* 42, 174. Also quoted in P. Brooks, 'Martin Luther and the Pastoral Dilemma', in P. Brooks (ed.), *Christian Spirituality in Honour of Gordon Rupp* (London: SCM Press, 1975), 95-117 (113).

[69] *LW* 1, 16; *WA* 42, 13. See R. Kolb, '"What Benefit Does the Soul Receive from a Handful of Water?": Luther's Preaching on Baptism, 1528-1539', *Concordia Journal* 25 (1999), 346-63 (358), where he speaks of the word as God's creative instrument. For a full discussion of Luther's understanding of the word of God, see J. Pelikan, *Luther the*

action or deed of God. God's word is causative, speaking reality into existence in his covenants. The prophets speak, and in their speaking the deed of God is accomplished. 'In the case of God to speak is to do, and the word is the deed.'[70] What God says becomes actual, and not mere language. God's word acts and accomplishes his will. The gospel, writes Bayer, is '*promissio* (promise), a *speech act* that delivers forgiveness of sins, life and salvation.'[71] The justifying word God utters in the mass is indeed the action he performs through the created elements of bread and wine. It is a word of address that ultimately transforms the reality of the addressee. God's word is his instrument of power, which assumes created forms. Luther claimed that God has chosen elements of his created order, which are intrinsically good, to effect his saving will. Such an understanding runs contrary to Western culture, which, under the grip of the influence of ancient Greece, tends to differentiate the spiritual from the material, and elevate the spiritual above the material. In contrast, Luther, thinking Hebraically, rejects this so-called platonic spiritualism; he affirms that differentiation occurs between God the Creator and his created order, not between the spiritual and material, since both belong to the created order. Animated by this biblical worldview or vision, he presumed that God has attached his recreating word to Christ's flesh, to human language in oral and written form, to the sacramental elements, all of these being vehicles or instruments of God's power. Kolb expounds on this:

> God ordains what is beneficial and what is not, Luther affirms. God has always used such external signs for different purposes. He revealed His will to Gideon through a fleece (Judges 6:37). He confirmed kings in office by anointing them with oil. David recognized God's guidance in the rustling of the breeze under the pear tree (2 Sam. 5:24). 'Christ gave all such signs not only for the sake of love but also to confirm people in the faith, that they might believe in him and through him in God ... The whole of salvation history unfolds through the external signs: Mary's virginity, Pilate's administration, the Church, the word.' Finally, Luther confirms his position (on sacraments) by reversing the question against his opponents. 'You cannot give me a single example of a person who was made a Christian or received

---

Expositor: Introduction to the Reformer's Exegetical Writings (Luther's Works, Companion Volume; St. Louis: Concordia, 1959), 54-70.

[70] *LW* 12, 33; *WA* 40, II, 231 (Ps. 2, 1532). See R. Jenson, *Systematic Theology*, Vol. II, *The Works of God* (Oxford: Oxford University Press, 1999), 159-60, where he quotes Luther's *Ennaratio in Genesis, 17*: 'Sun, moon, heaven, earth, Peter, Paul, I, you, etc., are all words of God, or perhaps rather syllables or letters in context of the whole creation ... In this way the words of God are embodied realities (*res*) and not mere language.' Cf. S. Paulson, *Luther for Armchair Theologians* (Louisville: Westminster John Knox, 2004), 69-73.

[71] See M.C. Mattes, *The Role of Justification in Contemporary Theology* (Grand Rapids: Eerdmans, 2004), 156, where he analyzes Oswald Bayer's theology of the gospel as speech act.

> the Holy Spirit apart from something external … He always grasps something physical as a means by which he deals with you, something that is beneficial.'[72]

For Luther, the sacraments are likened unto the Incarnation. Just as God meets us in the human person of Jesus, so he meets us in his sacramental signs. The sacraments are just ordinary bread and wine, but 'what a glorious majesty lies hidden beneath these things.' 'The glory of God is precisely that for our sake he comes down into the very depths, into human flesh, into the bread, into our mouth, our heart, our bosom.'[73] This, too, is linked with Luther's theology of the cross (*theologia crucis*) in which God reveals himself in what seems weak and foolish, the opposite of power and might.

Luther's Optimism of Grace: 'To receive God's word in many ways is so much better'

The gospel of Jesus Christ is conveyed by the means that God has ordained as the vehicles of the economy of salvation. This sermon made it clear that the sacramental action of God effects forgiveness, new life, comfort, and strength in believers. Luther extolled the power of the word of God as fundamental to an understanding of reality. To him, God's word is causative, determining the way things are. Its efficacy so thrilled Luther that he was never tired of teaching on this subject. This was most evident in his *A Short Order of Confession Before the Priest for the Common Man* (1529), where Luther, as part of the order of confession of believers to their pastors, had the pastor ask the parishioner why he desired to receive the sacrament after he had just received absolution. The parishioner was to answer that he desired to strengthen his soul with God's word and sign. In reply, the pastor asks whether absolution has not already bestowed grace. To which the parishioner retorts, 'So what! I want to add the sign of God to his word. To receive God's word in many ways is so much better.'[74] To Luther, there are five forms of the word of God, all of which are revelatory of a God who delights in overwhelming us with these proofs of his mercy and love for us (*pro nobis*). All these means are indicative of Luther's optimism of grace, in which God endlessly and lavishly fills our hearts with his favor in many different ways. Each of these is an extension and an application of the gospel. In the *Smalcald Articles* III:IV (1537), Luther wrote,

> We shall now return to the gospel, which offers counsel and help against sin in more than one way, for God is surpassingly rich in his grace: First, through the spoken word, by which the forgiveness of sin (the peculiar function of the gospel)

---

[72] Kolb, '"What Benefit Does the Soul Receive from A Handful of Water?"', 357; Ngien, 'Theology of Preaching in Martin Luther', 31.

[73] *LW* 37, 73 ('That the words of Christ "This is My Body" etc shall stand firm against the fanatics, 1527'). See also E. Schlink, *Theology of Lutheran Confessions* (Philadelphia: Fortress Press, 1961), 160-61.

[74] *LW* 53, 118.

> is preached to the whole world; second, through Baptism; third, through the holy sacrament of the altar; fourth, through the power of the keys; and finally, through the mutual conversation and consolation of brethren. Matt. 18:20, 'Where two or three are gathered,' etc.[75]

The sacraments are separate instances of the word of God, which convey to the church God's unwavering promises, and grace is common to them all, bestowing upon believers forgiveness of sins, life, and salvation. Sacraments have no other content than the gospel: the message of forgiveness. They are God-given signs in which God himself is present and active. They assure us that we are the objects of God's supra-abundant grace, that the divine wrath has been placated. Both law and gospel are of this same word: 'The creative word of God sustains the Christian life; it annihilates sin and sinner, meaninglessness and despair; it creates something new – order out of chaos, life out of death, resurrection out of crucifixion.'[76] The banquet, Luther's metaphor for the Lord's Supper,[77] is God's own action on our behalf. In it, Christ announces the refreshment of our faith through the words of institution.

Luther disagreed with Zwingli who regarded thanksgiving and public profession of faith as the core of the sacrament. In his *Ratio Fidei*, Zwingli called the sacrament a 'supper of thanksgiving,' an event where believers express thanks to God 'for the kindness conferred on us in his Son.' At the same time, the Lord's Supper was the occasion to give public testimony to their faith, since it is a visible act where believers bear witness that 'they have been previously received into it (the Church) invisibly.' He declared about the mass, 'I believe, indeed, I know that all the sacraments are so far from conferring grace that they do not even convey or distribute it.'[78] By making these two aspects – thanksgiving and public confession – primary, Zwingli transformed the sacrament into a sacrifice, the gift of God into a human work. Lutherans emphasized the sacramental element (God's work) and not the sacrificial element (our work): 'The sacraments were ordained not only to be the marks of profession among men, but especially to be signs and testimonies of the will of God toward us.'[79] For Zwingli, nothing really happened in the Eucharist

---

[75] 'Smalcald Articles III: IV', in *BC*, 310. Also cited in R.P. Bucher, *The Ecumenical Luther: The Development and Use of His Doctrinal Hermeneutic* (St. Louis: Concordia Academic, 2003), 126. See also *LW* 26, 399.

[76] M. Marty, *The Hidden Discipline* (St. Louis: Concordia, 1962), 90.

[77] *LW* 42, 176, where Luther used the analogy of a 'banquet' for the Lord's Supper.

[78] H.E. Jacobs (ed.), *The Book of Concord* (2 vols; Philadelphia, 1883), 2, 198 and 200, as cited in T.G. Tappert, 'Meaning and Practice in the Reformation', in Lehmann (ed.), *Meaning and Practice of the Lord's Supper*, 92. Cf. Steinmetz, *Luther in Context*, 82-84.

[79] See *Augsburg Confession*, XIII, 1; cf. *Apology*, XXIV, 68, as cited in Tappert, 'Meaning and Practice in the Reformation', 93. Cf. J.F. White, *Sacraments in Protestant Practice and Faith* (Nashville: Abingdon, 1999), 18-20; L.J. Vander Zee, *Christ, Baptism and the Lord's Supper* (Illinois: IVP, 2004), 174-75. Both Luther and Calvin share the Augustinian conviction that the sacramental signs and spiritual reality are inseparably one. For the eucharistic theology of John Calvin, see B.A. Gerrish, *Grace and Gratitude*

except in the mind and faith of the communicants; for Luther, as for Augustine, the sacramental signs and the spiritual reality are not separated, in that the signs carried the freight of what God had promised in them, namely the saving power of Christ's body and blood. What God promises, he truly does: he hides in the created elements in order to effect his recreative power to save. Therefore Luther could call Christ a 'sacrament,' as Augustine did, a pure gift of God in human form: 'If I were to speak according to the usage of the Scriptures, I should have only one single sacrament (Christ), but with three sacramental signs.'[80]

Furthermore although both public preaching and the sacrament share the same gospel content, Luther saw a fundamental difference between the preached word and the sacramental word. The former is directed to the congregation in general, whereas the latter conveys the word of promise to individuals in particular. The peculiar worth of the sacrament and its advantage over the preached word lie in its affirmation of individuality, that the promise of the sacrament is bestowed upon individuals with spiritual profit to them. This is beyond the scope of public preaching, at least for a person who is under temptation, since it is addressed to all without distinction. In the sacrament, the content of the word reaches the particular individual so that the sermon is indeed grasped as their own. Luther wrote,

> However, a distinction has to be made here. When I preach his death, it is an open and public proclamation, in which I am addressing myself to no one individually; whoever grasps it, grasps it. But when I am distributing the sacrament I designate it for the individual who is receiving it; I give him Christ's body and blood that he may have forgiveness of sins, obtained through his death, and preached in the Christian community. This is something more than the public sermon; for although the same thing is present in the sermon as in the sacrament, here there is the advantage that it is directed to definite individuals. In the sermon I do not point out or portray any particular person, but in the sacrament, it is given to you and to me in particular, so that the sermon comes to be your own.[81]

(Minneapolis: Fortress Press, 1993). Luther and Calvin, as Fredrick Dale Bruner writes, steer in between Zwingli on the one side and Rome on the other: 'Luther and Calvin believed that both the Roman church on the right and the Zwinglians and Anabaptist churches on the left made the Lord's Supper too much a place *where believers did things for God* – either by offering Christ to God (Rome) or by offering their deep devotion to God (the Radical Protestants). The Main direction of the Supper, in both of these views, was up.' See his *The Churchbook, Matthew 13–28* (Dallas: Word, 1990), 958.

[80] *LW* 36, 18; cf. B. Hanson, *Grace That Frees: The Lutheran Tradition* (Maryknoll: Orbis, 2004), 130; Siggins, *Martin Luther's Doctrine of Christ*, 63-64.

[81] *LW* 36, 348-49; *WA* 19, 504-505, as cited in Althaus, *Theology of Martin Luther*, 347. Cf. H. Sasse, *We Confess the Sacraments* (trans. N. Nagel; St. Louis: Concordia, 1984), 11-15.

*Order of Salvation (*ordo salutis*): God's Forgiveness and Our Repentance*

As regards the order of salvation, is forgiveness by God logically prior to our repentance, or repentance logically prior to forgiveness?[82] To resolve this, we are necessarily confronted by the question: how does God forgive our sins? Does God forgive only when we repent? Some would say that God cannot forgive if we do not repent. And if God forgives the unrepentant, would he not be charged with condoning their sins? What are we to make of the liturgies of the Church which speak to the effect that 'whoever repents of his sins may be forgiven.' Is it theologically accurate to speak of God's forgiveness in this way, that our repentance is the prerequisite of God's forgiveness? Though it is not entirely wrong to speak of it in this way, there is a hidden danger in it, for it may lead people to feel that repentance is something we must do in order to obtain, earn or deserve God's forgiving grace. In that case, repentance becomes a 'work' necessary for salvation, in which case we are no longer saved by grace alone. If repentance is a work necessary to achieve God's forgiveness, then we are confronted with an acute problem that haunted Luther then and haunts our conscience now: how much work is necessary for salvation? In the popular mind, repentance is defined as feeling sorrow for our sins. But to what extent are we really sorry for what we have done amiss, and to what degree are we simply sorry about the consequences of the sin? For instance, the child caught stealing money is very sorry, sorry for being caught and having to suffer the punishment for it, but not necessarily sorry for their criminal offence. Also if forgiveness is based on feeling sorrow, how can we be certain that we feel the right kind of sorrow for our sins? It is true that the Bible links forgiveness and repentance. But there is no evidence that repentance is a cause of God's grace. For Jesus certainly pronounced forgiveness when there was no sign of repentance. At the cross, he uttered, 'Father, forgive them, for they know not what they do' (Luke 23:34). Those who crucified Jesus showed no signs of repentance; on the contrary, they were getting much sadistic pleasure out of torturing him. Likewise Jesus shocked the Pharisees by proclaiming the opposite of what they wanted to hear, that the paralytic's sins had been forgiven, despite no sign of repentance by the paralytic (Mark 2:5; Matt. 9:2; Luke 5:20). In the parable of the prodigal son in Luke 15, the son was forgiven by the father. Was he forgiven only when he returned home, or because he returned home? Neither! The father's attitude was always one of forgiveness, independent of the son's disposition towards him. If anyone had known the mind of the father, he would have gone to the son in the far country with this good news: your father has forgiven you, let's go home. The truth of the matter is that the father's attitude towards the son was not changed by the son's returning home. The only change was that the son, by coming home, put himself in a position to recognize or appropriate the father's forgiveness, not cause or condition it. The most succinct explanation of this was found in

[82] W.E. Hordern, *Living by Grace* (Philadelphia: Westminster, 1975), 70-82. The author is indebted to Hordern's formulation of Luther's evangelical order of salvation, which puts forgiveness of God before repentance.

Luther's *Large Catechism*, where he commented about the petition for forgiveness in the Lord's Prayer:

> Here again there is great need to call upon God and pray, 'Dear Father, forgive our debts'. Not that he does not forgive sin even without and before our prayer; and he gave us the gospel, in which there is nothing but forgiveness, before we prayed or even thought of it. But the point here is for us to recognize and accept this forgiveness.[83]

Luther caught this vision of God's forgiveness as unconditionally given. It does not wait for us to repent or to pray for it. God's forgiveness is thus prior to our repentance and prayer. His forgiving grace does not waver, and it refuses to abandon us. His love for us is completely realistic and unconditional, based at every point on the prior knowledge of the worst about us so that no future discovery about us could ever disenchant God in the way we so often become disillusioned about ourselves. The father has forgiven his son even in the far country, even before he repents, or before he feels sorry, or before he comes to his senses. But the son cannot be reconciled insofar as he remains aloof in the far country. He has to come home and 'accept' his father's forgiveness. Faith, as Paul Tillich aptly defined it, is 'accepting our acceptance.'[84] Forgiveness is already there, and all we need to do is to receive it and accept it. Nevertheless our acceptance by God does not depend upon our accepting his grace, for we are already accepted by God in Jesus Christ. It is a gift given to us. If our accepting causes God's acceptance of us, then our salvation is not by grace alone. Therefore any understanding of salvation in a legal context in which we have to do something meritorious so as to earn God's forgiveness was not part of Luther's theology of grace. There is a causal relationship between forgiveness and repentance, Luther maintained. But it is never our repentance that causes God's favour; rather, it is God's forgiveness that causes our repentance. To invert the evangelical order of grace, making repentance prior to forgiveness, is to destroy *sola gratiae* (grace alone), for it regards God's grace as conditional upon what we do. For Luther, God cannot be made gracious. The indicatives of grace are prior to the imperatives of obedience. Thus salvation must be understood in the evangelical context, in which the priority of the gospel and primacy of God's justifying words reign so supremely that they effect a change in us, moving us towards repentance and faith.

Hearing God's pronouncement of his forgiveness can be a very powerful motive for us to seek reconciliation with him. For instance, when someone has broken a relationship, the word that the wounded party has forgiven the guilty one can serve as a strong impetus causing the offender to seek reconciliation. Our repentance is not a condition of grace, but only a response to grace. Whereas 'legal repentance' takes the form, 'Repent, and if you do, you will be forgiven,' 'evangelical repentance' takes this form, 'Christ has given himself for you for the forgiveness of your sins;

---

[83] 'The Large Catechism', in *BC*, 432.

[84] Hordern, *Living by Grace*, 78.

therefore, repent! Receive his forgiving grace in repentance.'[85] The latter is Luther's – the gift is primary, and the response secondary. By putting the emphasis on the primacy of the word, Luther gave priority to the responsive rather than causative character of faith.

The justifying word, 'I forgive you,' is the content of the gospel, whereas repentance is our response to the gospel, not our causing it. '[O]nly as the word is maintained as the work of God, does faith retain the character of receptivity or reception of other gifts.'[86] This, too, is in accord with Luther's sacramental theology, in which God gives himself in his Son. In the Eucharist, Christ spoke the justifying word which effects forgiveness in us. The words of Christ's institution summon from us an unconditional response of faith and repentance; they foment a sacramental piety, which is not contingent upon any human invention of pious works or pious desire. A conversion (repentance and faith) that is not rooted in God's justifying *word-act*, specifically in the mass, is not true conversion. The sacrament is purely God's action on our behalf, to which we respond with gratitude and thanksgiving. Unlike Zwingli who stressed the signifying character of the sacrament for which thanksgiving was rendered, Luther saw the causative character of God's word in it as the source of gratitude. We thank God for coming into our lives and redeeming us as the recipients of the inestimable benefits promised in Christ's last will. It is precisely by our unworthiness that we become the object of God's grace. Therefore when faced with doubts or a lack of assurance, Luther did not ask, 'How is your devotional life or prayer life? How about your good works?', instead he exhorted believers to heed Christ's words, the very 'sum and substance of the whole gospel.' He encouraged believers to accept and affirm God's word of promise given in Jesus Christ through the mass (and other means), quite apart from any emotions they might experience. We are to hear Christ's words, by which our identity is forged and by which we are transformed into images of the one whose innocence we receive in a happy exchange for our sins. In the mass, we experience the power of his re-creating word at work. In Pannenberg's estimation, 'We (thereby) receive a new identity, but we do not possess it separately, in our separate existence apart from Christ, but only "in Christ", which is to say in faith that unites us with

[85] See J.B. Torrance, *Worship, Community and the Triune God of Grace* (Illinois: IVP, 1996), 54. Although Torrance's exposition of the evangelical order of grace is based on Calvin's *Institutes*, Book 3, the substances coincide with Luther's understanding. Modern Lutheran pietists, in their emphasis on 'conversional piety', have in some ways inverted the order of salvation, making repentance prior to forgiveness. For further discussions, see R.E. Olson, *The Story of Christian Theology: Twenty Centuries of Tradition and Reform* (Downers Grove, IL: IVP, 1999), ch. 29; J. Weborg, 'Pietism: "The Fire of God Which ... Flames in the Heart of Germany"', in F.C. Senn (ed.), *Protestant Spiritual Traditions* (New York: Paulist, 1986), 183-216.

[86] C.P. Arand, *That I May Be His Own: An Overview of Luther's Catechisms* (St. Louis: Concordia Academic, 2000), 167.

Christ, with the Christ "outside ourselves".'[87] With his emphasis on the objective nature of God's work for us in Christ, Luther shunned the inward experiences of a subjective nature as a legitimate basis of assurances of any place before God. Not by introspection but only by ex-centricity – by looking outside ourselves (*extra nobis*) to God's 'speech act' in Jesus Christ can we find assurance. Our inner experience must not become primary, in which case we begin to turn away from faith in Christ to trust in ourselves. When this happens, we are reverting to righteousness by works as the outcome.[88] To Luther, the objective word of Christ is the anchor of faith, and the landmark of true piety. Faith cleaves to the sacrament, trusting that God's word be done unto it.[89] It is an anathema to attack Christ's words, for to do so is to attack the gospel itself; to deny Christ's words is to deny his justifying action on us, thus nullify the power and use of the sacrament.

> Everything happens on these words [of institution]. Every Christian should and must know them and hold them fast. He must never let anyone take them away from him by any other kind of teaching, even though it were an angel from heaven (Gal. 1:8). They are the words of life and salvation, so that whoever believes in them has all his sins forgiven through that faith; he is a child of life and has overcome death and hell. Language cannot express how great and mighty these words are, for they are the sum and substance of the whole gospel.[90]

---

[87] W. Pannenberg, 'Luther's Contribution to Christian Spirituality', *Dialog* 40 (2001), 248-89 (287).

[88] W.E. Hordern, *Experience and Faith: The Significance of Luther for Understanding Today's Experiential Religion* (Minneapolis: Augsburg, 1983), 99.

[89] See *LW* 42, 174, where he advised the communicants to pray, 'Do unto me according to your words.'

[90] *LW* 36, 277; *WA* 11, 432.

CHAPTER 5

The Theology and Practice of Prayer: God's Initiative and Human Appropriation

Distinctive to Luther's *Personal Prayer Book* is the order in which he placed the Lord's Prayer after the Ten Commandments and the Creed, viewing it as the exercise of faith to the law–gospel distinction.[1] This stands in sharp contrast to the most common medieval order from 1450 to 1500: the Lord's Prayer, the Creed, and the Ten Commandments, the rationale of which consists in that 'the Lord's Prayer in the rosary was useless without the faith of the Creed, and the faith of the Creed was of no effect without the keeping of the commandments.'[2] Luther consciously reversed this order, accentuating the priority of the gospel as the source of life and power for morality. However, this does not imply that he was constructing a new vision of salvation in which the keeping of the law is denied its rightful place. Rather, the law, whose function is to show us that we by ourselves are powerless to fulfill God's will, finds its fulfillment in the gospel. The structure and content in which prayer is done corresponds to the way in which God's revelation of himself comes to us, moving from the Decalogue (law) to the Creed (gospel), and ending with the Lord's Prayer (the appropriation of the creedal benefits). The logic of this order is that in God's encounter with the sinner, law (Decalogue) precedes gospel (Creed). The sinner must first meet the moral imperative and be crushed by it prior to being ready to hear the gospel. The Lord's Prayer then is the exercise of faith, which responds to the creedal announcement of the word of grace in the gospel. This divine order with the same rationale is carried over into Luther's *Catechisms*, which he did not consider as textbooks of doctrine but as daily resources for personal devotions. His *A Simple Way to Pray* is an extension of his *Catechisms*, indicative of Luther's lifelong commitment to their proper use. Thus the substance of his catechetical writings will also enter our discussions. Although Luther's writings on prayer are basically catechetical and devotional in focus, they are not devoid of rich theological content.[3]

The key motive for prayer is God, since it is God who draws us to himself. 'Just as God was in Christ reconciling the world unto Himself, so in prayer God

---

[1] *LW* 43, 3-45; cf. 'The Small Catechism' and 'The Large Catechism', in *BC*, 337-461.

[2] *LW* 43, 13.

[3] K.W. Stevenson, *The Lord's Prayer: A Text in Tradition* (Minneapolis: Fortress Press, 2004), 158.

condescends into the world of human asking and thanking and draws man back into his own world.'[4] Luther's theology of prayer is centered wholly on the infallible word of God, from beginning to end. However, the word of God appears in various forms, as in command, promise, Christ's own words, and other portions of Scripture. These are the selected instruments of divine power, which God uses to achieve his saving purpose. 'The creaturely words, whether written or spoken, are for him [Luther] rather the vehicle or media of the Divine creative Word, by which God addresses Himself directly and personally to us.'[5] On account of his word, prayer is our response to God's invitation: his word is not the response to our prayer. Fundamental to the nature of God is his glory to give: it is god-like to bestow gifts with extravagance and generosity. Correspondingly, in prayer, our actual relation to God is revealed, that we are always the receivers of what he lavishly gives. God is the causative factor in moving us to pray, to seek what we need from him, not from ourselves. This he does through his four ordained avenues: command, promise, words, and faith, all are God's gifts to us. These constituents, which receive elaboration in his *Large Catechism*, are summarized in Luther's exposition of the opening phrase of the Lord's Prayer – 'Our Father' – in his letter to Master Peter the Barber, *A Simple Way to Pray*:

> O Heavenly Father, dear God, I am a poor unworthy sinner. I do not deserve to raise my eyes or hands toward thee or to pray. But because thou hast *commanded* us all to pray and hast *promised* to hear us and through thy dear Son Jesus Christ hast taught us *both how and what to pray*, I come to thee in *obedience to thy word, trusting* in thy gracious promise. I pray in the name of my Lord Jesus Christ together with all thy saints and Christians on earth as he has taught us: Our Father who art, etc., through the whole prayer, word for word.[6]

God's Command and his Paradoxical Action

It is of God's own accord that we are to pray. In *The Large Catechism*, Luther appealed to the Second Commandment, 'You shall not take God's name in vain,' as the basis for grounding prayer in God's command. 'The first thing to know is this: It is our duty to pray because God has commanded it.'[7] In his exposition of the Second Commandment in *The Small Catechism*, he likewise saw the command to pray embedded in the prohibition not to use the name of God in vain: 'We should not use his name to curse, swear, practice magic, lie or deceive, but in every time of need call upon him, pray to him, and give him thanks.'[8] It is pre-eminently in this commandment that Luther found the 'ought' of prayer. Just as it is required of us to

---

[4] Marty, *Hidden Discipline*, 65-66.

[5] Watson, *Let God Be God*, 152.

[6] *LW* 43, 194-95; 'The Large Catechism', in *BC*, 420–22.

[7] 'The Large Catechism', in *BC*, 420.

[8] 'The Small Catechism', in *BC*, 342.

praise God's holy name, so it is 'our duty and obligation to pray if we want to be Christians.'[9] This 'creaturely obligation [to pray] grounded in our nature as human creatures' is understood in the same light as the obligations to honor our parents, obey civil authorities, love our spouses, and help our neighbors in need.[10] As with all of the Commandments, the command to pray (the Second Commandment) is an outflow of the First Commandment, and connects us with it. 'Prayer, therefore, is as strictly and solemnly commanded as are all the other commandments, such as having no other God (the First Commandment), not killing, not stealing, etc.'[11] So the solemnity of Luther's advice on this command cannot be ignored:

> Consider this command well, and impress it on your consciousness, so that you will not think that you may pray or not pray at your discretion, as though it is not a sin if you did not pray but were sufficient to let others pray. No, you must know that God has earnestly enjoined prayer under the pain of incurring His greatest disfavor and punishment, just as He commanded you not to have other gods but to confess and proclaim, to praise and to extol Him. And he who transgresses this commandment must know that he is no Christian and no member of God's kingdom.[12]

Luther repudiated the anthropocentric understanding of prayer held by two groups of people. On the one hand, the 'vulgar' regarded prayer merely as a matter of personal choice. To pray or not to pray made no difference: they claimed in a somewhat pious manner that if God did not heed their prayers they were better off not praying at all. For fear of making false and hypocritical prayers, they lapsed into the habit of never praying, sometimes with the hope that someone else would perform a vicarious act of prayer on their behalf, since their prayer did not move the heavens. Some prayed only in moments of need. Others showed their ignorance by considering prayer as the last resort: when all else failed, why not try prayer? All these attitudes – prayer as a matter of personal choice, an act of desperation or the result of a fatalistic resignation – contributed to the scarcity of prayer. This group of people did not please God because they regarded prayer from the human point of view. Prayers such as theirs were evoked not by God's command but by impulse or needs or circumstances. On the other hand, the 'sinners' were often so crushed by the weight of the law that they felt unworthy to pray. So they fled from God, thinking that they had merited nothing but divine wrath and condemnation. They reasoned that only those who were holier than they were and had earned favour with God, the saints or the elite, could truly pray in a way that God would hear. Luther wrote,

---

[9] 'The Large Catechism', in *BC*, 421.

[10] C.P. Arand, '"The Battle Cry of Faith": The Catechism's Exposition of the Lord's Prayer', *Concordia Journal* 21 (1995), 42-65 (47).

[11] *LW* 43, 29; 'The Large Catechism', in *BC*, 420-21. Cf. H. Lehmann, *Luther and Prayer* (Milwaukee: Northwestern, 1985), 18.

[12] *LW* 24, 389.

> Against such thoughts we should respect this commandment and turn to God so that we may not provoke his anger by such disobedience. By this commandment he makes it clear that he will not cast us out or drive us away, even though we are sinners; he wishes rather to draw us to himself so that we may humble ourselves before him, lament our misery and plight, and pray for grace and help. Therefore we read in the Scriptures that he is angry because those who are struck down for their sin did not return to him and assuage his wrath and seek grace by their prayers.[13]

Just as he did in his interpretation of the Ten Commandments, so Luther framed the command to pray within the context of God's terrible threats and comforting promises: 'God will not have this commandment treated as a jest but will be angry and punish us if we do not pray, just as he punishes all other kinds of disobedience. Nor will he allow our prayers to be frustrated or lost for, if he did not intend to answer you, he would not have ordered you to pray and backed it up with such a strict commandment.'[14] From this, it is clear that the command to call upon God parallels the paradoxical action of God in performing an alien work under the law in order to achieve his proper work under the gospel. As an alien work, the command to pray carries with it the force of a threat: 'You shall and must obey' or you incur 'God's wrath and displeasure'; as a proper work, the command takes on the force of promise which drives us to God: 'By this commandment he makes it clear that he will not cast us off or drive us away even when we are sinners; he wishes rather to draw us to himself' so that we might humbly seek his forgiving grace for our misery and plight. The God who commands us to pray is the one who wants to help. In these contradictory activities, God performs the alien work of humbling us by means of the law so that we might be driven to him for grace and help through the promise. The negative aspect of the command (God's threats) is revealed so that we might cling to God's mercy, the positive aspect of the command (God's promise). God's threats and promises represent the two ways in which the command is heard. When only the negative aspect of the command is heard, we meet a terrifying God who would destroy us for our sin, in which case we will be lost eternally. But when the negative aspect of the command is heard alongside the positive aspect, it leads us to seek grace by our prayers. To those who are struck down by the law, the word of promise comes as a powerful consolation, causing them to ask God for grace and help. God desires to help and therefore requires that we ask for it. Abiding in these two words is God's determination to remain the God to whom we look for all good and in whom we find refuge in every hour of need. Prayer, which flows from the First Commandment, ultimately takes us back to it. By calling upon God, we make known the peculiar significance of his place and standing as God in our lives. That is, we allow him 'alone' to be our God, worthy of trust and praise.[15]

So any thoughts of deferring prayer take us away from the First Commandment, and thus from God, the one who wishes himself 'alone' to be our God. In prayer, we

---

[13] 'The Large Catechism', in *BC*, 421.

[14] 'The Large Catechism', in *BC*, 422; cf. 368.

[15] 'The Large Catechism', in *BC*, 365.

indicate how much God is worth to us ('Is he alone worthy of my trust?') as well as how much we value the First Commandment ('Do I take it as seriously as I take God?'). In Arand's apt words, 'in prayer, the hegemony of God is at stake in our lives.'[16] Precisely by prayer, we extol the pre-eminence of his ontological status as God in our lives. In the command to pray (the Second Commandment), as in the First Commandment, God declares his sovereignty over all creation, and remains 'the true God' to whom our hearts cling for all good.[17] The Second Commandment (prayer) takes us back to the First Commandment, and puts it into operation. Prayer is thus a practical way in which we perform the First Commandment. Whoever considers the First Commandment considers God 'alone' as God. If God is God in our lives, we pray as the outcome. The life of prayer helps cultivate 'the habit of commending ourselves each day to God – our soul, body, wife, children, servants, and all that we have – for his protection against every conceivable need.'[18] Those who do not call on God when trouble strikes do not consider God as God, and hence disobey the First Commandment. Conversely, those who let God be God, the origin and goal of life, would make prayer the first business of the morning and the last at night. This explains why Luther encouraged parents to teach their children to pray shortly and pointedly: 'Lord God, protect me!' He admonished parents to continue the custom of saying grace before and after meals, and saying other prayers for both morning and evening so that the First and Second Commandments should constitute their daily routine and constant practice. Hence, appended to the end of Luther's *Small Catechism* were blessings before meals, thanksgivings after meals, and morning and evening prayers.[19]

Luther steered both the ignorant and sinners away from consideration of themselves, from seeking within themselves some pre-existent materials which might form a basis or legitimate reason to pray. Instead he directed them to look outside themselves and to consider God's command. Prayer was not optional, but so earnestly commanded that all prayers must be based on obedience to God, irrespective of who the believer was, whether sinner or saint. Worthiness or unworthiness had nothing to do with the effectiveness of prayer. 'God does not regard prayer on account of the person, but on account of His word and the obedience accorded to it.'[20] Depending solely on this commandment, believers were to come to God just as they were – unworthy, distracted, and miserable sinners. They might be assured that the prayer they offered was no less precious, holy, and pleasing to God than those of St. Paul and the saints. In the command, God 'demands this glory from us that we should put our petitions to Him, as a child does to his father.'[21] Prayer reflects 'no

[16] Arand, 'Battle Cry of Faith', 50. Cf. Luther's 'Commentary on Psalm 118, 1530', *LW* 14, 61, where it is stated that 'he who does not call on God or pray to him in trouble certainly does not consider him to be God.'

[17] 'The Large Catechism', in *BC*, 365; cf. *LW* 43, 14.

[18] 'The Large Catechism', in *BC*, 374.

[19] 'The Small Catechism', in *BC*, 353-54.

[20] 'The Large Catechism', in *BC*, 422.

[21] *LW* 21, 146.

other purpose than that it befits obedience and the commandment of God.'[22] It rests on God's initiative, which seeks obedience as an appropriate response, that which is proper to an intimate relationship between God and his creatures.

On account of God's command, Luther accentuated the priority of prayer over all other affairs or works, however important and necessary they were. For him, as for Jerome, everything a Christian does is prayer.[23] In his exposition of the *Sermon on the Mount* (1521), Luther placed prayer just one step lower than the office of the ministry (preaching and teaching), affirming that

> prayer is the chief work of a Christian and an inseparable part of the sermon. He [God] also wants to indicate that, because of all the temptations and hindrances we face, nothing is more necessary in Christendom than continual and unceasing prayer that God would give His grace and His Spirit to make the doctrine powerful and efficacious among us and among others.[24]

Similarly, keenly aware of the assaults (*Anfechtungen*) that may come from the devil, the world, or the flesh, Luther in his *A Simple Way to Pray* advised that prayer be the way the Christian should begin and end each day. Prayer is a plea for God's aid. It becomes a defense against these afflictions or assaults. Hence Luther warned against breaking the habit of true prayer, thereby giving way to the devil who besets believers, and the flesh which so readily tempts to sin. He wrote, 'Guard yourself carefully against those false, deluding ideas which tell you, "Wait a little while. I will pray in an hour; first I must attend to this or that." Such thoughts get you away from prayer into other affairs which so hold your attention and involve you that nothing comes of prayer for that day.'[25] To overcome the sluggishness and laxity of human nature, Christians must dedicate themselves to the discipline of regular prayer. This Christ himself taught in Luke 11, 'Pray without ceasing' (cf. Ps. 1:1, 2). Bonhoeffer's words on the discipline of prayer resonate with Luther's view:

> I need a firm discipline of prayer. We are fond of prayer as our fancy takes us, for a short time, for a long time, or even not at all. That is willfulness. Prayer is not a free offering to God, but the bounden duty that He requires. We are not free to carry

---

[22] *LW* 21, 146.

[23] Cf. Jerome, *Commentary on Matthew*, book 4 under Matt. 25:11, as cited in *LW* 43, 193.

[24] *LW* 21, 228-29. See D.P. Scaer, 'Luther on Prayer', *Concordia Theological Quarterly* 47 (1983), 305-15 (307), where he linked together prayer and the *Anfechtungen* (assaults).

[25] *LW* 43, 193.

on as we wish. Prayer is the day's first service to God. God claims our time for his service.[26]

God's Promise, the Clothed God, and the Trinity

We should be all the more eager to pray because God has promised to hear our prayers, as he says in Psalm 50:15, 'Call upon me in the day of trouble, and I will deliver you,' and Christ says in Matthew 7:7, 8, 'Ask and it will be given to you.' The promise of God elicits from us the appropriate response of prayer and praise; it is no empty solicitude; what he promises, he truly does. The command and promise are bound together, and are not to be seen in isolation from one another. In every instance, his command is accompanied by his own promise; what he commands, he too promises. Yet his promise is unconditional, and our sole duty is to ask. In his exposition of John 16:24, 'Ask, and you will receive, that your joy may be full,' Luther again linked together the command and the promise:

> And just as it is the purpose of Christ's promise and assurance to make us eager and willing, so this command should constrain and compel us. If I want to show my love for Christ and be obedient to Him, I have an obligation to pray, no matter how unworthy I may be.' In Christ, God's gracious promise and bountiful blessings have reached their consummate expression. Thus Luther emphasized that we 'consider the promise contained in Christ's words: "Truly, truly, I say to you, if you ask anything of the Father, He will give it to you in My Name." Lay hold of these words, and impress them on your heart.

The promise Christ makes and confirms with an oath enables us to combat our sluggishness and apathy; it impels us to begin to pray from the heart.

> [I]n all fairness we should blush with shame before ourselves and really fear God's terrible judgment if we attach so little importance both to His command and to His solemn promise and allow them to fall on deaf ears. It will do no good to excuse yourself and say: 'I really did not know whether I am worthy' or 'I lacked the desire, and it was inconvenient for me' or 'I had to attend to other business'.[27]

Failure to pray is, therefore, the result of our unwillingness to be earnestly motivated and rightly empowered by the infallible promise of Christ. Prayer is both a privilege and a responsibility. It is because of God's promise that we are driven to pray; it is because of God's command that we dare not disobey. The promise without the command is empty, as is the command without the promise. In his exposition of the *Sermon on the Mount* (1522), Luther intimated that with the words 'Our Father'

---

[26] See D. Bonhoeffer, *The Way to Freedom* (New York: Harper & Row, 1963), 57-58, as cited in F.E. Rohrbough, 'A Lutheran Understanding of Prayer', *Andrews University Seminary Studies* 38 (2000), 69-75 (71).

[27] *LW* 24, 389-90.

God 'warns us to remember both his command and promise,' since together they constitute the basis of our communion with him.[28]

> Such promises certainly ought to awaken and kindle in our hearts a desire and love to pray. For by his word God testifies that our prayer is heartily pleasing to him and will assuredly be heard and granted, so that we may not despise or disdain it or pray uncertainly.
>
> This you can hold up to him and say, 'I come to Thee, dear Father, and pray not of my own accord or because of my own worthiness, but at thy commandment and promise, which cannot fail or deceive me.'[29]

Luther's theology of prayer is thus a concrete application of the Reformation doctrine of justification. Just as in justification we are declared righteous on account of God's efficacious word, so in prayer we have his word that he will certainly answer and heartily grant us what we ask for. In his *On Rogationtide Prayer and Procession* (1519), Luther asserted

> Our prayer must not be based upon or depend upon our worthiness or that of our prayer, but on the unwavering truth of the divine promise. Whenever our prayer is founded on itself or something else, it is false and deceptive, even though it wrings your heart with its intensive devotion or weeps sheer drops of blood.[30]

In his explanation of the opening words of the Lord's Prayer in his *Personal Prayer Book*, 'Our Father who art in heaven,' Luther again considered the word of God, ascribing to it the power by which 'Christendom, and every Christian soul' are born. The word of God 'creates true Christians, who know Christ and who deeply savor him.'[31] Without the word of God, both faith in God and our prayer to him are impossible. The word of God awakens faith in us and kindles in us a love to pray. Luther asked that we pay attention to the external word of God, in this instance, his promise that he will attend to our needs. He understood the words 'Our father who art in heaven' as God's tender invitation to us to 'believe that he is our dear Father and we are his dear children so that with all boldness and confidence we may ask him as dear children ask their dear father.' This is reflected in his prayer recorded in his *Personal Prayer Book*:

> Moreover, since you are not a physical father here on earth but a spiritual father in heaven, not like an earthly, mortal father who is not always dependable and cannot be of help by himself, show us what an immeasurably better Father you are and

---

[28] *LW* 21, 146.
[29] 'The Large Catechism', in *BC*, 423.
[30] *LW* 42, 88-89.
[31] *LW* 42, 56.

teach us to regard earthly fatherhood, fatherland, friends, possessions, body and blood as far less in value than you.[32]

Through our rebirth by means of the word, we acknowledge the creator God as our true Father, who grants us the privilege of prayer. 'With this type of Father we are given the privilege of request, and we need not be afraid to exercise that privilege.'[33]

The Trinity and the Creed

Whereas the command to pray takes us back to the Ten Commandments, the promise that God hears us and is 'our dear Father' leads us to the Creed. In his *Large Catechism* (1529), Luther introduced the Creed into a passage that connected it with the Ten Commandments, viewing the Creed as the fulfillment of the Ten Commandments. Because the Ten Commandments demand too high a level of conduct for anyone to reach, the Creed is 'given in order to help us to do what the Ten Commandments require of us ... Therefore it is necessary to learn this part [the Creed] as it is the other, so that we may know where and how to obtain strength for this task.'[34] Likewise Luther introduced the Lord's Prayer with a passage that related it to the Creed, seeing the Lord's Prayer as an appropriation of God's infinite blessings that the Creed offers. Consequently, nothing is more necessary than 'to call upon God incessantly and drum into his ears our prayer that he may give, preserve, and increase in us faith and obedience to the Ten Commandments and remove all that stands in our way and hinders us from fulfilling them.'[35] There is in Luther's thinking a movement from the crushing power of the Ten Commandments to the Creed, the summary of the gracious activities of the triune God for us (*pro nobis*), and finally to the Lord's Prayer, the appropriation of the creedal blessings procured for us through the Trinity. The order in which prayer is done reflects the way in which God's revelation of himself comes to us. The Ten Commandments teach what we ought to do; the Creed teaches what God does for us and bestows upon us. We are first confronted by the Ten Commandments with their stern demands. It shows forth our inability to please God because of our sinful predicament. God's wrath and displeasure still condemn us because we by ourselves could not fulfill the law's demand. But the Creed comes, bringing us 'pure grace and making us upright and pleasing to God.'[36] The Creed draws us into God's triune life, to God's fatherly forgiveness and love in Christ, which, by the Spirit's working, we embrace in faith. Finally, the Lord's Prayer teaches us to pray for the full actualization of our new,

---

[32] *LW* 43, 30.

[33] J.W. Voelz, 'Luther's Use of Scripture in the *Small Catechism*', D.P. Scaer and R.D. Preus (eds), *Luther's Catechisms – 450 years: Essays Commemorating the Small and Large Catechisms of Dr. Martin Luther* (Fort Wayne: Concordia Theological Seminary, 1979), 55-64 (62).

[34] 'The Large Catechism', in *BC*, 419.

[35] 'The Large Catechism', in *BC*, 420.

[36] 'The Large Catechism', in *BC*, 420.

God-given status as God's beloved. This order with the same rationale echoes that of Luther's earlier *Personal Prayer Book* (1522), where he claimed that the Ten Commandments, the Creed, and the Lord's Prayer are 'the essentials of the Bible.' They summarize the total content of Scripture with such brevity and clarity that we are without excuse regarding the things necessary for salvation. 'God's particular order of things' is thus woven into the fabric of the Christian life, as indicated in Luther's Foreword to his prayer book:

> Three things a person must know in order to be saved. First, he must know what to do and what to leave undone. Second, when he realizes that he cannot measure up to what he should do or leave undone, he needs to know where to go to find the strength he requires. Third, he must know how to seek and obtain that strength. It is just like a sick person who first has to determine the nature of his sickness, then find out what to do or to leave undone. After that he has to know where to get the medicine which will help him do or leave undone what is right for a healthy person. Third, he has to desire for this medicine and to obtain it or have it brought to him.
>
> Thus, the commandments teach a man to recognize his sickness, enabling him to perceive what he must do or refrain from doing, consent to or refuse, and so he will recognize himself to be a sinful and wicked person. The Creed will teach and show him where to find the medicine – grace – which will help him to become devout and keep the commandments. The Creed points him to God and his mercy, given and made plain to him in Christ. Finally, the Lord's Prayer teaches all this, namely, through the fulfillment of God's commandments everything will be given him. In these three are the essentials of the entire Bible.[37]

To elaborate, the Creed is trinitarian in structure and substance. It accentuates the principle of correspondence between God's 'essence' (who God is) and 'work' (what he does for us) – this knowledge is open only to the eyes of faith. A theology of glory (*theologia gloriae*) seeks painstakingly, by means of human reason or speculation, to discern the true identity of God and what he thinks and does, yet to no avail. But in the Creed we are given this revelation in richest measure. 'In these three articles God himself has revealed and opened to us the most profound depths of his fatherly heart, his sheer, unutterable love.'[38] The Creed proclaims the threefold self-giving nature of God. 'Through this knowledge we come to love and delight in all the commandments of God (including prayer) because we see that God gives himself completely to us, with his gifts and his power, to help us keep the Ten Commandments: the Father gives us all creation, the Son all his works, and the Holy Spirit all his gifts.'[39] Each person contributes to the fulfillment of the Ten Commandments.

---

[37] *LW* 43, 13-14. Cf. G.G. Krodel, 'Luther's Work on the Catechism in the Context of Late Medieval Catechetical Literature', *Concordia Journal* 25 (1995), 364-404 (374-75).

[38] 'The Large Catechism', in *BC*, 419; Kolb, *Teaching God's Children His Teaching*, ch. 4, 2-4.

[39] 'The Large Catechism', in *BC*, 420. Cf. Arand, *That I May Be His Own*, 134-40.

In the First Article, the Father creates all creaturely things in order to serve us, and we in turn use them to his glory. 'He gives us all these things so that we may sense and see in them his fatherly heart and his boundless love towards us. Thus our hearts will be warmed and kindled with gratitude to God and a desire to use all these blessings to his glory and praise.'[40]

In the Second Article, the Father gives us his Son in order to acquire grace for us through the efficacious activities of the Son's suffering and dying on the cross in order that we might fulfill the Ten Commandments. As stated in Luther's *Small Catechism* concerning this Article, 'Jesus Christ ... has redeemed me, a lost and condemned creature, delivered me and freed me from all sins, from death, and from the power of the devil, not with silver and gold but with his holy, precious blood and with his innocent sufferings and death, in order that *I may be his*, live under him in his kingdom, and serve him in everlasting righteousness, innocence and blessedness.'[41]

In the Third Article, the Holy Spirit teaches us to understand the redemptive deed of Christ and helps us to receive and preserve it to our advantage. All three persons work in full unity externally (*ad extra*) as the one God who takes pleasure in giving more generously than we are in willing to pray. Since it is God's nature to give, as the Creed affirms, our position before him is one of receiving, for we cannot give from what is not our own. So whether we stand before God as creatures as in the First Article, or as sinners as in the Second and Third Articles, 'we are always the receivers' of God's supra-abundant grace.[42] So 'there is no need for you to persuade Him with your words or to give him detailed instructions ... Whatever He gives us will be in excess of our understanding and hopes.'[43] Prayer is not an occasion when we instruct God about our needs, but rather is God's reminder to us of our needs and of the blessings he lavishly gives.

This teaching appears in Luther's *An Exposition of the Lord's Prayer for Simple Layman* (1519), where he regarded the seven petitions as 'seven reminders of our wretchedness and poverty by means of which man, led to a knowledge of self, can see what a miserable and perilous life he leads here on earth.'[44] The purpose of these petitions is 'so that we never have any excuse not to pray.'[45] The Lord's Prayer awakens us out of slumber concerning our need so that we learn to expect God to answer our prayers. Jesus' teaching on prayer calls for a radical reversal in our attitude to prayer, turning us away from ourselves to God: 'When my heart is turned to Him and awakened in this way, then I praise Him, thank Him, take refuge with Him in my need, and expect from Him. As a consequence of all this, I learn more

---

[40] 'The Large Catechism', in *BC*, 413.

[41] 'The Small Catechism', in *BC*, 345.

[42] H. Girgensohn, *Teaching Luther's Catechism* (trans. J.W. Dobertsein; Philadelphia: Muhlenberg, 1959), 52-53.

[43] *LW* 21, 144.

[44] *LW* 42, 27.

[45] 'The Large Catechism', in *BC*, 436.

and more to acknowledge what kind of God He is.'[46] Prayer is a means of grace, that which brings us God's grace rather than that which earns his favor.

Meditation on the Creed in this way becomes an occasion for our joyful reception of God's grace, since God answers our prayer with his promise that he will turn towards us with forgiveness and acceptance at all times. 'God therefore wishes you to lament and express your need and wants, not because he is unaware of them, but in order that you may kindle your heart to stronger and greater desires and spread your cloak wide to receive many things.'[47]

The Second Article of the Creed (God the Son) speaks of our right and privilege, as God's new creation, to pray. This is a crucial point: God may require prayer in the commandments, but as desperately wicked sinners, we may hold back or even flee from him, after having been defeated by the law for our innumerable sins. As a remedy, Luther, in his *Exposition of the Lord's Prayer for Simple Layman* (1519), turned to the Christological basis of prayer, that the knowledge of God as our true Father and his promises to hear us belong to us solely on account of the Son of man: 'In his skin and on his back we too must ascend.'[48] This reflects Luther's theology of the cross, in which God hides precisely in the opposite of himself, in Jesus' humanity, to reveal and accomplish his saving will. Just as God has chosen to meet us in Jesus of Nazareth, 'in his skin,' so we come before him in his name, ascending 'on his back' to the inner world of the divine. Here we observe in Luther's Christology a movement from 'below to above': 'from Christ as man to Christ as God and thereby to God.'[49] All other ways or means to establish a salvific relationship with God are doomed to failure because outside of God's 'clothed' word there is futile speculation. Luther was conscious that matters of the divine are necessarily beyond the gaze of sinful mortals. With Augustine, he believed that 'God lowers himself to the level of our weak comprehension and presents himself to us in images, coverings, as it were, in simplicity adapted to a child, that in some measure it may be possible for him to be known by us.'[50] He warned against any speculative incursion into the majesty of the 'naked' God, and led us to biblical revelation in which God has clothed his word and promises. Such a revelation of God forms the basis for true trust in God, making 'the ascent to God' (prayer) possible.[51] As a true theologian of the cross, Luther observed 'this general rule: to avoid as much as possible any questions that carry us to the throne of the Supreme Majesty. It is better and safer to stay at the manger of Christ the man. For there is a great danger in involving oneself in the mazes of the Divine Being.'[52] Earlier in his *Theses for the Heidelberg Disputation* (1518), Luther indicated that although we are forbidden to see

[46] *LW* 21, 44.

[47] 'The Large Catechism', in *BC*, 424.

[48] *LW* 42, 23.

[49] Althaus, *Theology of Martin Luther*, 181.

[50] *LW* 2, 45.

[51] See *LW* 10, 121, where, in his first lectures on the Psalms, Luther designated 'especially earnest prayer' as the 'ascent of the mind to God.'

[52] *LW* 2, 45.

God's 'face,' we, like Moses, are permitted to see God's 'backparts,' a visible piece of the divine mystery.[53] Thus whoever seeks God in any form other than as 'the clothed deity,' the incarnate Son of God, does not find the true God but only the enemy. The God who hides himself, the naked God or the 'absolute God,' remains absolutely hidden in his inscrutable and impassible being, from whom we must flee to the God of mercy who has appeared in Jesus Christ. The naked God does not concern us because clothed in his word and with his word he is offered, worshipped, and proclaimed, and therefore is accessible. God's essence is accessible insofar as God defines his hiddenness in his self-revelation in Jesus' cross and resurrection. God in his own life corresponds to the incarnate and crucified Christ. God 'wants us to learn of the revealed word painstakingly,' wherein he hides himself as a witness to his steadfast love.[54] He does not wish us to approach him in his absolute hiddenness, for to seek to address God directly results in despair and destruction. In his exposition of Psalm 51:1, Luther declared that the absolute God and human creatures are the 'bitterest of enemies':

> From this absolute God everyone should flee who does not want to perish ... Human weakness cannot help being crushed by such majesty ... We must take hold of this God, not naked but clothed and revealed in His word; otherwise despair crushes us ... The absolute God is like an iron wall, against which we cannot bump without destroying ourselves. Therefore Satan is busy day and night, making us run to the naked God so that we forget His promises and blessings shown in Christ and think about God and the judgment of God. When this happens, we perish utterly and fall into despair.[55]

Not the absolute hiddenness, but the precise hiddenness of God in his opposite, that is, 'in his skin and on his back,' is the presupposition and basis of true prayer. 'This God, clothed in such a kind appearance and, so to speak, in such a pleasant mask, that is to say, dressed in His promises – this God we can grasp and look at with joy and trust.'[56] In reality God's promises, made known throughout the Bible, and supremely and fully in Jesus Christ, constitute the true foundation for prayer. Without God's promises, all certainty, consolation and hope vanish, making prayer for forgiveness, new life, and help ineffective. God, clothed in the person of Jesus, draws near to us with his promises of help and mercy so that we can ask, counting on receiving what we need for body and spirit. That 'our father' is our 'dear Father' is rooted in the promise of grace and victory in Christ. This confession has Christ's death and resurrection as its basis. Jesus Christ, by his death and resurrection, conquers sins, death and the devil '*in order that I may be his*.'[57] In Christ, God has turned towards us with love and acceptance, thus abolishing his distance from us

[53] *LW* 31, 50.

[54] *LW* 3, 139.

[55] *LW* 12, 312.

[56] *LW* 10, 312.

[57] See C.P. Arand, '"That I May Be His Own": The Anthropology of Luther's Explanation of the Creed', *Concordia Journal* 21 (1995), 28-41.

(which would mean divine wrath for us) so that we might turn back to him. God's blessing in coming to us is radically opposed to the curse of his remaining at a distance from us. The contradictory nature of this is found in Christ, but resolved for those who believe.[58] Because God does not remain at a distance from us, we too must not remain at a distance from him. In Christ, the distance between God and us is abolished. By the same token, God ceases to be a terrible judge, but is our dear Father, who in Christ promises to hear us and give us his grace. To pray 'Our Father' is to pray 'in the name of our Lord Jesus Christ.' God encourages us to believe that he is our beloved Father so that in Christ we may ask things of him boldly and confidently as beloved children do to their beloved fathers. In that light, Luther uttered the following prayer:

> O Almighty God, in your unmerited goodness to us, and through the merit and mediation of your beloved Son, Jesus Christ, you have permitted, and even commanded and taught us to regard you and call upon you as one Father of us all. You have done so although instead you could rightly and properly be a severe judge over us sinners since we have acted so often against your divine and good will and have aroused your wrath. Now through your mercy implant in our hearts a comforting trust in your fatherly love, and let us experience the sweet and pleasant savor of a childlike certainty that we may joyfully call you Father, knowing and loving you and calling on you in every trouble. Watch over us that we may remain your children and never become guilty of making you, dearest Father, our fearful judge, changing ourselves, your children, into your foes.[59]

Whereas the Second Article grants us the right and privilege to pray, the Third Article (God the Holy Spirit) provides for us the strength and confidence to pray. Just as we cannot by our own reason or power believe in Jesus, so neither can we by our own reason or strength come before God in prayer.[60] Prayer seeks what we need from God, not from ourselves. It is a confession of our need and helplessness, calling out for God's grace. 'Yet to call out in my need is to die, to confess my inability and to seek help from God.'[61] With respect to the life of faith and prayer, it ties the Holy Spirit closely to Christ. The work of the Holy Spirit is to communicate to us the gospel: in Christ's cross and resurrection divine mercy has conquered divine wrath, if only we believe. Redemption is completed, and the benefits Christ has acquired and won for us by his sufferings, death, and resurrection belong to us in faith. But this work remains hidden, and is of no use to us unless God causes us to perceive and receive it. If the Holy Spirit had not come to offer and apply to us this treasure of salvation, the work of Christ would have been all in vain. Thus he who spurns knowing the Father in the Son loses all knowledge of God. It is by the Holy Spirit that we are led to see God in the flesh, in whom the Father is mirrored. The God who came to us in Christ is indeed the same God who

---

[58] Ngien, *Suffering of God according to Martin Luther's 'Theologia Crucis'*, 124.

[59] *LW* 43, 29.

[60] *LW* 43, 211; 'The Small Catechism', in *BC*, 345.

[61] Arand, 'Battle Cry of Faith', 60.

comes as the Holy Spirit. Christ accomplishes redemption, but the Holy Spirit carries on his work without ceasing until the Last Day. God has revealed himself and opened to us his sheer, boundless love. Moreover, none could come to recognize the Father's love were it not for the Lord Christ, who is 'a mirror' of God's fatherly heart.[62] Apart from Christ we know nothing but an angry and severe judge. But neither could we know of Christ's heart had it not been revealed by the Holy Spirit. We do not know the Father revealed in the First Article except through the Son revealed in the Second Article; nor can we know of Christ except through the Holy Spirit revealed in the Third Article.[63] And with the help of the Spirit, we are enabled to pray and seek what we need from God. Here we discern a logical order, beginning with the First Article, moving through the Second to the Third Article, and finally concluding with the Lord's Prayer.[64] The Lord's Prayer is thus the bridge between the objective works of the triune God and the subjective realization in our daily life of the benefits procured for us through the Trinity. All three Persons work together as one God, giving himself completely and all his gifts unconditionally.[65] While God invites us to believe the gospel that he is our true and dear Father through the work of Christ, the Holy Spirit enters our hearts prompting us to cry 'Abba Father.' 'Working through the Spirit, Father and Son stir, awaken, call and beget new life in me and in all who are his. Thus the Spirit in and through Christ quickens, sanctifies, and awakens the spirit in us and brings us to the Father, by whom the Spirit is active and life-giving everywhere.'[66]

Words for Use in Prayer and a Four-stranded Schema of Prayer

God not only commands us to pray and promises to meet us in our prayers, he also grants us the words we are to use in our prayer. This was already stated in the opening address of the Lord's Prayer in *A Simple Way to Pray*, where Luther wrote, 'thy dear Son, our Lord Jesus Christ, has taught us both *how and what to pray*.'[67] Based on Matthew 6:9, Luther taught that 'we should be encouraged and drawn to pray because, in addition to this commandment and promise, God takes the initiative and puts into our mouths the very words we are to use.'[68] Prayer has been a central part of the Jewish religion. Just as John the Baptist had taught his disciples to pray,

[62] 'The Large Catechism', in *BC*, 419, as cited in F. Hebart, 'The Role of the Lord's Prayer in Luther's Theology of Prayer', *Lutheran Theological Journal* 18 (1984), 1-17 (8). Cf. *LW* 42, 8 (Meditation on Christ's Passion, 1519), where Luther pictured Christ as the 'earnest mirror.'

[63] 'The Small Catechism', in *BC*, 345-47. Cf. T.J. Wengert, '"Fear and Love" in the Ten Commandments', *Concordia Journal* 21 (1995), 14-27 (20).

[64] For the transition from the Third Article to the Lord's Prayer, see 'The Small Catechism', in *BC*, 345-47.

[65] *LW* 43, 28.

[66] 'The Large Catechism', in *BC*, 423.

[67] *LW* 43, 194.

[68] 'The Large Catechism', in *BC*, 423.

so Jesus teaches his own disciples, who came to him, asking, 'Lord, teach us to pray, as John taught his disciples' (Luke 11:1). What is new about the Lord's Prayer is *how and what* we are to pray, not that we pray. Instead of offering a polemical treatise on prayer, Jesus taught the disciples his own words of prayer, God's way of showing us how to communicate with him. This in turn dispels any hint of agnosticism about what and how to pray. We are given the very words we are to utter and the way we are to pray. It is God who takes the initiative to establish the divine–human encounter. He seeks to draw us into his own world by 'kindling fire in our hearts' through the words we are to use.[69] This is the very purpose of recitation or reading of the word of God: to warm our hearts to pray. We are to turn to the word of God, as it is expressed especially but not exclusively in the words of Scripture. 'Nothing is so effectual against the devil, the world, flesh, and all evil thoughts as to occupy oneself with the word of God, talk about it, and meditate on it.'[70]

For this reason, Luther took very seriously the discipline of daily recitation and meditation. In his *A Simple Way to Pray*, he disclosed his personal practice of prayer in the order which is similar to that of his *Catechisms*: the Ten Commandment–the Creed–the Lord's Prayer:

> First, when I feel that I have become cool and joyless in prayer because of other tasks or thoughts (for the flesh and the devil always impede and obstruct prayer), I take my little psalter, hurry to my room, or, if it be the day and hour for it, to the church where a congregation is assembled and, as time permits, I say quietly to myself and word-for-word the Ten Commandments, the Creed, and some words of Christ (including the Lord's Prayer) or of Paul, or some psalms, just as a child might do.[71]

Luther prepared for prayer by first reciting the Ten Commandments, the Creed, and certain portions of Scripture. His practice was to recite the Lord's Prayer, after which he meditated slowly on one petition or more. Then, as time permitted, he would meditate on the Ten Commandments and do the same with the Creed. By means of repetition he used the word to free himself from all distractions. Luther's underlying principle was that the heart needs to be nurtured and shaped for prayer. This is achieved by the word of God, the instrument of God's power of which the Lord's Prayer is one means which God uses as 'flint and steel to kindle a flame in the heart' for him.[72] Part of the potential problem is that we know the Lord's Prayer by heart so that praying its petitions becomes a matter of routine, devoid of actual reflection upon it. We become so accustomed to the words that we no longer

---

[69] *LW* 43, 209.

[70] 'The Large Catechism', in *BC*, 359-60.

[71] *LW* 43, 193. Cf. S. Peura, 'The Essence of Luther's Spirituality', *Seminary Ridge Review* (Winter 2000), 16-33 (20-21), where he argued that Luther began by meditating on the Ten Commandments or the Creed before meditating on the Lord's Prayer. This is the exact opposite of Luther's practice. Peura's position is one of *theosis*, which speaks of salvation as an essential participation in God.

[72] *LW* 43, 209.

perceive how each petition could open an entire world of meaning and provide an agenda for both praying and living.[73] To correct this, Luther urged the one who would pray not to embark on an empty repetition of phrases, but to meditate on each petition individually, in isolation, kneeling or standing with their hands folded and eyes towards heaven. This too was the constant practice that Luther imposed upon himself: 'This in short is the way I use the Lord's Prayer when I pray it. To this day I still suckle at the Lord's Prayer like a child and as an old man eat and drink from it and never get my fill. It is the very best of prayers, even better than the Psalter, which is so very dear to me.'[74] Enough time for repetition and thoughtful reflection is given, until the heart is rightly stirred and inclined towards God. When that happens, 'the Holy Spirit preaches here, and one word of his sermon is far better than a thousand of our prayers.'[75] And he who would pray should be content with any good thoughts emerging from one petition, and disregard all others in order to listen to the 'sermon of the Spirit.'[76] Luther's letter of instruction contains sample reflections for each petition. To cite the sixth one, 'And lead us not into temptation,' as an example:

> O dear Lord, Father and God, keep us fit and alert, eager and diligent in thy word and service, so that we do not become complacent, lazy, and slothful as though we had already achieved everything. In that way the fearful devil cannot fall upon us, surprise us, and deprive us of thy precious word or stir up strife and factions among us and lead us into other sin and disgrace, both spiritually and physically. Rather grant us wisdom and strength through thy Spirit that we may valiantly resist him and gain the victory. Amen.[77]

After praying the Lord's Prayer, Luther exhorted the Christian to move on to the Ten Commandments and the Creed. He did not hesitate to offer very down-to-earth instructions on a method of approach to daily prayer, although his emphasis was on the content of prayer. In a well-structured manner, meditation on each commandment or article of the Creed is centered on four distinctive types of responses, which Luther called 'a garland of four strands': instruction, thanksgiving, confession, and petition.[78] Each of these, when woven with the others, creates a delightful 'garland' of praise to God. Below is Luther's illustration in detail for the first commandment, 'I am the Lord your God ... You shall have no other gods before me.'

---

[73] Kolb, *Teaching God's Children His Teaching*, ch. 5, 3-4.

[74] *LW* 43, 209.

[75] *LW* 43, 198.

[76] *LW* 43, 191.

[77] *LW* 43, 197.

[78] *LW* 43, 200; cf. R. Maas, 'A Simple Way to Pray: Luther's Instructions on the Devotional Use of the Catechism', in R. Maas and G. O'Donnell (eds.), *Spiritual Traditions for the Contemporary Church* (Nashville: Abingdon, 1990), 162- 69 (164-66).

The First Strand: Instruction

Here I earnestly consider that God expects and teaches me to trust him sincerely in all things and that it is his most earnest purpose to be my God. I must think of him in this way at the risk of losing eternal salvation. My heart must not build upon anything else or trust in any other thing, be it wealth, prestige, wisdom, might, piety, or anything else.

The Second Strand: Thanksgiving

Second, I give thanks for his infinite compassion by which he has come to me in such a fatherly way and, unasked, unbidden, and unmerited, has offered to be my God, to care for me, to be my comfort, guardian, help, and strength in every time of need. We poor mortals have sought so many gods and would have to seek them still if he did not enable us to hear him openly tell us in our own language that he intends to be our God. How could we ever – in all eternity – thank him enough!

The Third Strand: Confession

Third, I confess and acknowledge my great sin and ingratitude for having so shamefully despised such sublime teachings and such a precious gift throughout my whole life, and for having fearfully provoked his wrath by countless acts of idolatry. I repent of these and ask for his grace.

The Fourth Strand: Petition

Fourth, I pray and say: 'O my God and Lord, help me by thy grace to learn and understand thy commandments more fully every day and to live by them in sincere confidence. Preserve my heart so that I shall never again become forgetful and ungrateful, that I may never seek after other gods or other consolation on earth or in any creature, but cling truly and solely to thee, my only God. Amen, dear Lord God and Father. Amen'.[79]

In like manner, the same fourfold configuration applies in Luther's contemplation on the Apostles' Creed, the three articles of which correspond to the three Persons of the divine majesty. When praying the Creed, Luther imitated the practice of Augustine, who also exhorted Christians to 'say the creed daily. When you rise, when you compose yourself to sleep, repeat your creed, render it to the Lord, remind yourself of it, be not irked to say it over.'[80] Luther treated the Creed in the same

[79] *LW* 43, 200-201.

[80] See Augustine, *Serm.* 58, II, *PL* 38, 399-400, as cited in Maas, 'Simple Way to Pray', 166.

manner as he did the Decalogue, making it into a garland of four strands. As an example, his treatment of the second article points to the soteriological thrust of his Christology, that Christ suffers and dies for us (*pro nobis*):

The First Strand: Instruction

Again a great light shines forth and teaches us how Christ, God's son, has redeemed us from death which, after the creation, had become our lot through Adam's fall and in which we would have perished eternally. Now think: just as in the first article you were to consider yourself one of God's creatures and not doubt it, now you must think of yourself as one of the redeemed and never doubt that. Emphasize one word above all others, for instance, Jesus Christ, *our* Lord. Likewise, suffered for *us*, arose for *us*. All this is ours and pertains to us; that *us* includes yourself, as the word of God declares. (Italics are Luther's.)

The Second Strand: Thanksgiving

Second, you must be sincerely grateful for such grace and rejoice in your salvation.

The Third Strand: Confession

Third, you must sorrowfully lament and confess your wicked unbelief and mistrust of such a gift. Oh, what thoughts will come to mind – the idolatry you have practiced repeatedly, how much you have made of praying to the saints and of innumerable good works of yours which have opposed such salvation.

The Fourth Strand: Petition

Fourth, pray now that God will preserve you from this time forward to the end in true and pure faith in Christ our Lord.[81]

There is a doctrinal logic behind the order of Ten Commandments–Creed–Lord's Prayer, that we must first encounter the moral imperative of the law and be struck down by it before being made ready to hear the word of grace in the gospel. The Lord's Prayer leads us to an appropriation of the fulfillment of the Ten Commandments through the Creed. The antithetical unity of law and gospel forever abides in the Christian life. The believer learns from the law what cannot be accomplished by human efforts, and henceforth looks at sin 'only within the picture of grace … [which] is nothing else but that of Christ on the cross.'[82] The good news

[81] *LW* 43, 210-11.

[82] See *LW* 42, 104-106 (Sermon on Preparing to Die).

that our sins are forgiven in Christ is a sweet sound to the ears of faith and this same rationale is reflected in the order in which the strand of thanksgiving is placed before that of confession in prayer. That thanksgiving is logically prior to confession presupposes that God's grace has already been bestowed upon us, and therefore we begin on a note of thanksgiving because the divine agency of grace is the root of all human activities, including gratitude. In this, Barth's words might reflect Luther's thinking: 'Grace evokes gratitude like the voice an echo. Gratitude follows like thunder lightning.'[83] Thus any deviation from this pattern would signal disaster, for it places us solely under the crushing weight of the law without the consolation of the gospel. By the same token, confession is a response to the prior experience of God's grace, not a condition of it. The sins God reveals through the alien work of the law are ours, for which Christ died. The sins we confess, we cast them upon Christ to receive the *pro nobis* effects (e.g., forgiveness) of his activity on the cross (see italics under 'Instruction').

That being the case, Luther never intended this procedural approach to be a rigid formula to be followed, but rather as an aid to contemplation. He warned against 'a mindless repetition' – a mechanical usage of the four-stranded scheme, devoid of content. He did not want anyone to feel bound by his words or thoughts. Close to the end of his exposition of the Ten Commandments in his *A Simple Way to Pray*, he also stressed the need for spiritual sensitivity to the good thoughts that should lie behind such contemplation. He wrote, 'if in the midst of such thoughts the Holy Spirit begins to preach in your heart with rich, enlightening thoughts, honor him by letting go of this written scheme; be still and listen to him who can do better than you can.'[84] 'It is enough to consider one section or half a section which kindles fire in our heart. This the Spirit will grant us and continually instruct us in when, by God's word, our hearts have been cleared and freed of outside thoughts and concerns.'[85] Should anyone wish to improve on his schema, he added, let them do so:

> Let him meditate either upon all the commandments at one time or on as many as he may desire. For the mind, once it is seriously occupied with a matter, be it good or evil, can ponder more in one moment than the tongue can recite in ten hours or the pen write in ten days. There is something quick, subtle, and mighty about the mind and soul. It is able to review the Ten Commandments in their fourfold aspect very rapidly if it wants to do so and is in earnest.[86]

---

[83] See K. Barth, *Church Dogmatics* (Edinburgh: T&T Clark, 1960), IV/1, 41, as cited in M. Boulton, '"We Pray by His Mouth": Karl Barth, Erving Goffman, and a Theology of Invocation', *Modern Theology* 17 (2001), 67-83 (70). Cf. Senn, 'Lutheran Spirituality', *Protestant Spiritual Traditions*, 36, who concurs with Barth on this point: gratitude corresponds to grace.

[84] *LW* 43, 201.

[85] *LW* 43, 209.

[86] *LW* 43, 207.

Not the natural desire of the heart, but the desire of the kindled heart is the springboard for prayer.[87] This God-ward desire is not a human invention but God's creative work. The 'I–thou' (Buber's phrase) relationship with God, which we cannot produce, is the Spirit's work, igniting a flame in our hearts for him.[88] Thus once the heart is rightly warmed to prayer, certain formula or words or syllables may be laid aside in order to give way to the Holy Spirit. When the Holy Spirit makes the words shine in our hearts, we must pause and listen silently as to his sermon.

Luther made a distinction between an outward, sham prayer which is characterized by 'the mouth's thoughtless mumbling and chattering' and an inward, genuine prayer, which 'reflects innermost desires, its sighing and yearning.'[89] The former makes hypocrites, the latter produces true saints. In order that prayer be genuine, it must stem from the heart. Secondly, true sincere prayer demands the discipline of concentration and singleness of heart. This too is directed against those whose mouths babble and minds wander to other thoughts – a tendency so peculiar to mere external prayer, of which Luther repented. 'But, praise God, it is now clear to me that a person who forgets what he has said has not prayed well. In a good prayer one fully remembers every word and thought from the beginning to the end of the prayer.' Hence a prayer that arises from 'a cold and unattentive heart' is 'a more ridiculous kind of buffoonery.'[90]

Thus, for Luther, prayer is thoroughly dialogical, an 'I–thou' relationship in which we as the human partner are fully engaged both in mind and heart with God. In the moments of an I–thou encounter, the attention is held; the mind does not wander off; the heart is enflamed and made ready to express its yearnings, joys, and sorrows to God.

> So, a good and attentive barber keeps his thoughts, attention, and eyes on the razor and hair and does not forget how far he has gotten with his shaving or cutting. If he wants to engage in too much conversation or let his mind wander or look somewhere else he is likely to cut his customer's mouth, nose, or even his throat. Thus if anything is to be done well, it requires the full attention of all one's senses and members, as the proverb says, '*Pluribus intentus*, minor est ad singula sensus' – 'He who thinks of many things, thinks of nothing and does nothing right.' How much more does prayer call for concentration and singleness of heart if it is to be a good prayer![91]

---

[87] Hanson, *Grace That Frees*, 102.

[88] For a discussion of Buber's 'I–thou' theology, see McGrath, *Christian Theology*, 270-73.

[89] *LW* 43, 198.

[90] *LW* 43, 199. Cf. Hanson, *Grace That Frees*, 98-99.

[91] 'The Large Catechism', in *BC*, 436.

Faith: 'Amen' as the Condition of Efficacy

Faith must be present in order for the command, promise, and words of prayer to be efficacious. It is summed up in our willingness to say 'Amen', believing that our prayers will surely be heard.

> But the efficacy of prayer consists in our learning also to say 'Amen' to it – that is, not to doubt that our prayer is surely heard and will be granted. This word is nothing else than an unquestioning affirmation of faith on the part of one who does not pray as a matter of chance but knows that God does not lie since he has promised to grant his requests. Where such faith is wanting, there can be no true prayer.[92]

True prayer is done in faith, wholeheartedly adding 'yes' to it, and boldly believing against all appearances that our cries reach heaven. Further, Luther added that we are not to think we are praying alone, but the whole of Christendom, all devout saints, is standing there beside us, praying together with us in the common, united petition, creating a garland of praise to God.[93] Prayer warriors, past and present, must have their eyes fixed on God's promise, relying totally on it, not on their own deeds or worthiness. We come with a child-like faith, laying hold of 'a certainty and a truth' that God has heard our prayers. 'Behold, this is the importance that God attaches to our being certain that we do not pray in vain and that we must not in any way despise our prayers.'[94] Even if God does not grant our prayers in accordance with our wish, we dare not doubt that God has heard them. Prayer must be spoken in the assurance that its petitions are acceptable to and heard by the heavenly Father, 'for he himself commanded us to pray like this and promised to hear us.'[95] Thus those who conclude their prayers with a firm 'Amen' do not remain awake, tossing back and forth on the pillow, worrying about tomorrow's needs. This is the true meaning of 'Amen'.[96]

> Therefore, take note that a prayer is not good and right because of its length, devoutness, sweetness, or its pleas for temporal or eternal goods. Only that prayer is acceptable which breathes a firm confidence and trust that it will be heard (no matter how small and unworthy it may be in itself) because of the reliable pledge and promise of God. Not your zeal but God's word and promise render your prayer good. This faith, based on God's words, is also the true worship; without it all other worship is sheer deception and error.[97]

In Luther's view, there are two kinds of faith. There is a faith which is simply the acceptance of what is propositionally true about God.[98] In Buber's term, this faith

---

92 'The Large Catechism', in *BC*, 436.
93 *LW* 43, 198.
94 'The Large Catechism', in *BC*, 436.
95 'The Small Catechism', in *BC*, 348.
96 *LW* 43, 198.
97 *LW* 42, 77.
98 *LW* 43, 24.

puts God in an 'I–it' context, treating God merely as 'an item of knowledge' to be grasped intellectually.[99] This is not true faith. On the contrary, true faith grasps God, trusting in him and acting on the conviction that what has been promised by God in his word is an unquestionable certainty and undeniable truth. The true definition of faith Luther articulated in his opening remarks on the Creed in his *Personal Prayer Book*:

> Only a faith that ventures everything in life and in death on what is said (in Scripture) of God makes a person a Christian and obtains all he desires from God. No corrupt or hypocritical heart can have such a faith; this is a living faith as the First Commandment demands: I am your God; you shall have no other gods.[100]

Whenever faith is wanting, our prayer becomes a shame and pretense, a 'mere jabbering and babbling' of the mouth without the involvement of the heart.[101] We must not pray aimlessly, supposing that it suffices to say the words, whether God hears them or not, in which case we stake prayer on luck or chance, not on faith. In his exposition of Psalm 90, Luther pointed out that true prayer necessarily proceeded from the heart, as in Moses, who, 'in true faith of the heart, prays and says, "Thou art our Dwelling Place".' However, Moses' prayer cannot emerge from the heart 'without faith and without the gift of the Holy Spirit.'[102] Faith and prayer form such a unity that 'if we conclude our prayer with the word "Amen" spoken with confidence and strong faith, it is surely sealed and heard.'[103] When our prayers are spoken with genuine trust toward God in our hearts, doubts no longer abide; neither a 'No', nor a 'Perhaps' can vitiate the certainty of God's 'Yes' to our petitions.[104] Since 'Amen' (faith) is essential to true prayer, a mere recital of the words of a prayer is of no benefit if the heart is lacking. Speaking of the Lord's Prayer, Luther instructed, 'It would be better to pray one Lord's Prayer with a devout heart and with thought given to the words, resulting in a better life, than for you to acquire absolution through reciting all other prayers.'[105] Unfortunately, some had become so reliant on the prayers of the saints that they no longer derived from them the desired spiritual benefit or blessings. 'They nullify it, for they utter it merely with their lips and not with their hearts, because they will not believe that they are heard until they know, or imagine that they know, that they have prayed well and worthily. Thus they build on themselves.'[106]

---

[99] *LW* 43, 24.
[100] *LW* 43, 24-25.
[101] *LW* 21, 142.
[102] *LW* 13, 87-88.
[103] *LW* 42, 76.
[104] *LW* 43, 38.
[105] *LW* 42, 22.
[106] *LW* 42, 77.

A good prayer is marked not by so many words, but rather by 'a turning to God frequently and with heartfelt longing, and doing so without ceasing.'[107] Luther advised against heaping up empty phrases as the Gentiles did, thinking that they would be heard for their many words (cf. Matt. 6:7). Such lengthy prayer was a 'reckless and worthless prattle, the sort of thing that would come from people who supposed that they would not be heard otherwise.' He denounced the false manner of prayer espoused by the inhabitants of the monasteries and cloisters as well as the clergy. For they turned prayer into 'a mere work, to be judged on the basis of size and length, as though this made it a precious accomplishment.' They wore themselves out everyday with lengthy prayers, and by singing and reading their canonical times at night. As a result, they were suffering from 'the gentile delusion' that the more praying they performed 'the holier and greater an act of worship' would be. Such prayers, Luther charged, were worthless because they were 'the slave labor of their mouths or their tongues.' But true prayer, according to Jesus himself, is the language of faith, which stems from the heart. 'For God does not ask how much or how long you have prayed, but how good the prayer is and whether it proceeds from the heart.'[108] Therefore faith – a confident trust in God's word – is the *sine qua non* of praying, that is, without faith, prayer is of no avail. *Amen* is the condition of effective prayer. Just as faith is necessary in the order of salvation (*ordo salutis*) – justification, sanctification, and perseverance, etc. – so it must permeate the life of prayer in order for it to be effective.[109]

That prayer and faith are inextricably bound together corresponds to Luther's exposition of the First Commandment. The command to pray contains within itself the demand for a 'true faith and confidence of the heart' that expects nothing but all good things from God. As stated above, prayer is essentially of the heart, not of the lips. Faith-heart-prayer is directed to the one true God, who alone is good, and out of whom flows nothing evil but all good. Luther linked the prayer of faith with the true nature of God, for faith and God are bound together. Almost in an Anselmian fashion, Luther defined God as 'that to which your heart clings and entrusts itself' – the ultimate reality.[110] God as such is the superlative, belonging to a totally different ontological order. The supremacy of God requires us to fly straight to him, and cling to him alone as the true God, worthy of our total trust. God invites us to believe in order that we might ask. Faith, which is so crucial to our prayers, is not our gift to God, but only our acceptance of what God gives to us. Conversely, to do otherwise, such as to pray without a clinging faith, is to commit the sin of idolatry, looking elsewhere, to other gods as the ultimate reality. Essentially, to pray in faith is to practise the First Commandment, with our hearts turned towards no one else but God alone for all good. With a strong 'Amen', we grasp the meaning of God's words

---

[107] *LW* 43, 12.

[108] *LW* 21, 142-43.

[109] For a discussion of the order of salvation (*ordo salutis*), see A.A. Hoekema, *Saved by Grace* (Grand Rapids: Eerdmans, 1989), 14; Bruce A. Demarest, *The Cross and Salvation: The Doctrine of Salvation* (Wheaton, IL: Crossway, 1997), 36-44.

[110] 'The Large Catechism', in *BC*, 365.

encapsulated in the First Commandment: 'Whatever good thing you lack, look to me for it and seek it from me, and whenever you suffer misfortune and distress, come and cling to me. I am the only one who will satisfy you and help you out of every need. Only let your heart cling to no one else.'[111] By praying in faith, we honor God alone as the true God, who not only demands prayer of us but also will hear our petitions. Prayer is our response to God's fatherly invitation to us to believe that, in a real sense, he is our true and dear Father before whom we come with all boldness and confidence as beloved children do to their earthly parents. Hence, the human creature does not 'create the conditions of human and worldly existence, he discovers them already here – before he prays. But through our prayer this reality (God), existing before us "without our prayer" and gives us a gift, enters our own existence. Through prayer we can perceive what is already there.'[112] In other words, 'the praying individual is himself taken into God's reality as a reality accepted by the one who prays in faith.'[113] Prayer assumes as our own everything that is already there for us (*pro nobis*), the pre-existent gifts we don't create but only appropriate in faithful prayer. What is invoked in prayer is the pre-existent blessings God seeks to give to us, and which belong to us through faithful prayer. God would have us pray 'in order to have us acknowledge and confess that He is already bestowing many blessings upon us and that He can and will give us still more.'[114] The increasing awareness and appropriation of God's gifts are 'done among us,' as Luther said clearly, 'that God would lead us to realize this and to receive' his blessings.[115] He bids us pray for faith to receive his gifts. Prayer acquires the 'for us' (*pro nobis*) effects of Christ's saving work on the cross. Because God has turned towards us with his gifts, we now turn towards him, without doubting that he is *pro nobis*, and his gifts rightly belong to us, if we but believe. The so-called admirable change (*commercium admirabile*), through which Christ absorbs our sin and death, and communicates to us his divine properties such as righteousness, wisdom, and eternal life, occurs as an outcome of a faithful ('Amen') contemplative exercise. This explains why Luther constantly drew attention to the importance of the word 'Amen', for 'this word expresses the faith that we should have in praying every petition.'[116] '"*Amen*" is nothing but an expression of the faith of the person who doesn't doubt or pray on the off-chance, but knows that God doesn't lie, because he has promised to give.'[117] Thus truly to come in faith is the condition of the efficacy of our prayer.

---

[111] 'The Large Catechism', in *BC*, 365.

[112] V. Vajta, 'Luther als Beter', in H. Junghans (ed.), *Leben und Werk Martin Luthers von 1526 bis 1546: Festgabe zu seinem 500: Geburtstag* (Göttingen: Vangenhoeck & Ruprecht, 1983), vol. 1, 285, quoted in Arand, 'Battle Cry of Faith', 58-59.

[113] Vajta, 'Luther als Beter', vol. 1, 285, as quoted in Hebart, 'Role of the Lord's Prayer', 11.

[114] *LW* 21, 144.

[115] *LW* 21, 144.

[116] *LW* 42, 76.

[117] 'The Large Catechism III: 119, 120', as cited in Hebart, 'Role of the Lord's Prayer', 11.

Conclusion

Luther's theology of prayer is thus a direct implicate of the doctrine of justification. The crux of Luther's thinking on prayer is the double movement: the God–humanward and humanity–Godward movement. In his movement towards us, the triune God comes as giver of himself and all his gifts and, correspondingly, in our movement towards him, we come as the recipients of his blessings in Christ through the ministry of the Spirit. God's gracious promises in Christ find their subjective realization in us through the Spirit's working so that we, by faithful prayer, may have God as the true God, and possess all the good things he has as our own. All three Persons work in full unity, the Spirit drawing us into the inner world of the divine in order that we might perceive and enjoy God's fatherly promises in Christ. Like David, when our conscience is beset by sin, we take 'hold of God the Promiser with the help of the Spirit,' and know 'that in God there remained a hope of forgiveness for sinners.' Being wrapped 'in the bosom of God who is called Grace and Mercy,' we approach him boldly and confidently, not doubting that he wills to manifest his grace to us. 'This is true theology,' which Psalm 51:1 indicates: 'According to Thy abundant mercy blot out my transgressions.'[118] Prayer is a means of grace, that which brings us God's grace rather than that which earns his favour. Prayer as such is not our creation, but is a gift of God. True piety thus consists in obeying God's command, believing God's promise, using the words God offers, and expressing the faith God gives.

[118] *LW* 12, 323.

CHAPTER 6

A Method of Comfort: Temptation and *Theologia Crucis*

The Reformer's triadic rules – meditation (*meditatio*), prayer (*oratio*), and temptation (*tentatio/Anfechtung*) – governed the way Luther read theology, and shaped his distinct piety. It was precisely the third rule, which Luther referred to as 'the touchstone,' that made a good theologian out of him, as it continually drove him back to God in meditation and prayer.[1] Luther confessed, 'I did not learn my theology at one time, but I had to meditate deeper and deeper. Then my *Anfechtungen* carried me thither. For this [theology] cannot be acquired without experience.'[2] The experience of temptation continues as a perennial feature of an authentic Christian life.[3] The word *Anfechtung* (or *tentatio*) has no exact English equivalent. Roland Bainton defined it as 'all the doubts, turmoil, pang, tremor, pains, despair, desolation, and desperation which invade the spirit of man.'[4] The concept of temptation, McGrath expands accurately, is constituted by two aspects, distinct but inseparable: the '*objective*' assaults of spiritual forces upon the believer and the '*subjective*' anxiety and doubt within him as the outcome of these assaults.[5] Death, the devil, the world, and hell are the immediate sources of these terrifying assaults upon people. But most emphatically Luther grounded temptation theologically, viewing God as the ultimate source of it: temptation is God's alien work, which is intended to break down people's self-confidence, and reduce them to a state of doubt and despair in order that they may finally turn to him for aid. It is for this reason that Luther regarded *Anfechtung* as a 'delicious despair,' for hidden in it is precisely its opposite – God's delightful comfort.[6]

Above all, the liberating power of God's objective words and works, rather than the subjective responses or feelings of people, is the Reformer's anchor in times of trial. The sufferer must allow the majesty of God's word to dictate their praying,

---

[1] *LW* 34, 286-87.

[2] *Table Talk* 1, 352, as cited in Bornkamm, *Luther's World of Thought*, 73.

[3] See E. Grislis, 'The Experience of the *Anfechtungen* and the Formulation of Pure Doctrine in Martin Luther's Commentary on Genesis', *Consensus* 8 (1982), 19-31.

[4] R. Bainton, *Here I Stand* (Mentor Book; New York: Abingdon, 1950), 42. See also *LW* 48, 28, n. 10, as cited in *LW* 42, 181, n. 2.

[5] McGrath, *Luther's Theology of the Cross*, 170.

[6] See *WA* 5, 381, 18-19; 619.27, as cited in McGrath, *Luther's Theology of the Cross*, 171.

reading, or singing. This chapter is restricted to a few of Luther's letters of comfort, where he applied with variations his paradigmatic principles in his council to those who suffered the assaults of temptation on body, mind, and soul. His theology of the cross, that God is always manifest in ways that we do not expect or places which, at first glance, seem disappointing or inappropriate, was central to his advice to people when they experienced suffering. The Reformer's ability to steer away from the prevalent theology of glory or triumphalism – which believes that God is most clearly found in the successes, certainties and victories of life – is praiseworthy. The antinomy between the negative aspects of the assaults of God as hidden and the gracious activities of God as revealed occurs in Christ, but is resolved for those who believe. Temptation is the alien work that God does by means of the law so that he might achieve his proper work by means of the gospel: both are works done for the justification of the sinner. With this Luther championed the theology of justification that faith alone justifies, without human works. In the final analysis, what matters most to him was not didactic, what believers could learn from these experiences of suffering, but rather soteriological, what God intended for them in this awesome manner.

The Method of Comfort: Six Paradigmatic Principles

The oldest extant copy of the treatise *Comfort When Facing Grave Temptations* was included in a book printed in 1545. It also appeared in a handwritten collection of Luther's sermons edited by John Poliander, dated 1521.[7] Luther laid out six basic principles when giving comfort.

First, the person who is being tempted should consider only God's words offered to him in God's name, and not be affected by their inner feelings.[8]

Second, the person who is being tempted should recognize that they are not alone in their trials, but are surrounded by the entire body of Christ of which they are members, each member suffering the same trials.[9]

Third, the believer should not wish for swift deliverance from temptations, but cheerfully and willingly submit to God's fatherly will in the same way that Christ did: 'If I am to drink this cup, dear Father, may your will, not mine, be done' (Luke 22:42).[10]

Fourth, the believer should look up to God, in the firm belief that there is 'no stronger medicine' than praising the God hidden by the sufferings of the believer. This is borne out in David's words, 'I will call upon the Lord and praise him, and so

---

[7] *LW* 42, 181-82. John Poliander (1486–1541) was secretary to John Eck, Luther's opponent at the Leipzig Debate. He was so impressed by Luther that he gave up his position at the St. Thomas School in Leipzig to study theology at Wittenberg. Cf. *LW* 42, 170, n. 3.

[8] *LW* 42, 183.

[9] *LW* 42, 183.

[10] *LW* 42, 183.

shall I be saved from all that assails me' (Ps. 18:3). Praising God dispels the evil spirit of gloom and makes the heart leap for joy.[11]

Fifth, the believer should count these trials as a privilege, of which many have been deprived. Luther advised those who were being tempted to thank God for their election in this way, for God's blessings are given to those whom God deems worthy of such assaults. Here, Luther returned to the principle of the theology of the cross, in which God hides his blessings under the appearance of what appears as contrary to those blessings. His 'yes' is hidden in his 'no.' God forbids believers to pry into this hidden arena, for such an attempt would incur only harm. It suffices for the one who is assailed to know that trials are 'the best sign' of God's infinite goodness.[12]

Finally, the believer should lay hold of the constancy and reliability of God's triune character. It is divine to give us gifts extravagantly, as a good father does to his beloved children. Therefore the believer must never doubt the promise of the truthful and faithful God but firmly believe that God will hear their petitions and give them good gifts as he has promised.[13] In support of this argument, Luther cited Matthew 21:22; Mark 11:24; and Luke 11:9-13, the same texts he used as the basis of approaching God in prayer. God's promise is no empty word; what he promises, he truly fulfills. Faith lays hold of the divine promise, thus allowing it to be realized in the lives of believers. Luther's basic rule is this: to know God aright is to know him from below, that is, from the incarnate Christ – his human life, cross, and resurrection; and to know Christ aright is to know him 'alone' as the 'mediator' of God's grace – this is revealed by the Holy Spirit whom the heavenly Father gives to those who ask him.[14] Luther insisted on a movement from below, that those who are tempted should avoid dealing 'directly with God' (i.e., the hidden God) but begin with Christ, and through him ascend to the fatherly heart of God to receive his gifts.[15]

The proper usage of God's word, especially the Psalms, as a method of comfort, is integral to Luther's letters of spiritual counsel. As an illustration, he cited Psalm 142, the only Psalm which was not discussed in any of his other works, as a text of encouragement for those who are undergoing severe temptations.[16] As part of the exposition of Psalm 142:6, the Poliander text adds, 'That is, not only do people assail me, but the devil also is a clever accuser and deft jurist against my sins, and I, poor fellow that I am, cannot quote Scripture sufficiently against him. He wants to turn your mercy into nothing and my sins into mountains.'[17] These temptations drive David back to God in meditation and prayer so that he rests totally on God's provision. According to the heading for the Psalm, David's message from the cave,

[11] *LW* 42, 184.

[12] *LW* 42, 183-84.

[13] *LW* 42, 186.

[14] *LW* 42, 186.

[15] *LW* 42, 186.

[16] *LW* 42, 184, n. 5.

[17] *WA* 7, 788, as cited in *LW* 42, 185.

written out of distress, terror, complaint, and loneliness, is a great consolation to the wounded soul. After confession, this Psalm ends in an unwavering promise that the person assailed by temptation is supported by the company of the righteous, and is sustained by a gracious God who deals bountifully with him. Hidden in these assaults are the promises of divine comfort and divine help against evil, which we embrace in faith. To be visited by trials is by far better than to be without trials, for the latter, Luther asserted elsewhere, is the most dangerous trial.[18] It was because Luther had experienced the blessings of doubts and temptation that he could call them 'God's embraces.'[19] McGrath writes,

> Far from regarding suffering or evil as a nonsensical intrusion into the world (which Luther regards as the opinion of a 'theologian of glory'), the theologian of the cross regards such suffering as his most precious treasure, for revealed and yet hidden in precisely such sufferings is none other than the living God, working out the salvation of those whom he loves.[20]

Luther warned that before these inner assaults subside, they might magnify to a greater intensity after the believer receives the medicine of God's word. When that happens, the believer must not do anything except simply wait and abide by the aforementioned principles. However grievous the temptation, the greater is the assurance that the devil will soon be vanquished. The devil is hurling his strongest punches now, but is very close to losing his power over Christians. Luther drew an analogy from the Old Testament: the force of Pharaoh's persecution of the Israelites was not as severe as when it was nearing its end (Exod. 1:8-14). In the same way, a patient may feel extremely sick while taking medicine before the effects of its healing power are felt. Circumstances may become bitter before they become better. Therefore the one who is assaulted should face these grave temptations with a hopeful and cheerful spirit, holding fast to the promise that victory is very nearly his portion.[21] Such promise spurs him to a fuller faith in Christ.

These six principles are restated in various forms. They are woven into Luther's pastoral pieces as he sought to deal with the essence and varied manifestations of temptation in his people. The following letters, chronologically placed, are illustrations of this.

'A Letter of Consolation to All who Suffer Persecution Because of the Word of God' (1522)

Hartmut von Cronberg, a nobleman of Franconia, a member of the Diet, and a devout layman, was so sympathetic to the Reformer's evangelical cause that he

---

[18] *LW* 44, 47 and 63, as cited in *LW* 42, n. 3.

[19] *WA* 40, II, 582, 5 (Psalm 45, 1532), as cited in Bornkamm, *Luther's World of Thought*, 73.

[20] McGrath, *Luther's Theology of the Cross*, 151.

[21] *LW* 42, 186.

renounced a stipend of 200 guilders from the emperor in protest against the Edict of Worms.[22] He sent Luther his two letters: *An Open Letter to Emperor Charles V*, as a defence of Luther at Worms; and *A Letter to Mendicant Orders*, as a plea for the mendicants to give Luther's doctrine a favourable hearing for his doctrine was that of Christ.[23] The present letter, addressed to Cronberg, was written probably in late February 1522, while Luther was still hiding in the Wartburg.[24] Luther never intended it for publication. It was Cronberg who published it four times. As a result, Luther suffered persecution from Duke George of Saxony who had obtained a copy of it. Luther's allusion to a bitter foe of the Reformation, whom he regarded as 'that bladder,' was changed by Cronberg in subsequent versions to identify the Duke by name.[25] This alteration escalated the antagonism between Luther and Duke George.

What excited Luther was Cronberg's true faith and bold confession, in that Christ looms large in his writings. God's word resides so earnestly and firmly in his heart that it emboldens him to extol and confess it in speech, deeds, and writing, before all and against all odds, especially before exalted and brilliant minds. Cronberg's unusual ability to perceive the truth of the gospel Luther attributed to the Holy Spirit who 'reveals what has been given us and teaches us to interpret the spiritual truths' (cf. 1 Cor. 2:14).[26] He was duly esteemed by Luther as the man who is endowed with the Holy Spirit, and thus is imbued with the true knowledge of God's word. This letter to Cronberg shows Luther's awareness of what lay ahead for him and the gospel's cause: the suffering for the believer and the persecution by her enemies. The letter contains several helpful pointers to consolation.

The majesty of God's word reigns and is the source of comfort and joy when facing persecutions. Admittedly, Luther thanked God for mercifully opening his eyes to the truth of the infallibility of God's word, as declared in Isaiah 55:11: 'God's word does not go forth in vain.' No papal condemnation and persecution can thwart the joy he gained from someone grasping the truth of God's word and praising it. He found great solace in his daily discovery that God's word has been recognized so zealously by people, and is openly confessed.[27]

Luther acknowledged that persecution is a permanent reality in the world that is at enmity with God. The world is full of persecutors who severely oppose God's word, and thus God's people, as stated in Matthew 24:9, 'You must be hateful to all nations for my name's sake.' Luther cautioned believers about the opposition of the world to the word so that the Christian might not be overwhelmed by it, a negative experience that might arise as a result of obedience to God's word. 'It is the nature of the divine word,' Luther intimated, 'to be heartily received by few, but ruthlessly

---

[22] *LW* 42, 59. Cf. Luther's Letter to Melanchthon, 12 May 1521, in *WABr* 2: 332-33; *LW* 48, 215-17.

[23] *LW* 43, 64, n. 4.

[24] *LW* 43, 60.

[25] *LW* 43, 59.

[26] *LW* 43, 61.

[27] *LW* 43, 61-62.

persecuted by many.'[28] Persecution is thus a negative sign of the word of God at work.

This noble word naturally creates an unquenchable 'thirst' in those who receive it. Inevitably this thirst cannot be quenched, and impels the one who receives the word to confess it publicly, as David said in Psalm 116:10, 'I believe, therefore I speak.'[29] Just as faith seeks understanding, so faith seeks confession. God's word must not only be believed, as many have done, but also be confessed so that the whole world may hear it. The thirst for the salvation of God's people, or the desire to attest to the word of God at work, is a sure proof of genuine faith. Just as true faith is active in love, so it is active in a 'thirsty speech,' characterized by an inner compulsion to speak the word. This thirst is not abated by its speaking, but is made worse by persecution, as Christ's thirst on the cross was with gall and vinegar. St. Paul also felt the evangelical compulsion to speak, and wished that he might be cut off from Christ for the sake of his Jewish Brethren (cf. Rom. 9:3). A theologian of the cross anticipates 'vilification, the shame, and persecution' as the direct consequence of his 'thirsty speech.' This kind of suffering flows not from the Christian's condition as *totus peccator* (the complete sinner), but from their communion and identification with the crucified Christ. 'Wherever Christ is,' Luther wrote, 'Judas, Pilate, Herod, Caiaphas, and Annas will inevitably be also, so also his cross. If not, he is not the true Christ.'[30] Suffering is not denied, nor is it confessed as a judgment for sin. Rather it is placed upon Christ who hallows it as a negative proof of a genuine faith.

The evangelical thirst for the salvation of his enemies so dominated Luther that nothing, not even death, could deflect him from that. Here, he repeated what he had taught in his previous writings, especially *Sermon on Preparing to Die* and *Fourteen Consolations*. On account of Christ's triumphant act, death is no threat to the Christian, but a promise of life. The more the enemies rage against him, the more they destroy themselves for they are not well-provided for in divine matters. But what works against the believer as death actually works for him, for he has 'a Lord who holds the death and life of all (his) adversaries in his hand' (cf. Phil. 1:18; Rom. 14:9), and who comforts his hearts with his word, 'Be of good cheer, I have overcome the world' (John 16:33). When threatened with death by persecutors, the believer falls back on Christ and their union with him. Just as Christ is Lord and victor over death, the believer who is in Christ too is lord and victor over death. The Christian does not wander about in the Garden, looking for Christ with Mary Magdalene, as if Christ has not risen and ascended to the Father for them (cf. John 10:17). Instead they rest confident in 'the almighty resurrection of Christ,' a strong bulwark which can withstand any terrifying force or momentary power of the wretched foes.[31] They too find joy in Christ, knowing that death is nothing but the death of sin and the death of death itself. Then the believer's faith remains immovably certain that they will live even if their enemies inflict every woe upon

[28] *LW* 43, 62.

[29] *LW* 43, 62.

[30] *LW* 43, 62, 63.

[31] *LW* 43, 62, 63-64.

them and kill them. In view of the eschatological victory, Luther exhorted the Christian to be kindly disposed to their adversaries, even though they resented their being so. In lieu of revenge, the Christian should pity them for storing up earthly treasures for themselves for the gloomy and terrifying day of God's wrath (Rom. 2:5). They should pray for them, even when they gave them death in exchange for the life they sought to communicate. This is what Luther himself did for Duke George, praying that he, the principal foe of the cross, might be transformed from a Saul into a Paul (Acts 9:1-22).

Luther then digressed from the counsel he gave Cronberg to his confession of the pain he felt from the Wittenberg leaders, who ridiculed him and made fun of his efforts. He considered the vilification of the gospel by the Wittenbergers as a vicious satanic attack, and the hardest test he had ever undergone. He queried aloud whether the events at Wittenberg were his arrogant and foolish act, resulting in self-inflicted suffering. This reflection was only momentary, for he then wrote very confidently concerning Christ's triumphant act on the cross, in the resurrection, and at the ascension. Luther reverted to the central doctrine of justification, in which faith transcends both good and sinful deeds. So neither should we boast of our good deeds, nor despond in our wrongs. 'For the Father of all mercy has granted us faith, not in a wooden but a living Christ, who is Lord over sin and innocence, who can support and preserve us even if we fell into many thousands of sins every hour.'[32] The devil has not succeeded in tearing Christ from the right hand of God. Christ remains enthroned and, as Lord, he presides over all things, both negative and positive; therefore the believer, in a joyous exchange, also is lord over 'sin, death, the devil, and everything.' All that Christ is and achieves are communicated to the believer – this truth cannot be undone.[33]

Luther deplored the sin committed at Worms, where God's word was reviled, and consciously condemned without a hearing, that is, without a discussion of his doctrine.[34] He deeply feared that God's impending judgment and dreadful wrath might swallow up the entire German nation for deserting the divine truth and serving the pope with a fatal diet. His heart was filled with concern that God might withdraw his precious word completely from Germany to its own detriment. The Jews, who wilfully condemned God's Son, were consigned to a permanent hardening of heart that they never ceased to blaspheme him, and trashed his blessings. This, Luther said, was borne out in Psalm 109:17, 'He did not like blessing; therefore it shall be far from him.' Likewise, the German nation had condemned the gospel and St. Jerome, and shed innocent blood, for instance, that of John Huss at the Council of Constance (1414–18). The same thing had happened at Worms, when the papists hated and reviled Christ and, even though they had not shed the blood of Luther, he felt that in their hearts they were continually killing him. For fear that the German nation might reap its just desserts from the hidden God at the last days, Luther closed

---

[32] *LW* 43, 62, 65.

[33] *LW* 43, 62, 65.

[34] Cf. *LW* 32, 105-31, as cited in *LW* 43, 66, n. 13.

this section of his letter with an earnest prayer that God might preserve it from falling into such a permanent state of blindness or hardness of heart and lose sight of Christ, in whom and with whom believers are lord over all things, negative and positive.[35]

Finally, Luther elevated the preaching of the word of Christ above all else. Acting as the agent of God's word rather than the agent of any human being constitutes the essence of true Christianity. Luther did not allow himself or any leader to rise above God's word and dictate what is divine truth or falsehood. Although people believe because of his preaching, its efficacy lies in the power of God's word, not in the artistry of the preacher. True Christians possess a spirit of keen delight and active love for God's word, as this was so deeply reflected in Cronberg. Not offended by God's word, they adhere to it even if it comes from someone who denies and forsakes it. Luther ascribed 'an almost sacramental quality' to preaching so that when the word of God is preached, no one is exempted from its benefits.[36] The word of God remains free to be heard by all, including those under condemnation for heresy.[37] God's grace is not merely proclaimed in the word of God but also imparted by it to the believer. God hides in the preached word, as in other words, to communicate his saving grace. It is in the agency of human language, the spoken word, where God's immanence is felt clearly and definitely. The preached word demands a decision, just as every word spoken by people demands it. When Christ comes through preaching, he must be received wholeheartedly. To do otherwise is to commit the sin of impiety, as the Germans had at Worms. To revile God's word, for Luther, is to forfeit God's blessings hidden in it (cf. Ps. 109:17); those who condemn the gospel condemn themselves to the hell of God-forsakenness, putting themselves beyond the reach of God's grace. The one who denies the gospel is cursed, for they incur God's dreadful judgments. In contrast, the one who is not offended by God's word, but loves it dearly, and confesses it boldly is blessed. The conservative character of the Reformer shines forth in his unmixed adherence to the pure word of God, even against all that contrasts with it. The sacramental objectivity of the word of Christ demands a joyful allegiance, despite the subjective conditions, merits, or demerits of the preacher:

> [True Christians] are the ones who are not affected by whatever base, horrible, and shameful things they hear about me or about our associates, for they believe not in Luther but in Christ himself. The word has them, and they have the word. They pay no heed to Luther, whether he be a knave or a saint. God can speak through Balaam as well as Isaiah, through Caiaphas as well as through Peter, yes, even through an ass. I subscribe to their opinion. I myself do not know Luther either, nor do I want to know him, nor do I preach anything about him, but about Christ. The devil may

[35] *LW* 43, 67.

[36] George, *Theology of the Reformers*, 91.

[37] *LW* 39, 22; *WA* 6, 75; cf. *LW* 35, 396.

> take him [Luther] if he is able to, but if he keeps his hands off Christ, all is well with us.[38]

Luther saw Christ coming to him through Cronberg's pen, and he wished that his own missive would have the same effect, that Cronberg would see Christ through his pen, and fill his heart with an unending joy. This was the positive note on which Luther ended his letter.

'To all Christians in Worms' (1523)

Even before Luther had been pronounced a heretic at Worms in 1520, the inquisitors had been zealously pursuing those who sympathized with his evangelical doctrine and severe repression continued after the issue of the Edict of Worms. In 1521, the pro-Lutheran spirit was surprisingly high in the city of Worms, and so impressed were its citizens that nine out of ten of them supported Luther, and the remainder proclaimed the slogan, 'Down with Rome!'[39]

Luther's letter, 'To all Christians in Worms,' was written to an evangelical church that had been established in the city after the diet. Very little is known about its immediate occasion but it seems evident that what had happened to the adherents of the evangelical faith in Brussels was on Luther's mind as he addressed believers in Worms. The letter was published shortly after its receipt in the city.[40]

Luther expressed his joy that the gospel had taken root in Worms. He admonished believers that they should have a strong and active faith, grounded in love, lest they abandon 'the sublime, precious, and salutary gospel and begin to loathe it.' Just as the Jews grew tired of the daily gift of manna in the wilderness (Num. 11:20), so some Christians had become tired of the newly revived gospel so that they had relegated it to 'an item of news,' which they discussed ardently but carnally.[41] This they did in order to satisfy their curiosity, rather than appropriating the gospel as indispensable daily sustenance for their souls.

Luther warned against the devil's trickery, which had made the citizens believe that they knew everything. They had had enough of the gospel, their ears itching to hear something other than or in addition to its message of grace. Believers ought not to be amazed, Luther warned, if they received treatment similar to that experienced by the prophets of old and Christ. The prophets and apostles suffered because of the word of God. 'Christ himself had to suffer and be maligned as a perverter of the nation before Pilate because he taught differently than their scribes had done for so long.'[42] Christians should therefore rejoice, if they, like the prophets and apostles,

---

[38] *LW* 43, 68.

[39] *LW* 43, 74, where Luther is cited by P. Kalfoff (ed.), *Die Depeschen des Nuntius Aleander vom Wormser Reichstage 1521* (Halle: S.M. Niemeyer, 1897), 43.

[40] *LW* 43, 75. There was persecution in Brussels, which came as a result of true confession of evangelical faith.

[41] *LW* 43, 78.

[42] *LW* 43, 78-79.

suffered as had Christ himself, for they knew for certain that they had God's word on their side, a fact denied to their enemies. Their source of comfort in suffering was the power of 'God's word, which overcomes everything.'[43] In contrast, their enemies had nothing but the approbation of the people and the old customs (religious practices) of the multitudes for their support. Thus they were deprived of God's delightful comfort, a benefit given exclusively to the new, small flock at Worms, who heartily adhered to God's word against all odds.

Luther assured believers that they were blessed when people hated and reviled them on account of the Son of Man (Luke 6:22-23). This was what conformity to the image of the crucified Christ meant: just as God's only Son, their master, had to suffer in this way, so must those who belonged to his household. 'The servant is not above his master' (Matt. 10:24-25). Hostility came as the world's inevitable response to whatever was of God. The world hated whatever came from God but loved whatever was of its own. Anything the world did not hate was surely not of God. This Christ himself declared in John 15:19, 'If you were of the world, the world would love its own, but because you are not of the world, and because I have chosen you out of the world, therefore the world hates you.' Suffering was caused by a natural but violent response of the world to the Christian world-view. In his *Commentary on First Epistle of Peter* (1522), Luther stated that there are two conflicting world-views: Christians should orientate themselves towards the 'heavenly inheritance' and were called to forsake 'worldly reason, wisdom and holiness as nothing.'[44] But the world could not stand such a repudiation and, as a result, the Christian must endure condemnation and tribulation, just as Christ had promised. The configuration of the Christian life was 'faith, hope and the holy cross,' not 'faith, hope and love.'[45] Luther encouraged steadfastness under severe repression and persecution, the result of the world's opposition to the word of God. This was the comfort with which Christians should strengthen each other. They should know that they are not alone in their trials, but partakers of the fellowship of the prophets and Christ himself who shares his followers' pain. By facing temptation, Luther continued, they should see themselves solely 'in Christ' where peace was their very portion. They should edify each other with Christ's words, 'Be of good cheer, I have overcome the world ... in me you have peace' (John 16:33). This was the message that Luther sent to prepare Christ's flock for persecution.

'A Christian Letter of Consolation to the People of Miltenberg' (1524)

In 1522, a separate church had been established in the town of Miltenberg. Patronage of this parish had found favor with the mayor, council, and citizens of the town. Thus the church had the liberty to choose their own pastor. John Drach, who had matriculated in Erfurt and was well known among the humanist circle of the

---

[43] *LW* 43, 78.

[44] *LW* 30, 16; *WA* 12, 271, 35-37.

[45] *LW* 30, 16; *WA* 12, 271, 35-37.

university city, assumed the pastorate. Along with his humanist circle, Drach was sympathetic to Luther. When Luther passed through Erfurt in April 1521, on his journey to appear before the Diet of Worms, Drach had taken part in the public reception.

While pastor at Miltenberg, Drach translated his faith into action, and his work won him the respect and affection of the mayor, the council, and the populace. Simultaneously, he also attracted the bitter enmity of the twelve altar priests of the *Halbstift.*[46] These priests, who had experienced a decline in their revenues and prestige, laid a formal charge of heresy against Drach, which eventually led to his excommunication at a hearing in Aschaffenburg. The congregation in Miltenberg was so enraged at the decree of excommunication which had been read during the service (8 September 1523) that it revolted against the altar priests because of their injustice. Drach had intervened to preserve the priests from being lynched. They had appealed to the civil authorities for safety and, with the help of the episcopal officers and armed Catholic farmers, they had moved against the town. Finally, the town was seized once again by the old hierarchical order, and the congregation lost its right to call its pastor. The attempt to re-catholicize the town was so effective that, except for a small, hard core of remnants, it stamped out the Reformation and Lutheranism permanently.

Drach had petitioned Archbishop Albrecht of Mainz, who had jurisdiction over the affairs of Miltenberg, but to no avail. He then escaped episcopal arrest and, in January 1524, arrived in Wittenberg, where he had met Luther. Shortly afterwards, in response to the information given him by Drach, the Reformer wrote an open letter to the church in Miltenberg clearly defining a proper response to persecution.

The uniqueness of this letter lies in the contrast Luther made between worldly comfort and Christian comfort. The former originates with people, while the latter originates with God. Worldly comfort, which Luther regarded as false and pernicious, quenches all the fruits that proceed from the proper endurance of suffering and the cross in dependence upon God and his word.[47] Worldly comfort may be seen and felt temporally, and Christian comfort, though it cannot be seen and felt, consists in patience and hope. 'Worldly comfort, however, insists on seeing and feeling what the afflicted desires and will have nothing to do with patience. But here (we find that) patience is to have a place in hope along with the comfort of the Scriptures.'[48] Worldly comfort, which includes revenge against the sources of persecution, is completely unprofitable and harmful to the Christian and their cause. Worldly vengeance and comfort did not befit the Christian but their enemies who 'comforted themselves beautifully' by avenging themselves through various vicious means. Such viciousness did not console but lead them into destruction, the ultimate end of consolation that comes from the devil:

---

[46] *LW* 43, 100.
[47] *LW* 43, 103.
[48] *LW* 43, 103-104.

> But what sort of comfort is that? Does that comfort involve any hope? or Patience? or Scripture? Really, instead of patience they used their fist; instead of patience they manifested a spirit of vengeance; instead of hope they visibly vented their spite on you. They can feel the object of their desires. Whence comes such consolation? Not from God! It must surely come from the devil. And that is true indeed. But what will be the end of comfort that issues from the devil? Paul says what it is: '*Quorum Gloria in confusionem*' – 'Their end is destruction' (Phil. 3:19).[49]

It befitted the Christian to discard the worldly comfort that came from the devil, for nothing was to be gained from either slaying the wicked or gloating over their defeat. The Christian should cling to God's 'rich and proud consolation' accredited to him for suffering for the sake of God's word. Hidden worldly comfort was 'destruction.' But hidden in Christian comfort was the promise of God's blessing, as St. Peter declared, 'You are blessed if you suffer for righteousness' sake?' (1 Pet. 3:14). So blessed and proud was such suffering for Christ that even an emperor would willingly forsake his empire to assume it; he too would gladly regard his empire as filth in comparison with the comforting treasure hidden in his suffering for Christ's sake.[50]

The end of vengeance was worldly (devilish) comfort, whereas the end of patient suffering was Christian (divine) comfort. God used the devil as an instrument of wrath and destruction so that the work of the devil should become God's alien work. Insofar as worldly comfort worked to the Christian's advantage, it led him to divine comfort, corresponding to the distinction between God's alien work in the law and his proper work in the gospel. As such, worldly comfort would truly destroy the Christian, as it destroyed the persecutors, if he and his enemies did not flee to the comfort of God in Christ. As alien work, devilish comfort effected the opposite of divine comfort and resulted in divine judgment, from which the Christian must flee to the gospel of grace for divine comfort. Thus Luther advised,

> Look beyond this (vengeance and worldly comfort) and behold your salvation and their misery. You have a good, secure conscience and a just cause. They have a bad and uncertain conscience and a blind cause, the injustice of which they do not yet realize. Thus you have the comfort of God with patience in hope, taken from the Scriptures; whereas they have the comfort of the devil, consisting of vengeance in open malice.[51]

In lieu of worldly, physical vengeance, the Christian should count the persecutors as the object of Christian pity. They were to be sincerely pitied because they did not possess a clear conscience in their cause, and they received their gloomy and devilish comfort only from their malice, vengeance, and wantonness. Instead, the people of Miltenberg should thank God and rejoice that they had been 'found worthy to know

---

[49] *LW* 43, 104-105.
[50] *LW* 43, 104-105.
[51] *LW* 43, 106.

and to hear his word and to suffer for it; be pleased to know that [their] cause is God's word and that [their] comfort derives from God.'[52] The Christian's cheerful mind and thankful spirit would do more harm to the devil, the author of his distress, than any physical violence thrown at his raving foes, the devil's underlings. The one verse that peeved the devil and terrified him was Psalm 8:2, 'You have established virtue from the mouths of babes and sucklings that you might put an end to the enemy and avenger.' Luther explained:

> This verse not only threatens sadness and grief for him, but also his destruction; and that not by great force, which would shed honour on him, but by weak and feeble sucklings. It smarts and pains this mighty and haughty spirit no end to hear that his immense power, his horrible ranting, his mad vengeance are to be destroyed not with power but through the weakness of infants, and [to hear] that he will not be able to stave this off. Let us lend a hand to this end and earnestly apply ourselves to that task.[53]

Like weak infants, Christians are unable to talk but God speaks through their mouths. Unable to act, they rest totally on God's word that does everything. God's word would prevail over the gates of hell (Matt. 16:18) and thwart the devil's onslaught, effecting 'a happy victory and conquest ... without sword or fist.' Nothing pained the devil more than that his aim to incite Christians to sadness and depression so as to render them unfit for God had been defeated by God's word. This was 'his real hell': 'the persecution results in our joy and our praising God and extolling his word,' the precise opposite of the devil's goal.[54]

The rejection of vengeance as a Christian response to suffering was Luther's lifelong position, which governed his later views towards the peasants and events at Münster. His religious conviction was based on the Scriptures, not on speculation. As proof of this, he ended this letter with a German translation of Psalm 119 (120) and his explanatory notes on it. He sought to interpret this Psalm in a way that had an immediate bearing on the situation in Miltenberg. The sufferers were encouraged to cry to God for help, and pray that the preachers might preach the word in faith and with might. True Christians were characterized by an active love for God's word and the natural compulsion to preach mightily what they believed. 'Glowing coals of the juniper tree are the true Christians, who show forth God's word – this is what is meant by the term "sharper arrows" – with their life.'[55] The word of God was not spreading as fast as it should, which Luther blamed on the church's indolence in asking for God's help. When facing raving foes, the Christian should meet them not with worldly comfort but Christian comfort. Luther summarized his stance:

> Thus the only recourse left to you, as this psalm indicates, is to turn to the Lord in your distress, cry to him about these evil tongues, and earnestly and fervently pray

[52] *LW* 43, 106.
[53] *LW* 43, 107.
[54] *LW* 43, 107.
[55] *LW* 43, 108.

> for staunch marksmen who aim sharp arrows [God's Word] at the devil, hit him, and do not miss their mark, and to ask for glowing coals [true Christians] of the juniper tree which kindle the misled and blind people with fervour and fire and illumine them with a good life, to the glory and honour of God's name. If you do that, you will soon discover how effectively you are avenged on the devil and his scales. It will make your heart rejoice.[56]

Luther's dictum remained the same throughout his adult life: 'God's word should not, must not, and shall not be bridled.'[57] God's word reigns, and conquers everything. And nothing could undo that!

'Whether One May Flee from a Deadly Plague' (1527)

On 2 August 1527, the plague, known as the Black Death, invaded Wittenberg.[58] On 15 August, the Elector John relocated the university to Jena, then to Schlieben, where it remained until April 1528. Unmoved by the elector's order and the plea of his friends, Luther chose to remain in Wittenberg to care for the sick.[59] His house became a hospital for the sick and the distressed. His own illness and depression contributed to his tardiness in writing this pamphlet as a response to Johann Hess, pastor at Breslau, who asked Luther twice for advice as to whether Christians should flee the epidemic. The martyrdom of Leonhard Kaiser on 16 August of the same year had pre-occupied Luther so that he had spent much time writing his eulogy and his *Letter of Consolation to the Christians at Halle*. However, a Dominican's letter in Leipzig that mocked the Wittenbergers for fleeing the plague had stimulated Luther to finish 'Whether One May Flee from a Deadly Plague'. It was printed nineteen times and received a wide circulation during the period of the epidemic.

In beginning his letter, Luther said that God had for some time disciplined and scourged him so severely that he was unable to read and write. This confession spoke volumes about the struggles he had experienced during this period. This was borne out in his letter to Amsdorf on 1 November 1527, where Luther wrote of his struggles and the sick in his house: 'So there are battles (*Anfechtungen*) without and terrors within, and really grim ones.'[60]

Luther's concerns were with who might or might not flee the plague. Church and state should be obedient to God's plain mandate. Preachers and pastors must remain steadfast before the anguish of death. This was required by Christ's command, 'A good shepherd lays down his life for the sheep but the hireling sees the wolf coming and flees' (John 10:11). They were most needed for comfort and strength at the hour of death. Only under circumstances where the spiritual services in one locality were plentiful should they encourage others to leave in order to avoid needless exposure to

---

[56] *LW* 43, 112.

[57] *LW* 43, 107.

[58] See R.S. Gottfried, *The Black Death* (New York: Free, 1983).

[59] *LW* 43, 115.

[60] *LW* 43, 116, where Luther's letter to Amsdorf, *WABr* 4, 275, 20-25, was quoted.

danger. In support of this, Luther quoted an historical antecedent, St. Athanasius, who fled that his life might be spared because many others were present to administer his office. The civil authorities, too, were under obligation to remain, as St. Paul had taught in Romans 13:4, 'The governing authorities are God's ministers for your own good.' Fleeing in times of need was tantamount to abandoning the entire community, exposing it to every conceivable kind of danger or disaster, and that was 'a great sin.'[61] This kind of disaster was what the devil sought to instigate wherever there was no civic order.

Similarly, what applied to church and state also applied to those who were engaged in service or duty toward one another. A servant must be duty bound not to leave his master unless given permission by his master. Likewise, a master should not desert his servant unless reasonable provisions were made for him. The Christian must not abandon his neighbor in troubles, unless he furnished a capable substitute to care for him. If not duty bound to his neighbors, the Christian should flee rather than tempt God by exposing himself to the contagion. Those who possessed a 'milk faith' and were fearful might properly flee in God's name as long as they had made adequate provision for others to provide nursing care for their neighbors who were in need. Such action certainly was no sin, for it was not contrary to God's will and the good of the neighbor. It befitted God's command that Christians should not hate their own flesh, but nourish and cherish it (Eph. 5:29), and that they should do their best to preserve body and life, and not neglect them (1 Cor. 12:21-26). However, those who were strong in faith and saw death as 'a little thing' should not flee but willingly suffer nakedness, hunger, and danger, without tempting God and without condemning the weaker ones who had taken flight. As proof that fleeing from death was not wrong in itself, Luther went on to cite several biblical examples: Abraham, a great saint, for fear of death, escaped it by pretending that his wife, Sarah, was his sister. This he did without adversely affecting his neighbor, and thus was not considered as sinning against him (Gen. 12:13); Jacob also fled from his brother Esau to avoid death at his hands (Gen. 27:43-45); David fled from Saul and from Absalom (1 Sam. 19:10-17; 2 Sam. 15:14), etc. Although these examples referred to death by persecution and not by pestilence, the same truth applied: death is death, regardless of how it might occur.

Luther warned against the extremists, who disdained the use of medication, or those who did not use it with discretion.[62] There were many means for counteracting death and the plague: medications, hospices, hospitals, municipal home cares. To ignore these gifts of God, Luther wrote, was to 'sin on the right hand.'[63] Whoever served his neighbour and contracted disease should take necessary precautions, such as sanitary practices and living in quarantine, to prevent its spread. However, each must attend church and hear God's word so that he might learn how to live and die. Each should make confession, and receive the sacrament every week.[64] 'Now if a

[61] *LW* 43, 121.
[62] *LW* 43, 131.
[63] *LW* 43, 131.
[64] *LW* 43, 134.

deadly epidemic strikes,' Luther advised, 'we should stay where we are, make our preparations, and take courage in the fact that we are mutually bound together.'[65] He did not deny the devil's participation in causing death through the plague. Nevertheless, death was fundamentally 'God's decree and punishment' for our sin to which we must patiently submit, even if this involved laying down our lives on behalf of our neighbour, yet doing so without tempting God.[66]

Luther followed the custom in antiquity, both among the Jews and pagans, to bury the dead outside the town. A cemetery ought to be located in a quiet, remote spot where people or cattle could not roam over it at any time. It ought to be a spiritual, remote place that inspired devout thoughts in those who visited it. Even Christ's tomb was located outside a city. 'Not only necessity but piety and decency' should persuade us to provide a burial ground outside a town.

> A cemetery rightfully ought to be a fine quiet place, removed from all other localities, to which one can go and reverently meditate upon death, the Last Judgment, the resurrection, and say one's prayers. Such a place should properly be a decent, hallowed place, to be entered with trepidation and reverence because doubtless some saints rest there. It might even be arranged to have religious pictures and portraits painted on the walls.[67]

The significance of this document lies in the emphasis Luther put on the kenotic life in dealing with the sick neighbor. Whoever left his needy neighbors to their misfortune was a murderer, as St. John taught, 'Whoever does not love his brother is a murderer' (1 John 3:15). In cases of emergency, Christians should boldly risk their health. They should be ready both to live and to die according to God's will, as St. Paul had said, for 'none of us lives to himself and none of us dies to himself' (Rom. 15 [14:7]). Like a firefighter, they should boldly risk saving lives as it were from the consuming fire. Just as Christ emptied himself of all to save Christians, they too should empty themselves of self-interest, self-protection, or security for the salvation of their neighbors. This too was taught in 1 John 3:16, 'If Christ laid down his life for us, we ought to lay down our lives for the brethren.' They should receive the sick neighbor in the same way as they would receive Christ or Mary. Basing his argument on Matthew 15:40 and 22:39, Luther asserted that the command to love the neighbor was equal to the great commandment to love God, and that what was not done on behalf of the sick neighbor was not done for Christ. To flee the neighbor in need, which Luther denominated as 'a disgraceful flight,' was to disregard God's command in dealing with them, and thus 'fall into sin on the left hand.'[68]

> If you wish to serve Christ and to wait on him, very well, you have your sick neighbour close at hand. Go to him and serve him, and you will surely find Christ in him, not outwardly but in his word. If you do not wish or care to serve your

[65] *LW* 43, 127.
[66] *LW* 43, 136-37.
[67] *LW* 43, 131.
[68] *LW* 43, 130-31.

> neighbour you can be sure that if Christ lay there instead you would not do so either and would let him lie there. The Christian who serves Christ must serve his neighbour, and find Christ in that neighbour ... whoever wants to serve Christ in person would surely serve his neighbour.[69]

'A Letter of Consolation to the Christians at Halle' (1527)

The year 1527 was a difficult year when Luther experienced frequent dizziness, acute headaches, and anxiety. His exhaustion resulted from the intense battle with the enthusiasts, the peasants' war, Erasmus, and the sacramentarians. The news that his friend George Winkler had been murdered deepened his sorrow. The writing of this letter was interrupted by a severe illness that lasted for weeks.[70] Thinking that he was about to die, Luther lamented that he had not been found worthy of martyrdom:

> O God, that I had been or may still be found worthy of such a testimony and death. What am I? What am I doing? How ashamed I am of myself when I read this story that I had not long already been found worthy to suffer (since I deserved it ten times more than from the world). Well, then, my God, if it is to be that way, so let it be. Thy will be done.[71]

Bornkamm argued that the recurring and oppressive thought that others had died a martyr's death because of a cause of which he had been the instigator may have been the source of Luther's agonizing temptation and suffering.[72] However, sensing a divine purpose in these tragedies, Luther wrote an extended statement of condolence to the orphaned congregation in Halle. He did not bemoan the reason for the pastor's death. Instead he summoned them to true comfort and joy that Christ had deemed their pastor worthy to die for his word. He pointed out that their pastor's blood might become a divine seed for a hundred true evangelical pastors who would not stop promulgating his evangelical faith. The devil could not bear to hear the divine truth proclaimed by preachers such as their pastor, just as the pope could not bear to listen to the many preachers who had arisen after the martyrdom of John Huss.[73] Their outcries continued to spread to the four corners of the earth as a result of their martyrdoms. Luther commended Winkler for having been obedient to the authorities, an exemplary model of which his congregation ought to be proud. In spite of the many ominous signs of what would happen to him, he had wished rather to imitate Christ's kenotic example, so that it could be said of him, 'He was obedient even unto death.'

---

[69] *LW* 43, 145.

[70] *LW* 43, 145.

[71] Cf. H. Bornkamm, *Luther in Mid-Career, 1521–1530* (Philadelphia: Fortress Press, 1983), 558, where he quoted *WA* 23, 474, 15-18.

[72] Bornkamm, *Luther in Mid-Career*, 558.

[73] Cf. *LW* 44, 194-98, where followers of Huss came into conflict with the Roman Church.

George Winkler had been condemned because he had taught the evangelical practice of administering communion in two kinds. Luther admonished the Halle congregation to continue in the truth as their pastor had done, not withholding the cup, as had been customary for the validity of reception in both kinds was upheld by Scripture as well as Church law.[74] Patristic fathers, including Hilary, Cyprian, Irenaeus, Tertullian, and Chrysotom, had taught the custom.[75] Luther claimed that he had the clear, divine word of Christ in support of his teaching, without which Church laws would be of little support. He used canon law not so much to confirm his teaching as to refute his opponents, that is, using their own weapons against them to the enhancement of his evangelical faith. For instance, he quoted Pope Gelasius, who said in *de cones.., dis. II, Conperimus*:

> It has come to our attention that some, when they receive the sacred body, do not partake of the sacred blood. Because they are following a superstition, they should either receive the entire sacrament or stay away from the entire sacrament. For because it is a single sacrament it cannot be divided without great offence to God.[76]

Luther took a very pessimistic view of the future. The violent deaths of the faithful were foretastes of the impending disasters. Great misery was sweeping across Germany because unruly mobs were dividing Christians in mind and purpose.

> For what is certain in this life? Today we stand; tomorrow we fall. Today one has the true faith; tomorrow he falls into error. Today one hopes; tomorrow he despairs. How many good people fall into the error of the enthusiasts? How many will fall in the future through these sectarian errors. Here we stand in the words of Cyprian, 'daily and unceasingly under the spears and swords of the devils,' who day and night are on the prowl like ferocious lions and stab and strike among us – 'one sees their axes flash above one like woodsmen in the forest' ... These devils are simply determined to reduce the house of God, which is what we are, to dust and ashes.[77]

God acknowledged his special witnesses to the truth in that he removed them early from this evil world. Such had been the case of George Winkler: 'Being perfected in a short time, he fulfilled long years; for his soul was pleasing to the Lord, therefore he took him quickly from the midst of wickedness.'[78] This too was a sign of God's grace and mercy upon his elect and holy ones – such knowledge was open to the eyes of faith. 'It is a sure indication that a great catastrophe is at hand, which is to come upon this world and from which God has chosen to save his own lest they be caught in this world and perhaps even fall and be lost together with the

---

[74] *LW* 43, 149-60.

[75] *LW* 43, 156.

[76] See 'Decreti tertia pars de consecratione, dis. II, c. 12', as cited in *Corpus Iuris Canonici*, ed. H. Friedberg (Graz, 1955), vol. 1, col. 1218, as cited in *LW* 43, 155.

[77] *LW* 43, 160.

[78] *LW* 43, 162.

unbelievers, as Genesis 19[:24-29].'[79] In view of this, it was by far better that the pastor had died before he could have been seized by the devil and be lost forever. As a comfort to the people, Luther wrote reflectively of what their pastor would have said: 'If you loved me you would certainly rejoice that I was permitted to go from death to eternal life in this way.'[80]

'If Pastor George had been spared and perhaps had fallen into error and had been slain by the devil, how much more lamentable would that news have been to us! If he had to be slain, it is better that human weapons should have stabbed his earthly body in this world than that devilish weapons had slain soul and body for eternity.'[81] So the Halle congregation were to take comfort in this: death no longer posed any harm to the pastor, for he had escaped the devil. The evil work of the devil had become the alien work of God. God works through the devil's evil for the good of the faithful as its proper outcome. The negative assault of the devil, in the hand of the merciful God, effects ultimately the salvation of the believer. 'Therefore,' Luther wrote, 'it is much more fitting that we should praise and thank God for his grace because he calls our brothers away in such a wonderful and merciful fashion.'[82] In lieu of revenge, the congregation should pray for the persecutors that they would be saved through their prayers and kindnesses. Luther reassured the people that those who suffer for Christ's sake are blessed. He then reinforced his opinion that a true Christian, like the pastor, does not confront the cross of Christ in contemplative thought, nor as a spectator, but as a participant in suffering – that which is laid upon him by God, not self-chosen. With these words, he ended:

> It will not and cannot be otherwise than as written in Acts 14:22, 'Through many tribulations we must enter the kingdom of God.' It is unimaginable that Christ our head should wear a crown of thorns and die on the cross but that we should be saved without any suffering and with nothing but joy and delight. But if we are to suffer, then let it be suffering which God inflicts upon us and not that which we choose to bring upon ourselves, for he knows best what will serve and help us. What we choose for ourselves won't amount to anything.[83]

'That a Christian Should Bear His Cross with Patience' (1530)

The above quotation connects with Luther's *That a Christian Should Bear His Cross with Patience*. This piece may have been his brief notes to the Coburg *Sermon on Cross and Suffering* (1530). Many parallels between these two works are noted in the Weimar and American editions of Luther's works, a recognition of their close

---

[79] *LW* 43, 160.
[80] *LW* 43, 160.
[81] *LW* 43, 161.
[82] *LW* 43, 163.
[83] *LW* 43, 165.

relationship. This work reflects that of a matured Luther, who had seen the intrinsic linkage between his theology of the cross and a genuine Christian life.[84]

As had the ancient fathers, Luther allegorized the contrast between the tree in the Garden of Eden whence came sin and death and the tree of the cross on Golgotha whence came righteousness and life. In order to live, one must eat of the dead tree on Golgotha, or else remain in death.[85] There is in each person's heart 'a deeply rooted desire to seek life where there is a certain death and to flee from death where one has the source of life.'[86] To truly live, Luther said, one must find life in its opposite – death. Thus a true Christian desires the 'dead wood' of the cross, 'the image of death, suffering, and sorrow,' as opposed to the 'living wood' of Eden, 'the image of life, delight, and goodness.'[87] For hidden in these negative images of suffering and death are the positive images of comfort and eternal life. This discovery evokes Luther's praise of God: 'Thanks be to Christ who has not left me without the relic of the Holy Cross.'[88]

For Luther, the cross of Christ and of the Christian are distinguished but not separated.[89] The true theologian of the cross, thus the true church, does not confront the cross as a passive onlooker, but is themself drawn into this event so that they are faced with the demand of a life under the cross. That a yes to Christ's cross is a yes to the believer's cross is the true meaning of cruciform discipleship. Thus the vocation of the church is not to withdraw from the realities of the world and escape into the seclusion of a monastery, but to live out the cost of discipleship in everyday human life. Christians are called to be Christ-bearers, living a life in which Christ's work and burden, through the joyous exchange, become theirs. Cruciformity – the cross as the form of the Christian life – is the inevitable sign of true faith. However, it should not be the kind of suffering which is self-imposed, as the Anabaptists and those who sought righteousness through works taught, but imposed by God.[90] Since suffering proceeds from God, it must have a godly purpose. Christians must suffer not because of any vices or scandals, but so that they may be conformed to Christ. The holy cross serves for learning the faith and the word. It too subdues sin and pride. Therefore no Christian could thrive without suffering and trials, just as no one could without food or drink.[91]

In this writing, Luther locates the source of suffering not only in God but also in the devil. This must not be taken as an apparent contradiction. 'Because the devil, a

---

[84] See M. Edwards, 'The Older Luther', in G. Dunnhaupht, *The Martin Luther Quincentennial* (Detroit: Wayne State University Press, 1985), 43-62 (50), where he argues for a distinction between the 'young Luther' and the 'old Luther.' The period 1530–35 fits the 'old Luther.'

[85] *LW* 43, 183.

[86] *LW* 43, 183.

[87] *LW* 43, 183.

[88] *LW* 48, 307.

[89] Loewenich, *Luther's Theology of the Cross*, 113.

[90] *LW* 43, 184; cf. *LW* 51, 198.

[91] *LW* 43, 184; cf. *LW* 51, 207.

mighty, evil, deceitful spirit, hates the children of God.'[92] The assaults do come from the devil, a real and potent adversary against whom the Christian struggles throughout their adult life. Luther saw himself engaging in a relentless combat with the devil, in which he would be entirely lost were it not for Christ. As stated earlier, the devil could become an agent of divine power, through which God works an alien work for our sake.

After talking about the necessity and source of the cross, Luther now speaks of its entreaty. Here he brought out the implications of God's identification with suffering:

> The touch of Christ sanctifies all the sufferings and sorrows of those who believe in him. Whoever does not suffer shows that he does not believe that Christ has given him the gift of sharing in his own passion. But if anyone does not wish to bear the cross which God places upon him, he will not be compelled to do so by anyone – he is always free to deny Christ. But in so doing he must know that he cannot have fellowship with Christ or share in any of his gifts.[93]

This quotation yields three important statements about Christian suffering, all of which have a connection with Christian sanctification. First, our suffering is hallowed by Christ; second, to shun suffering is to shun the benefits of Christ's passion; third, there can be no fellowship with Christ without the cross. Inevitably suffering, for Luther, is the essential element in the Christian life, without which there can be no genuine faith in God, no living relationship with Christ, and no certain salvation. By now, Luther saw suffering as a legitimate mark of a true church, about which he wrote in his *Exhortation to All Clergy Assembled at Augsburg* (1530):

> For the right church must surely be the one which holds to God's word and suffers for it, as we do, praises God, and murders no one or leads no one away from God's word.[94]

Finally, Luther cautioned against responding to sufferings and trials according to our feelings and sight. Fellowship with God is ruined when we disregard the word and rely on what is visible. He counseled Christians never to let go of the word, as Eve had done. It takes great effort and care to disregard the visible waves of suffering and cleave to the word of the invisible God. 'This then is the true art, that in suffering and the cross we should look to the word and the comforting assurance, and trust them, even as He said, "In me you shall have peace, but in the world, tribulation" (cf. Jn. 16:33).'[95] Victory belongs to those who adhere to the word, with which they become indifferent to all feelings and thoughts and are not held captive by them.

---

[92] *LW* 43, 184; cf. *LW* 51, 206.

[93] *LW* 43, 184, 184-85; cf. *LW* 51, 207.

[94] *LW* 34, 39.

[95] *LW* 51, 205; cf. *LW* 43, 186.

'Comfort for Women Who Had a Miscarriage' (1542)

In 1541, John Bugenhagen, a close associate of Luther, wrote an interpretation of Psalm 29 as a dedication to King Christian II of Denmark. While reading it, Luther was caught by a reference to 'little children' in the text, whereupon he advised John to add in a comfort for women whose children had died at birth, or had been stillborn and could not be baptized. John agreed with Luther in principle, but was not disposed to change his text, except to attach as an appendix any statement Luther might have on the subject. This short piece dealt with the borderline question of the fate of children who die before they can be baptized, a gnawing question that besets the grieving mother. Written with pastoral concern, Luther averred that the miscarriage, through no fault of the mothers, is not a sign of God's wrath. True theology, for the Reformer, must observe this limit for a proper discourse about God: 'He who tries to explore the majesty will be crushed by the glory.'[96] With this, Luther advised that we should shun the speculative incursion into the ways of the hidden God, demanding from him why a child should have been stillborn. Such questioning was forbidden, as was the temptation to question the matter of election. God's judgment is beyond our gaze, and remains hidden from us. Mothers whose babies have been stillborn should take comfort in that they have done all they could during the pregnancy, and have faith that God's will is always better than theirs, though it may seem otherwise when seen from a human perspective. Instead of viewing God as angry towards them or those who are involved, they should view this 'misbirth' (*abortivum*) as a test to develop patience.[97]

Luther saw the basis for consolation in the yearning and unspoken prayers of the mother in which the Spirit was at work and in the faithful prayers of God's precious people. The believing Christian should rest in the hope that her heartfelt cry and deep longing to bring her child to be baptized will be pleasing to God as an effective prayer. In deepest despair, when she found herself unable to name or utter her wish, she could derive comfort from the intercession of the Holy Spirit, as St. Paul wrote in Romans 8:16-17, 'Likewise the Spirit helps us in our weakness; for we do not know how to pray as we ought (that is, as was said before, we dare not express our wishes), rather the Spirit himself intercedes for us mightily with sighs too deep for words. And he who searches the heart knows what is the mind of the Spirit'; and in Ephesians 3:20, 'Now to him who by the power at work within us is able to do far more abundantly than all that we ask or think.'[98] The mother's heartfelt and unexpressed yearning, which Luther called 'a true, spiritual longing,' becomes 'a great, unbearable cry in God's ears' that moves God to respond. This too had been the case with Moses, who was so overcome by grief and sorrow that his sighs and deep cries had caused the division of the Red Sea and its drying up, the drowning of Pharaoh with all his accomplices, and the salvation of the Israelites (Exod. 14:15).

---

[96] Cf. *LW* 43, 53 (A Letter to Hans von Rechenberg, 1522).

[97] *LW* 43, 247, n. 2. Luther cited 1 Cor. 15:8, where Paul called himself a misbirth, one untimely born.

[98] *LW* 43, 248.

Not knowing for what or how he should pray, in this case, not knowing how the deliverance might come about, Moses uttered a cry from his heart, which was found acceptable to God.

By prayer, Luther argued, Christians could accomplish impossible things, and receive things far greater than they could imagine, often to their astonishment afterward. In support of this view, Luther cited the conversion of St. Augustine, which he ascribed to the praying, sighing, and weeping of St. Monica, Augustine's mother, for him.

> [She] did not desire anything more than that he might be converted from the errors of the Manicheans and become a Christian. Thereupon God gave her not only what she desired, but, as St. Augustine puts it, her 'chiefest desire' (*cardinem desiderieius*), that is, what she longed for with unutterable sighs – that Augustine become not only a Christian but also a teacher above all others in Christendom. Next to the apostles Christendom has none that is his equal.[99]

Luther then advised the bereaved mother not to doubt the promise that God willed to be her God, and that she was precious in his sight. God had not confined his efficacious grace to the sacrament (i.e., baptism), but had made a covenant with his people through his word. Just as God hides in the sacramental words in order to bestow his efficacious grace, so he hides in his covenantal promise that he shall hear them. As his covenantal people, Christians should take to heart God's promise: to do otherwise is to deny God's very nature. Faith embraces God's intention: 'his promise and our prayer or yearning which is grounded in that promise should not be disdained or rejected, but be highly valued and esteemed.'[100] This means that Christians should comfort their fellow Christians in a way different from that in which they comfort unbelievers or the wicked. In times of trial, Luther advised, cleave to Christ, the one who promises and does not lie: 'All things are possible for him who believes' (Mark 9:23). Christians must adhere to God's promise, and pray in faith that his hidden intention shall triumph over what is opposed to it. With this, the bereaved mother should take comfort in the thought that God surely heeds her unspoken yearning, and will accomplish all things in better ways than she had hoped for or understood.

Furthermore, God would accomplish his saving will through the channel of another's intercession, even when there was no explicit sign of personal faith in the one for whom prayer is offered. Such a view finds support in the gospel where Christ raised the widow's son at Nain, as an answer to the prayers of the mother apart from the faith of her son (Luke 7:11-17). Also Christ freed the demonized daughter of the Canaanite woman not through the daughter's faith but through that of the mother (Matt. 15:22-28). For this reason Christians should avoid condemning stillborn infants for whom believers and Christians have devoted their prayers and yearnings. By faith, Christians should lay hold of God's promise that he will

---

[99] *LW* 43, 149.
[100] *LW* 43, 250.

accomplish far greater and better things than appear to the contrary, and not seek to understand why God does not prevent stillbirths.

Concluding Reflections

I shall conclude with reflections on three major themes that dominate Luther's thinking as he sought to teach about God's ways with people, especially those who are assaulted by evil: (1) the merciful intention of the hidden God; (2) preaching as an instrument of divine power and God's hiddenness in human language; and (3) the cross and the question of theodicy.

The Sunnier Side of God's 'painful grace': The Merciful Intention of the Hidden God

For Luther, the hidden God and the revealed God are simply different aspects of the one God. He wrote that God says, 'From an unrevealed God I will become a revealed God. Nevertheless I will remain the same God.'[101] Further, Luther regarded temptation as God's embracing of the believer, the negative, painful, and terrifying aspects of God as hidden, which truly condemn believers if they do not flee to the graciousness of God as revealed in Christ. These contrasting sides of God are paralleled by the distinction between God's alien work in the law and his proper work in the gospel. God is active both in suffering and temptation – they are God's alien work through which he effects his proper work: his merciful intention is hidden under its opposite – his alien work. Through temptations believers are constantly forced back to the foot of the cross. Both as the hidden deity and as the revealed deity, God directs us away from himself when we seek to grasp him in his impassible naked deity towards himself as he hides in his human life, cross, and resurrection. Luther advised those who were assailed by temptation and suffering to shun the immediacy of the hidden God and rely on the mediation of the incarnate Christ, the revelation of God, through whom the painful or passible embraces of the hidden God are conquered by faith: 'only by him alone are all our sins paid and God's grace given to us, lest he [the believer] presume to deal directly with God [i.e., the hidden/naked God] and without the mediator.'[102] To combat temptation, the believer must lay hold of the efficacious activities of the incarnate Christ, the merciful intention of the alien work, and thus of the hidden God.

Underlying these gloomy assaults is God's merciful intention, his proper work, in which the believer rejoices. 'The fundamental insight, recognized by faith alone, is that God's wrath is his penultimate, and not his final word.'[103] Insofar as sin and unbelief still exist, the wrath of God continues to abide in an authentic Christian life. However, in Christ God's mercy has conquered God's wrath so that it does not remain a permanent but only a temporary force. The terrifying assault of divine

---

[101] See *LW* 5, 45; *WA* 43, 459.

[102] *LW* 42, 186.

[103] McGrath, *Luther's Theology of the Cross*, 155.

wrath against a sinner is God's strange work under the law, nevertheless his death-causing work, from which believers must flee into the wonderful embrace of divine mercy, his final word. Behind the gospel lies the dark reality of the terrifying judgment, the opposite of justification. Such a situation cannot be healed unless faith comes to understand the merciful intention hidden under its opposite – the severity of God's wrath.

The paradox involved in temptation is seen in the justification of the believer. Those who are tempted must submit to the paradoxical actions of God: the assault of temptation are foreign to God's nature, but result in justification, an action which is intrinsic to God's very nature. God makes a person a sinner before he makes him righteous. God performs the alien work in the law by killing the sinner's self-sufficiency in order that he might experience God's proper work in the gospel as he clings to God's efficacious promises in Christ. Temptation reveals the futility of self-justification and the need of God's justification. Suffering comes upon the believer as a chastisement, not from a vindictive, wrathful God but from a gracious God. Underlying the divine chastisement is God's 'painful grace,' the purpose of which is to strangle the old Adam so that the believer might turn to God alone for every good.[104] As alien work, suffering leaves believers naked and helpless; as proper work, it instills a trusting and saving relationship with God. Thus it is through suffering, which strips believers of sin, that God creates within them the faith that justifies. Luther wrote in his Romans commentary,

> Therefore suffering comes, through which a man is made patient and tested; it comes and takes away everything he has and leaves him naked and alone, allowing him no help or safety in either his physical or spiritual merits, for it makes a man despair of all created things, to turn away from them and from himself, to seek help outside of himself and all other things, in God alone ...[105]

Through the experience of temptation, Luther came to understand the theology of justification by faith alone: hence, his right to be named a true theologian.

Preaching: An Instrument of Divine Power and God's Hiddenness in Human Language

True Christians and right preaching, for Luther, must be true to God's word, the very substance and sustenance of faith. God's word assumes several created forms, not the least of which is preaching. Just as God hides himself and his promise in the words of the sacraments to meet us there, so he does the same in the office of preaching. Like other words, preaching too is an instrument of divine power, through which God accomplishes and fulfills his grace. He does this in complete independence of the preacher's disposition. Luther declared,

---

[104] Tinder, 'Luther's Theology of Christian Suffering', 110, where he describes divine chastisement as God's 'painful grace.'

[105] *LW* 25, 291.

> God has opened my mouth and bidden me speak, and he supports me mightily ... Therefore, I will speak and ... not keep silent as long as I live, until Christ's righteousness goes forth as brightness, and his saving grace be lighted as a lamp ... For no matter what I may be personally, still I can boast before God with a good conscience that in this matter I am not seeking my own advantage ...[106]

The human preacher is God's chosen vehicle through whom his voice is heard and his presence is felt. The Church is not a 'pen house,' but a 'mouth house' where God's word is preached:

> For since the advent of Christ, the gospel, which used to be taken in the Scriptures, has become an oral preaching. It is the manner of the New Testament and of the gospel that it must be preached and performed by word of mouth and a living voice. Christ himself has not written anything, nor has he ordered anything to be written, but rather to be preached by word of mouth.[107]

So important was the preaching office that Luther elevated it as central to the liturgy. 'To hear mass means nothing else but to hear God's Word and thereby serve God.'[108] Therefore he insisted, 'One should not consider who is speaking but what he is saying: for if it is the Word of God how would God himself not be present.'[109] Unlike the Aristotelian God who hides in his aloof solitariness, Luther's God is the one who hides in human language in order to speak with us with efficacy. 'Hear, brother: God, the creator of heaven and earth, speaks with you through his preachers ... Those words of God are not of Plato or Aristotle but God himself is speaking.'[110] The God who speaks is the God who acts, as Luther wrote in his exposition on Psalm 2 (1532): 'In the case of God to speak is to do, and the word is the deed.'[111]

God must be apprehended in human speech because he so graciously wills to meet us in it. For Luther, wrote Peter Meinhood, human language is 'a divine order in which human speech and the divine spirit are brought together into a unity.'[112] Luther wrote,

---

[106] *LW* 45, 347-48; *WA* 15, 27-28.

[107] *WA* 10, I, 48, as cited in George, *Theology of the Reformers*, 91. On Luther as a preacher, see A.S. Wood, *Captive to the Word: Martin Luther: Doctor of Sacred Scripture* (Grand Rapids: Eerdmans, 1969), 85-94.

[108] *LW* 51, 262; *WA* 36, 354.

[109] *LW* 3, 3, 220; *WA* 43, 32.

[110] *WATr* 4, 531, no. 4812, as cited in Ngien, 'Theology of Preaching in Martin Luther', 32.

[111] *LW* 12, 33; *WA* 40, II, 231.

[112] P. Meinhold, *Luthers Sprachphilosophie* (Berlin: Lutherisches Verlagshaus, 1958), 13: 'einer göttlichen Ordnung, in der menschliche Rede und göttlichen Geist zur Einheit.'

> no difference is perceptible between the word of man and the word of God when uttered by a human being; for the voice is the same, the sound and pronunciation are the same, whether you utter divine or human words.[113]

> In the prophets the term 'voice' applies without exception to the 'voice of the Lord', so that we must accept every word which is spoken as if the Lord himself were speaking, no matter by whom it is spoken, and we must believe it, yield to it, and humbly subject our reason to it.[114]

There abides a correspondence between God hiding in his humanity to reveal himself and God hiding in human language to communicate with us. God's descent into human language is indeed God's way of relating to us, not in a foreign language, but in the language of common people. Henceforth when we hear God's Word spoken, we should obey it wholeheartedly because 'God does everything through the ministry of human beings.'[115]

Preaching has a dual aspect: it is indeed the minister's activity, but also God's activity. But when we hear a sermon, we do not hear the pastor. 'Of course, the voice is his, but the words he employs are really spoken by my God.'[116] God meets people through the agency of the human voice. 'Just as a man uses his tongue as a tool with which he produces and forms words, so God uses our words, whether gospel or prophetic books, as tools with which he himself writes living words in our hearts.'[117]

The uniqueness of Luther's theology of preaching lies in that preaching is not mere human speech about God; rather it is God's own speech to people, which corresponds to God's own action. God's word acts and thus accomplishes his will, but through the agency of human speech. Preaching then is not the preacher's discursive reflections about God and life, an exercise distinctive of the custom of the university, but is God's audible address to sinners in need so that he might confer good on them, and clothe them with Christ's righteousness. The preacher speaks and, in his speaking, the justifying action of God is accomplished. God creates through his opposite (i.e., the preacher) the object of his love – a people no longer under divine wrath. Preaching is not a rehashing of the old stories, nor is it a memorial speech about God's deeds. Wingren's words elucidate Luther's view:

> [P]reaching, in so far as it is Biblical preaching, is God's own speech to man, is very difficult to maintain in practice. Instead it is very easy to slip into the idea that preaching is only speech about God. Such a slip once made, gradually alters the picture of God, so that he becomes the far-off deistic God who is remote from the

---

[113] *LW* 4, 140; *WA* 43, 236.
[114] *LW* 25, 239-40; *WA* 56, 253.
[115] *LW* 3, 274: *WA* 43, 71.
[116] *LW* 22, 528; *WA* 47, 229.
[117] *LW* 10, 212; *WA* 3, 256.

> preached word and is only spoken about as we speak about someone who is absent.[118]

Such an understanding of preaching is the result of Luther's doctrine of the word of God. 'The "Word of God" was the speech of God.' Pelikan wrote of Luther, '"The God who speaks" would be an appropriate way to summarize Luther's picture of God.'[119] Luther's God is not an impassive deity, like those of the Greeks, but an ever-present deity who hides in human speech and who is active in preaching through the human voice. God actively speaks through human language only when the preacher remains true to Christ, obeys him, and seeks nothing but that God's word might be heard. Accordingly, faithful hearers will respond, 'Pay attention, we are hearing God's speech.'

> Right preachers should diligently and faithfully teach only the Word of God and most seek only his honour and praise. Likewise the hearers should also say: I do not believe my pastor, but he tells me of another lord, whose name is Christ: him he shows to me, I will listen to him, in so far as he leads me to the true Teacher and Master, God's Son.[120]

Above all, true preaching must be faithful to Christ, its very content. Insofar as preaching points to Christ, it is God speaking, and thus he must be heard and received. The Word of God remains free to be heard by everyone, even if it comes from its antithesis (e.g., the heretics).

On account of God's call, preachers assume only the 'right to speak,' not the 'power to accomplish.'[121] Its efficacy lies in the power of God's causative word, not in human performance or endowments. This understanding induces comfort in the preacher's conscience, especially when confronted with the assaults of uncertainty and crisis. Right preaching inculcates in the hearers the personified pledge, which assures Christians that they may rely on God for every good and flee to him in every need. It too condemns human pride and overconfidence, as preachers may be tempted to glory in the fruits of their labor, rather than in the causality of God's word. The finest gifts of God must not be turned in upon themselves for self-aggrandizement. Ultimately the glory is God's, since it is he who works efficaciously through the instrumentality of human speech. It is God's good pleasure to shine his word in the heart with the law and the gospel, but not without the external, spoken word. Preachers are 'God's co-workers' to achieve his purpose.[122] Consequently no humanly devised programs, or methods, typical of the consumerist culture, should

---

[118] G. Wingren, *The Living Word: A Theological Study of Preaching and the Church* (trans. V.C. Pogue; Philadelphia: Fortress Press, 1960), 19. Also quoted in H.S. Wilson, 'Luther on Preaching as God Speaking', *Lutheran Quarterly* 19 (2005), 63-76 (65).

[119] Pelikan, *Luther the Expositor*, 50.

[120] *LW* 51, 388; *WA* 51, 191.

[121] *LW* 51, 76; *WA* 10, III, 15.

[122] *WA* 17, II, 179, as cited in Althaus, *Theology of Martin Luther*, 40.

become substitutes for public preaching, the ordained means of divine grace and the indispensable sign of a true church.

If this was the case, Luther asked why all preaching was not equally effective. Why some hearers, not all, felt the saving power and significance of God hiding in the human voice and were converted to the gospel. His answer was, '[T]his has not been revealed to us but rather is to be left to the judgment of God.' The task of the preacher, he said, was to remain faithful to preaching and hearing, and 'leave the matter in God's hands; he will move whatever hearts he wills.'[123] With a confident trust, Luther heeded God's voice: 'just go on preaching; don't worry about who will listen ... You preach and let me manage.'[124]

Faith knows that it is God who works all in all. The 'whomever' or the 'whenever' is the Spirit's prerogative, about which men could do nothing except submit to God's working and timing.

Luther gave credence to the freedom of God's word so that control is taken out of the preacher's hand. The Holy Spirit works freely through the word in the manner appropriate to the specific context of the sermon. In contrast to the enthusiasts who emphasized human preparation to receive the Holy Spirit, Luther affirmed that God's word enters the heart of believers without any preparation or help on their part. There was only one 'true preparation' – to hear or read or preach the word.[125]

The conviction that God's Word never fails caused Luther to invest considerable value in the office and practice of preaching. Luther's view of God's speech as God's justifying deed created in him a 'thirsty speech,' which could not rest but impelled him to preach. The refreshing power of God's word had indeed carried him through an incredibly difficult and demanding life till the end. This was evident in his *The Last Sermon in Wittenberg* (1546), preached just three days before he died, where Luther interpreted Jesus' words, 'Come to me all who labor and are heavy laden,' to mean

> just stick with me, hold to my Word, and let everything else go. If you are burned or beheaded for it ... if things go badly, I will give you the courage to laugh ... Only come to me ... It will not be heavy for you but light and easy to bear ... [because] I myself am helping you.[126]

Speculative Theodicy or Theology of the Cross?

Luther's letters are not exercises of a speculative theodicy, if by that we mean a rational defense and justification of God in the face of the dreadful realities of evil and

---

[123] *WA* 39, I, 370; cf. 404 and 406, as cited in Althaus, *Theology of Martin Luther*, 39.

[124] *WA* 10, I, 2, 51, as cited in F. Meuser, 'Luther as Preacher of the Word of God', in McKim (ed.), *The Cambridge Companion to Martin Luther*, 136-48 (137).

[125] *WA* 12, 497, as cited in Althaus, *Theology of Martin Luther*, 41.

[126] *LW* 51, 391, as cited in Meuser, 'Luther as Preacher of the Word of God', 147.

suffering. He had no interest in abstract speculation as to why God permitted evil. This too was made plain in his letter to a man who lost his only son in an accident:

> It is characteristic of our human nature to think that what we wish is best and what God does is unsatisfactory. But it would not be good if our will is always done because we would then become too sure of ourselves. It is enough for us that we have a gracious God. Why he permits this or that evil to befall us should not trouble us at all.[127]

Luther's view is also shared by twentieth-century Catholic divine Karl Rahner, who insists on allowing 'God to be God' in the face of the agonizing mystery of pain and evil. Thus Rahner argues that

> in our present concrete state, the acceptance of suffering without an answer other than the incomprehensibility of God and his freedom is the concrete form in which we accept God himself and allow him to be God. If there is not directly or indirectly this absolute acceptance of the incomprehensibility of suffering, all that can really happen is the affirmation of our own idea of God and not the affirmation of God himself.[128]

As a theologian of the cross, Luther did not allow talk about God that comes too easily. He disavowed any talk that assumes it is always easy to know what God is doing or intending. This is precisely what the theologian of glory claims to do. But that person, according to Luther, is not worthy of the name 'theologian,' for he 'looks upon the invisible things of God as though they were clearly perceptible in those things which have actually happened.'[129] It is the tendency of our fallen nature to speculate upon the incomprehensible mystery of suffering, but God forbids it. God says 'No' to our demand for an account of his governance of the universe. Nevertheless, this 'No' does not come from an angry or impassible deity who resents our inquiries; rather it is a 'No' of a loving God who diverts us away from abstract speculation towards the concrete image of the crucified Christ. There, suffering is neither rejected nor glorified; it is both acknowledged and overcome. The cross is the *locus* where we witness God's deepest humiliation in his Son, and where we see God's 'suffering' love for us in which God is most God-like. This means Luther's

---

[127] Luther's *Letters of Spiritual Counsel*, 69, as cited in Tinder, 'Luther's Theology of Christian Suffering', 111-12.

[128] K. Rahner, 'Why Does God Allow Us to Suffer?', *Theological Investigations*, vol. 19 (New York: Crossroad, 1983), 207; J. Moltmann, *The Trinity and the Kingdom* (trans. M. Kohl; New York: Harper & Row, 1981), 49. Likewise Moltmann questions the apologetic value of theodicy. Because the theodicy question assumes some belief in God, he says, 'it is not really a question at all, in the sense of something we can ask or not ask, like other questions. It is faith and theology to make it possible for us to survive, to go on living, with this open wound. The person who believes will not rest content with any slickly explanatory answer to the theodicy.'

[129] *LW* 31, 52. See Forde, *On Being a Theologian of the Cross*, 81-87.

theology of the cross must not be converted into a speculative theodicy. The resolution of the problem of theodicy is to be sought nowhere except in God's salvific deed on the cross to overcome evil, and in his indwelling in the dark and shameful places of death, agony, or degradation. The problem of suffering is thus resolved not by theoretical edifices, but by practically adverting to a theology of the cross. Dorothy Soelle's words echo Luther's:

> God is no executioner – and no almighty spectator (which would amount to the same thing). God is not the mighty tyrant. Between the sufferer and the one who causes the suffering, between the victim and the executioner, God, whatever people make of this world, is on the side of the sufferer. God is on the side of the victim, he is hanged.[130]

Thus 'theodicy,' Kenneth Surin writes, 'resolves itself into *theophany*':[131] in the cross, we have a passionate God who is personally engaged in a protest against the evils of sin, death, and hell, and eventually conquers these foes. That God who is a suffering participant in human miseries is less likely to be criticized as a deceiver, executioner, sadist, and despot.[132] Luther's denial that God is impassible incites faith, and justifies a belief in a morally benevolent deity who creates a world with suffering in it. Although the cross is primarily about God's justification of the ungodly, the reverse is implied, that in God's justification of them he too justifies himself before the world as the one who moves towards them with acceptance and forgiveness. At Golgotha, God justifies himself as the one who so loves the world that he gave his only begotten Son to redeem us from sin, death, and hell, if we only but believe. For Moltmann, it is humanity's innocent suffering challenging God's justice that occasions the cross. In contrast, for Luther, as for Anselm, it is God's justice offended by the guilty, sinful humanity that occasions it.[133] Satisfaction occurs only through penal substitution, that Christ takes our place, and in a joyous exchange assumes all our debts and guilt. Christ in his righteous person dies the innocent death of a sinner, and thereby has achieved satisfaction, which we could not produce for ourselves. He is driven to this by his sheer, boundless love. This is far from a theoretical theodicy: if God, why evil? But this is Luther's theology of the cross, in which God's true identity as love is known, and known only in his saving relationship to us in the suffering and cross of Jesus Christ. To grasp God aright is to grasp him as he wills to be grasped, that is, not in power but in weakness, not in majesty but in lowliness, not in glory but in the shame of the cross of Christ. This

---

[130] D. Soelle, *Suffering* (London: Darton, Longman & Todd, 1975), 148.

[131] K. Surin, *Theology and the Problem of Evil* (Oxford: Blackwell, 1986), 118.

[132] Cf. Moltmann, *Crucified God*, 221; W. McWilliams, *The Passion of God: Divine Suffering in Contemporary Theology* (Georgia: Mercer University Press, 1985), 40.

[133] See B.F. Eckardt, Jr, 'Luther and Moltmann: The Theology of the Cross', *Concordia Theological Quarterly* 49 (1985), 19-28, for a discussion of the similarities and differences between Luther's and Moltmann's theology of the cross. Cf. Althaus, *Theology of Martin Luther*, 202-203.

theology crucifies all human speculations as to why evil occurs, and draws the sinner through Christ's heart into the heart of God, deeming him worthy as the object of his love. The love, which God is, creates, not out of any pre-existent salvific materials, but strictly out of nothing (*ex nihilo*) a people no longer under divine wrath. This flows forth intrinsically from the cross, as stated in Thesis 28 of Luther's *Heidelberg Disputation*: 'This is the love of the cross, born of the cross, which turns in the direction where it does not find good that it may enjoy, but where it may confer good upon the bad and needy person. "It is more blessed to give than to receive" (Acts 20:35), says the Apostle.'[134] Strohl remarks aptly:

> That God does not remove suffering and immediately make straight the rough places of our lives isn't for Luther a negative reflection either on the extent of God's power or the integrity of God's professed love for us. The absoluteness of that power is revealed in its extraordinary efficaciousness. God's power serves God's love, making itself susceptible to the suffering of creation so as to transform that suffering from within and able always to bring life out of nothingness.[135]

That being said, a truly biblical style of pastoral care does not encourage people to suffer. Luther repeatedly warned against creating our own crosses, but assured us of divine comfort when trials hit us. It does not befit pastors to make the management and removal of pain their chief aim, but the triumphalists, who believe that God is found only in success and the lives of victorious people. Rather through prayer, the proper usage of God's word and sacrament, and their exemplary presence, they enable the sufferers to see that suffering, painful though it can be, is grounded and hallowed by God. It is there where God is found most intimately with us and for us. Then our consolation and faith are firmly established, which makes it possible for us to continue living, even with open wounds.

---

[134] *LW* 31, 57.

[135] Strohl, 'Luther's "*Fourteen Consolations*"', 169-82 (180).

Bibliography

Primary Sources

Lull, T.F. (ed.), *Martin Luther's Basic Theological Writings* (Minneapolis: Fortress Press, 1989).

Luther, M., *The Bondage of the Will* (trans. J.I. Packer and O.R. Johnson; London: Clarke, 1957).

—, *D. Martin Luthers Werke: Kritische Gesamtausgabe* (100 vols; Weimar: Hermann Bohlau Nachfolger, 1883–).

—, *D. Martin Luthers Werke: Kritische Gesamtausgabe* (Briefwechsel, 11 vols; Weimar: Herman Bohlau Nachfolger, 1906–61).

—, *D. Martin Luthers Werke: Kritische Gesamtausgabe: Tischreden* (Weimar: Hermann Bohlau Nachfolger, 1912–21).

—, *Letters of Spiritual Counsel* (ed. T.G. Tappert; Library of Christian Classics, vol. 18; Philadelphia: Westminster, 1955).

—, *Luther's Works* (American Editions, 55 vols; ed. J. Pelikan and H.T. Lehman; St. Louis: Concordia; Philadelphia: Fortress Press, 1955–67).

Plass, Ewald M. (comp.), *What Luther Says: A Practical In-Home Anthology for the Active Christian* (St. Louis: Concordia, 10th edn, 1994).

Tappert, T.G. (trans. and ed.), *The Book of Concord* (Philadelphia: Muhlenberg, 1959).

Secondary Sources

Alfsvag, K., 'Who Has Known the Mind of the Lord? The Theological Significance of the Doctrine of the Hidden God,' *Luther-Bulletin* 12 (2003), 30-45

Althaus, P., *The Theology of Martin Luther* (trans. R.C. Schultz; Philadelphia: Fortress Press, 1966).

Anderson, H.G., J.F. Stafford, and J.A. Burgess(eds.), *The One Mediator, the Saints, and Mary* (Lutherans and Catholics in Dialogue 8; Minneapolis: Augsburg, 1992).

Arand, C.P., 'The Battle Cry of Faith: The Catechisms' Exposition of the Lord's Prayer,' *Concordia Journal* 21 (1995), 42-65.

—, *That I May Be His Own: An Overview of Luther's Catechism* (St. Louis: Concordia Academic, 2000).

—, '"That I May Be His Own": The Anthropology of Luther's Explanation of the Creed,' *Concordia Journal* 21 (1995), 28-41.

Aries, P., *Western Attitudes toward Death: From the Middle Ages to the Present* (trans. P.M. Ranum; Baltimore: Johns Hopkins University Press, 1974).

Avis, P., 'Luther's Theology of the Church,' *Churchman* 97 (1983), 104-11.

Bainton, R., *Here I Stand: A Life of Martin Luther* (Mentor Book; New York: Abingdon, 1950).

Barth, K., *Church Dogmatics* (ed. G.W. Bromiley and trans. T.E. Torrance; Edinburgh: T&T Clark, 1962–75).

Bastien, P.E., *Praying with Martin Luther* (Minnesota: Saint Mary's, 1999).

Bayer, O., *Living by Faith: Justification and Sanctification* (trans. G.W. Bromiley; Grand Rapids: Eerdmans, 2003).

Begalke, M.V., 'An Introduction to Luther's Theology of Pastoral Care' (PhD dissertation; Ottawa: University of Ottawa, 1979).

Bertram, R., 'Luther on the Unique Mediatorship of Christ,' in H.G. Anderson, J.F. Stafford, and J.A. Burgess (eds), *The One Mediator, The Saints and Many* (Minneapolis: Augsburg, 1992), 249-62.

—, '"Scripture and Tradition" in the Lutheran Confessions,' *Pro Ecclesia* 10 (2001), 179-94.

Bird, M.F., 'Justified by Christ's Resurrection: A Neglected Aspect of Paul's Doctrine of Justification,' *Scottish Bulletin of Evangelical Theology* 22 (2004), 72-91.

Boase, T.S.R., *Death in the Middle Ages: Mortality, Judgment and Remembrance* (London: Thames & Hudson, 1972).

Bonhoeffer, D., *The Communion of Saints: A Dogmatic Inquiry into the Sociology of the Church* (trans. R.G. Smith; New York: Harper & Row, 1963).

—, *The Cost of Discipleship* (trans. T.R.H. Fuller; New York: Macmillan, 1963).

—, *Letters and Papers from Prison* (ed. E. Bethge; New York: Macmillan, 1972).

—, *Sanctorum Communio: A Theological Study of the Sociology of the Church* (ed. C.J. Green; Dietrich Bonhoeffer's Works, 1; Minneapolis: Fortress Press, 1998).

Bornkamm, H., *The Heart of Reformation Faith: The Fundamental Axioms of Evangelical Belief* (trans. J.W. Doberstein; New York: Harper & Row, 1965).

—, *Luther in Mid-Career 1521–1530* (Philadelphia: Fortress Press, 1983).

—, *Luther's World of Thought* (trans. M.H. Bertram; St. Louis: Concordia, 1958).

Boulton, M., '"We Pray by His Mouth": Karl Barth, Erving Goffman, and a Theology of Invocation,' *Modern Theology* 17 (2001), 67-83.

Braaten, C.E., 'Let's Talk about the "Death of God",' *Dialog* 26 (1987), 209-14.

Braaten, C.E., 'The Problem of God-Language Today,' in C.E. Braaten (ed.), *Our Naming of God: Problems and Prospects of God-Talk Today* (Minneapolis: Fortress Press, 1989), 11–33.

Braaten, C.E., and R.W. Jenson (eds.), *Union with Christ: The New Finnish Interpretation of Luther* (Grand Rapids: Eerdmans, 1998).

Brecht, M., *Martin Luther: His Road to Reformation 1483–1521* (trans. J.L. Schaff; Minneapolis: Fortress Press, 1969).

—, *Martin Luther: Shaping and Defining the Reformation 1521–1532* (trans. J.L. Schaff; Minneapolis: Fortress Press, 1990).

—, *Martin Luther: The Preservation of the Church 1532–1546* (trans. J.L. Schaff; Minneapolis: Fortress Press, 1993).

Brokering, H. (ed.), *Luther's Prayers* (Minneapolis: Augsburg, 1994).

Brondos, D.A., '*Sola Fide* and Luther's "Analytic" Understanding of Justification: A Fresh Look at Some Old Questions,' *Pro Ecclesia* 13 (2004), 39-57.

Brooks, P., 'Martin Luther and the Pastoral Dilemma,' in P. Brooks (ed.), *Christian Spirituality: Essays in Honour of Gordon Rupp* (London: SCM Press, 1975), 95-117.

Brooks, P. (ed.), *Christian Spirituality: Essays in Honor of Gordon Rupp* (London: SCM Press, 1975).

—, *Seven-Headed Luther: Essays in Commemoration of a Quincentenary 1483–1983* (Oxford: Clarendon Press, 1983).

Brunner, Frederick Dale, *The Churchbook, Matthew 13–28* (Dallas: Word, 1990).

Bucher, R.P., *The Ecumenical Luther: The Development and Use of His Doctrinal Hermeneutic* (St. Louis: Concordia Academic, 2003).

Buehler, D.A., 'Caring, Curing, Calling: The Minister and the Ministry of Healing,' *LCA Partners* 3 (1981), 7-25.

Burgess, J.A., and M. Kolden (eds), *By Faith Alone: Essays on Justification in Honor of Gerhard O. Forde* (Grand Rapids: Eerdmans, 2003).

Burtness, J.H., 'As Though God Were Not Given: Barth, Bonhoeffer and the *Finitum Capax Infiniti*,' *Dialog* 19 (1980), 249-55.

Carlson, A.E., 'Luther and the Doctrine of the Holy Spirit,' *Lutheran Quarterly* 11 (1959), 135-46.

Cavanaugh, W.T., 'A Joint Declaration? Justification as *Theosis* in Aquinas and Luther,' *Heythrop Journal* 41 (2000), 265-80.

Chemnitz, M., *The Lord's Supper* (trans. J.A.G. Preus; St. Louis: Concordia, 1979).

Cocke, E.W., 'Luther's View of Marriage and Family,' *Religion in Life* 42 (1973), 103-16.

Cole, W.J., 'Was Luther a Devotee of Mary?' *Marian Studies* 21 (1970), 94-102.

Congar, Y., 'Considerations and Reflections on the Christology of Luther,' *Dialogue between Christians* (trans. P. Loretz; Westminster: Newman, 1966).

Demarest, Bruce A., *The Cross and Salvation: The Doctrine of Salvation* (Wheaton, IL: Crossway, 1997).

Ebeling, G., *Luther: An Introduction to His Thought* (trans. R.A. Wilson; Philadelphia: Fortress Press, 1972).

Eckardt, B.F., Jr., 'Luther and Moltmann: Theology of the Cross,' *Concordia Theological Quarterly* 49 (1985), 19-28.

Edwards, M., 'The Older Luther,' in G. Dunnhaupht, *The Martin Luther Quincentennial* (Detroit: Wayne State University Press, 1985), 43-62

Elder, E.R. (ed.), *The Spirituality of Western Christendom* (Kalamazoo: Cistercian, 1976).

Elert, W., *The Structure of Lutheranism*, Vol. 1, *The Theology and Philosophy of Life of Lutheranism* (trans. W.A. Hansen; St. Louis: Concordia, 1962).

Evans, G.R. (ed.), *A History of Pastoral Care* (London: Cassell, 2000).

Forde, G.O., 'Law and Gospel in Luther's Hermeneutic,' *Interpretation* 37 (1983), 240-52.

—, 'Luther's Theology of the Cross,' *Christian Dogmatics* (2 vols.; Philadelphia: Fortress Press, 1984).
—, *On Being a Theologian of the Cross: Reflections on Luther's Heidelberg Disputation, 1518* (Grand Rapids: Eerdmans, 1997).
—, *Theology Is for Proclamation* (Minneapolis: Fortress Press, 1990).
Forell, G.W., 'Justification and Eschatology in Luther's Thought,' *Church History* 38 (1969), 164-74.
Gaffin, R.B., 'Redemption and Resurrection: An Exercise in Biblical-Systematic Theology,' *Themelios* 27 (2002), 16-31.
George, T., *Theology of the Reformers* (Nashville: Broadman, 1988).
Gerrish, B.A., *Grace and Gratitude* (Minneapolis: Fortress Press, 1993).
—, '"To the Unknown God": Luther and Calvin on the Hiddenness of God,' *Journal of Religion* 53 (1973), 263–92.
Girgensohn, H., *Teaching Luther's Catechism* (trans. J.W. Dobertsein; Philadelphia: Muhlenberg, 1959).
Gorman, M.J., *Cruciformity: Paul's Narrative Spirituality of the Cross* (Grand Rapids: Eerdmans, 2001).
Gottfried, R.S., *The Black Death* (New York: Free, 1983).
Gould, J.B., 'Bonhoeffer and Open Theism,' *Philosophy and Theology* 15 (2003), 57-91.
Gray, M., *The Protestant Reformation: Beliefs, Practice, and Tradition* (Brighton: Sussex Academic Press, 2003).
Greaves, R.L., 'Luther's Doctrine of Grace,' *Scottish Journal of Theology* 18 (1965), 385-95.
Greene, L., *How Melanchthon Helped Luther Discover the Gospel* (Fallbrook: Verdict, 1980).
Grislis, E., 'The Experience of the *Anfechtungen* and the Formulation of Pure Doctrine in Martin Luther's Commentary on Genesis,' *Consensus* 8 (1982), 19-31.
—, 'Luther on Sanctification: Humility and Courage,' *Consensus* 9 (1983), 3-16.
—, 'Luther's View of the Hidden God,' *McCormick Quarterly* 21 (1967-68), 81-94.
Gritsch, E.W., and R.W. Jenson, *Lutheranism: The Theological Movement and Its Confessional Writings* (Philadelphia: Fortress Press, 1976).
Hagen, K., *A Theology of Testament in the Young Luther: The Lectures on Hebrews* (Leiden: Brill, 1974).
Hanson, B., *Grace That Frees: The Lutheran Tradition* (Maryknoll: Orbis, 2004).
—, *A Graceful Life: Lutheran Spirituality for Today* (Minneapolis: Augsburg, 2000).
Hebart, F., 'The Role of the Lord's Prayer in Luther's Theology of Prayer,' *Lutheran Theological Journal* 18 (1984), 1-17.
Heinz, J., '"The Summer That Will Never End": Luther's Longing for the "Dear Last Day" in His Sermon on Luke 21 (1531),' *Andrews University Seminary Studies* 23 (1985), 181-86.

Helmer, C., 'Luther's Theology of Glory,' *Neue Zeitschrift für Systematicsche Theologie und Religionsphilosophie* 42 (2000), 237-45.

—, 'More Difficult to Believe? Luther on Divine Omnipotence,' *International Journal of Systematic Theology* 3 (2001), 2-26.

Hendrix, S.H., 'Luther's Impact on the Sixteenth Century,' *Sixteenth Century Journal* 16 (1985), 3-14.

—, 'Martin Luther's Reformation of Spirituality,' in T. Wengert (ed.), *Harvesting Martin Luther's Reflections on Theology, Ethics, and the Church* (Grand Rapids: Eerdmans, 2004), 240-60.

Herms, E., *Luthers Auslegung des Dritten Artikels*_(Tübingen: Mohr, 1987).

Hinkson, C., 'Luther and Kierkegaard: Theologian of the Cross,' *International Journal of Systematic Theology* 3 (2001), 27-45.

Hoekema, A.A., *Saved By Grace* (Grand Rapids: Eerdmans, 1989).

Hoffman, B.R., *Luther and the Mystics: A Re-examination of Luther's Spiritual Experience and His Relationship to the Mystics* (Minneapolis: Augsburg, 1976).

Hordern, W.E., *Experience and Faith: The Significance of Luther for Understanding Today's Experiential Religion* (Minneapolis: Augsburg, 1983).

—, *Living by Grace* (Philadelphia: Westminster, 1975).

Janz, D.R., 'Syllogism or Paradox: Aquinas and Luther on Theological Method,' *Theological Studies* 59 (1998), 3-21.

Jenson, R., 'The Hidden and Triune God,' *International Journal of Systematic Theology* 2 (2000), 5-12.

—, *Systematic Theology*, Vol. 2, *The Works of God* (Oxford: Oxford University Press, 1999).

Johansen, J.H., 'Martin Luther on Scripture and Authority, and the Church, Ministry and Sacraments,' *Scottish Journal of Theology* 15 (1962), 350-68.

Jüngel, E., *Death: The Riddle and the Mystery* (trans. I. and U. Nicol; Edinburgh: St Andrew Press, 1975).

Jüngel, E., *The Doctrine of the Trinity: God's Being Is in Becoming* (Grand Rapids: Eerdmans, 1976).

—, *God as the Mystery of the World: On the Foundation of the Theology of the Crucified God in the Dispute between Theism and Atheism* (trans. D.L. Guder; Grand Rapids: Eerdmans, 1983).

—, 'Quae Supra nos, nihil ad nos,' *Entsprechungen: Gott-Wahrheit-Mensch* (Munich: Kaiser, 1980).

Junghans, H., 'Luther on the Reform of Worship,' in T. Wengert (ed.), *Harvesting Martin Luther's Reflections on Theology, Ethics, and the Church* (Grand Rapids: Eerdmans, 2004), 207-25.

Kalfoff, P., *Die Depeschen des Nuntius Aleander vom Wormser Reichstage 1521* (Halle: S. M. Niemeyer, 1897).

Kärkkäinen, V.-M., '"The Christian as Christ to the Neighbour": On Luther's Theology of Love,' *International Journal of Systematic Theology* 6 (2004), 101-17.

—, 'Evil, Love and the Left Hand of God: The Contribution of Luther's Theology of the Cross to Evangelical Theology of Evil,' *Evangelical Quarterly* 79 (2002), 215-34.

—, 'The Holy Spirit and Justification: The Ecumenical Significance of Luther's Doctrine of Salvation,' *Pneuma: The Journal of the Society for Pentecostal Studies* 24 (2002), 26-39.

—, 'Justification as Forgiveness of Sins and Making Righteous: The Ecumenical Promise of a New Interpretation of Luther,' *One in Christ* 37 (2002), 32-45.

—, *Pneumatology: The Holy Spirit in Ecumenical, International, and Contextual Perspective* (Grand Rapids: Baker, 2002).

Kelly, R., '*Oratio, Meditatio, Tentatio Faciunt Theologum*: Luther's Piety and the Formation of Theologians,' *Consensus* 19 (1993), 9-27.

—, 'The Suffering Church: A Study of Luther's *Theologia crucis*,' *Concordia Theological Quarterly* 50 (1986), 3-17.

Kimel, A.F., Jr., 'Eating Christ: Recovering the Language of Real Identification,' *Pro Ecclesia* 13 (2004), 82-91.

Kittelson, J.A., *Luther the Reformer: The Story of the Man and His Career* (Minneapolis: Augsburg, 1986).

Kleinhaus, K.A., 'Why Now? The Relevance of Luther in a Postmodern Age,' *Currents in Theology and Mission* 24:4 (December 1997), 488-95.

Kleinig, J.W., 'The Kindred Heart,' *Lutheran Theological Journal* 19–20 (1985–86), 142-54.

—, 'Luther on the Christian's Participation in God's Holiness,' *Lutheran Theological Journal* 19 (1985), 21-9.

Klugg, E.F.A., *Lift High This Cross: The Theology of Martin Luther* (St. Louis: Concordia, 2003).

—, 'Luther on the Church,' *Concordia Theological Quarterly* 47 (1983), 193-207.

—, 'The Sacramental Presence in Lutheran Orthodoxy,' *Concordia Theological Quarterly* 50 (1986), 95-107.

Kolb, R., 'Luther on the Two Kinds of Righteousness,' in T. Wengert (ed.), *Harvesting Martin Luther's Reflection on Theology, Ethics and the Church* (Grand Rapids: Eerdmans, 2004), 38-55.

—, *Martin Luther as Prophet, Teacher, and Hero* (Grand Rapids: Baker, 1999).

—, *Teaching God's Children His Teaching: A Guide for the Study of Luther's Catechism* (Hutchinson: Crown, 1992).

—, '"That I May Be His Own": The Anthropology of Luther's Explanation of the Creed,' *Concordia Journal* 21 (1995), 28-41.

—, '"What Benefit Does the Soul Receive from a Handful of Water?": Luther's Preaching on Baptism, 1528–1539,' *Concordia Journal* 25 (1999), 346-63.

Koslofsky, C.M., *The Reformation of the Dead: Death and Ritual in Early Modern Germany, 1450–1700* (Basingstoke: Macmillan, 2000).

Krispin, G.S., 'The Consolation of the Resurrection in Luther,' *Lutheran Theological Review* 2 (1989–90), 37-51.

—, 'A Study in Luther's Pastoral Theology,' *Logia* 10 (2001), 13-19.

Krodel, G.G., 'Luther's Work on the Catechism in the Context of Late Medieval Catechetical Literature,' *Concordia Journal* 25 (1999), 364-404.

Lage, D., *Martin Luther's Christology and Ethics* (Lewiston: Edwin Mellen, 1990).

Law, D.R., 'Descent into Hell, Ascension, and Luther's Doctrine of Ubiquitarianism,' *Theology* 107 (2004), 250-56.

Lazareth, W.H., *Luther and the Christian Home* (Philadelphia: Muhlenberg, 1960).

Lehmann, H., *Luther and Prayer* (Milwaukee: Northwestern, 1985).

Lehmann, H.T. (ed.), *Meaning and Practice of the Lord's Supper* (Philadelphia: Muhlenberg, 1961).

Lehmann, Martin E., *Luther and Prayer* (Milwaukee: Northwestern, 1985).

Lenker, J.N. (ed.), *Luther's Church Postil: Pentecost or Missionary Sermons* (6 vols.; Minneapolis: Lutherans in All Lands, 1907).

Leroux, N.R., *Luther's Rhetoric: Strategies and Style from the Invocavit Sermons* (St. Louis: Concordia Academic, 2002).

Lienhard, M., *Luther: Witness to Jesus Christ* (trans. E.H. Robertson; Minneapolis: Augsburg, 1982).

Lienhard, M., 'Luther and the Beginnings of the Reformation,' in J. Raitt (ed.), *Christian Spirituality II: High Middle Ages and Reformation* (New York: Crossroad, 1987), 268–99.

Lindberg, C., 'The Lutheran Tradition,' in R. Numbers and D. Amundsen (eds), *Caring and Curing: Health and Medicine in the Western Traditions* (New York: Macmillan, 1980), 173-203.

—, 'Prierias and His Significance for Luther's Development,' *Sixteenth Century Journal* 3.2 (1972), 45-64.

—, '"There Should Be No Beggars among Christians": Karlstadt, Luther, and the Origins of Protestant Poor Relief,' *Church History* 46 (1977), 313-34.

Lindberg, C.H., 'Luther's Concept of God: A Critique of Anders Nygren's Interpretation of Martin Luther' (PhD thesis; Ann Arbor, MI: University Microfilm International, 1965).

Lischer, R., 'Luther and Contemporary Preaching: Narrative and Anthropology,' *Scottish Journal of Theology* 36 (1983), 487-504.

Littell, F.H. (ed.), *Reformation Studies: Essays in Honor of Roland H. Bainton* (Virginia: John Knox, 1962).

Loewen, H., *Luther and the Radicals* (Waterloo: Wilfrid Laurier University Press, 1974).

Loewenich, W. von, *Luther's Theology of the Cross* (trans. H.J.A. Bouman; Minneapolis: Augsburg, 1976).

Lohse, B., *Martin Luther's Theology: Its Historical and Systematic Development* (trans. Roy A. Harrisville; Minneapolis: Fortress Press, 1999).

Maas, R., 'A Simple Way to Pray: Luther's Instructions on the Devotional Use of the Catechism,' in R. Maas and G. O'Donnell (eds), *Spiritual Traditions for the Contemporary Church* (Nashville: Abingdon, 1990), 162-79.

Maas, R., and G. O'Donnell (eds.), *Spiritual Traditions for the Contemporary Church* (Nashville: Abingdon, 1990).

Macchia, F.D., 'Justification through New Creation: The Holy Spirit and the Doctrine by Which the Church Stands or Falls,' *Theology Today* 58 (2001), 202-17.

Mackinnon, J., *Luther and the Reformation* (London: Longmans, Green, 1928), vol. 2.

Macleod, D., 'The New Perspective: Paul, Luther and Judaism,' *Scottish Bulletin of Evangelical Theology* 22 (2004), 4-31.

Marius, R., *Martin Luther: The Christian between God and Death* (Cambridge: Belknap Press of Harvard University, 1999).

Marshall, B.D., 'Justification as Declaration and Deification,' *International Journal of Systematic Theology* 4 (2002), 3-28.

Martin, J., 'An Abandonment of Hope: Martin Luther and the Jews,' *Churchman* 107 (1993), 331-38.

Marty, M.E., *Health and Medicine in the Lutheran Tradition* (New York: Crossroad, 1983).

—, *The Hidden Discipline* (St. Louis: Concordia, 1962).

Maschke, T., F. Posset, and J. Skocir (eds), *Ad Fontes Lutheri: Toward the Recovery of the Real Luther: Essays in Honour of Kenneth Hagen's Sixty-fifth Birthday* (Milwaukee: Marquette University Press, 2001).

Matheson, P., *The Rhetoric of the Reformation* (Edinburgh: T&T Clark, 1998).

Mattes, M.C., *The Role of Justification in Contemporary Theology* (Grand Rapids: Eerdmans, 2004).

Maxwell, D., 'Crucified in the Flesh: Christological Confession or Evasive Qualification,' *Pro Ecclesia* 13 (2004), 70-100.

McCue, J.F., 'Luther and the Problem of Popular Preaching,' *Sixteenth Century Journal* 16 (1985), 33-43.

McDonough, T., *The Law and the Gospel: A Study of Martin Luther's Confessional Writings* (Oxford: Oxford University Press, 1963).

McGrath, A.E., *Christian Theology: An Introduction* (Oxford: Blackwell, 3rd edn., 2001)

—, *The Intellectual Origins of the European Reformation* (Oxford: Blackwell, 1987).

—, *Luther's Theology of the Cross: Martin Luther's Theological Breakthrough* (Oxford: Blackwell, 1985).

—, '"The Righteousness of God" from Augustine to Luther,' *Studia Theologia* 36 (1982), 63-78.

McGrath, A.E. (ed.), *The Christian Theology Reader* (Oxford: Blackwell, 2nd edn., 2001).

McKim, D.K. (ed.), *The Cambridge Campanion to Martin Luther* (Cambridge: Cambridge University Press, 2003).

McNutt, J., 'Martin Luther as Human Being: Reflections from a Distance,' *Churchman* 108 (1994), 265-70.

McWilliams, W., *The Passion of God: Divine Suffering in Contemporary Theology* (Atlanta: Mercer University Press, 1985).

Meinhold, P., *Luthers Sprachphilosophie* (Berlin: Lutherisches Verlagshaus, 1958).

Meuser, F., 'Luther as Preacher of the Word of God,' in D.K. McKim (ed.), *The Cambridge Companion to Martin Luther* (Cambridge: Cambridge University Press, 2003), 136-48.

Meyer, R.Z., *This Faith is Mine: Meditations for Youth on Luther's Catechism* (St. Louis: Concordia, 1960).

Mildenberger, F., *Theology of Lutheran Confessions* (trans. E. Lueker; Philadelphia: Fortress Press, 1986).

Moltmann, J., *The Crucified God: The Cross of Christ as the Foundation and Criticism of Christian Theology* (trans. M. Kohl; New York: Harper & Row, 1977).

—, *The Trinity and the Kingdom* (trans. M. Kohl; New York: Harper & Row, 1981).

Moseman, C., 'Martin Luther on "Becoming a Christ to One's Neighbor",' *Presbyterion* 26 (2000), 93-104.

Mueller, G., 'Protestant Veneration of Mary: Luther's Interpretation of *The Magnificat*,' in J. Kirk (ed.), *Humanism and Reform: The Church in Europe, England, and Scotland, 1400–43: Essays in Honor of James K. Cameron* (Oxford: Blackwell, 1991), 99-111.

Nagel, N., '*Sacramentum et Exemplum* in Luther's Understanding of Christ,' in C.S. Meyer (ed.), *Luther for an Ecumenical Age* (St. Louis: Concordia, 1967), 172-99.

Nebe, A., *Luther as Spiritual Adviser* (trans. C.A. Hay and C.E. Hay; Philadelphia: Lutheran Publication Society, 1894).

Neufeld, F. vann, 'The Cross of the Living Lord: The Theology of the Cross and Mysticism,' *Scottish Journal of Theology* 49 (1996), 131-46.

Ngien, D., 'Chalcedonian Christology and Beyond: Luther's Understanding of the *Communicatio Idiomatum*,' *Heythrop Journal* 45 (2004), 54-68.

—, *The Suffering of God according to Martin Luther's 'Theologia Crucis'* (Bern: Lang, 1995).

—, 'Theology of Preaching in Martin Luther,' *Themelios* 28 (2003), 28-48.

—, 'Trinity and Divine Passiblity in Martin Luther's "Theologia Crucis",' *Scottish Bulletin of Evangelical Theology* 19 (2001), 31-64.

—, 'Ultimate Reality and Meaning in Luther's *Theologia Crucis*: No Other God, But the Incarnate, Human God,' *Andrews University Seminary Studies* 42 (2004), 383-405.

Noll, M.A., 'Martin Luther and the Concept of a "True" Church,' *Evangelical Quarterly* 50 (1978), 79-85.

Nugent, D.C., 'Mystical and Evangelical Theology in Martin Luther and St. John of the Cross,' *Journal of Ecumenical Studies* 28 (1991), 555-65.

—, 'What Has Wittenberg to Do with Avila? Martin Luther and St. Teresa,' *Journal of Ecumenical Studies* 23 (1986), 650-58.

Numbers, R.L., and D.W. Amundsen (eds.), *Caring and Curing: Health and Medicine in the Western Religious Traditions* (New York: Macmillan, 1986).

Nygren, A., *Agape and Eros* (trans. P. Watson; Philadelphia: Westminster, 1953).

Oberman, H.A., *The Harvest of Medieval Theology: Gabriel Biel and Late Medieval Nominalism* (Grand Rapids: Eerdmans, 1967).

—, *Luther: Man between God and the Devil* (trans. E. Walliser-Schwarzbart; New Haven: Yale University Press, 1989).

—, 'Luther and the *Via Moderna*: The Philosophical Backdrop of the Reformation Breakthrough,' *Journal of Ecclesiastical History* 54 (2003), 641-70.

O'Connor, M.C., *The Art of Dying Well: The Development of the Ars Moriendi* (New York: Columbia University Press, 1942).

Olmsted, R.H., 'Staking All on Faith's Object,' *Pro Ecclesia* 10 (2001), 135-58.

Olson, R.E., *The Story of Christian Theology: Twenty Centuries of Tradition and Reform* (Downers Grove, IL: IVP, 1999).

Owen, B., *Daily Readings from Luther's Writings* (Minneapolis: Augsburg, 1993).

Oyer, J.S., *Lutheran Reformers against Anabaptists* (The Hague: Martinus Nijhoff, 1964).

Pannenberg, W., 'Luther's Contribution to Christian Spirituality,' *Dialog* 40 (2001), 248-89.

Parsons, M., *Luther and Calvin on Old Testament Narratives: Reformation Thought and Narrative Text* (Lewiston: Mellen, 2004).

Pauck, W. (ed.), *P. Melanchthon and M. Bucer* (Library of Christian Classics, vol. 19; Philadelphia: Westminster, 1969).

Paulson, S., *Luther for Armchair Theologians* (Louisville: Westminster John Knox, 2004).

Pelikan, J., *Luther the Expositor: Introduction to the Reformer's Exegetical Writings* (Luther's Works, Companion Volume; St. Louis: Concordia, 1959).

Pelikan, J. (ed.), *Interpreters of Luther: Essays in Honor of Wilhelm Pauck* (Philadelphia: Fortress Press, 1968).

Perkins, D., 'The Problem of Suffering: Atheistic Protest and Trinitarian Response,' *St. Luke Journal of Theology* 23 (1979), 14-32.

Peters, T., *God – the World's Future* (Minneapolis: Fortress Press, 1992).

—, *Sin: Radical Evil in Soul and Society* (Grand Rapids: Eerdmans, 1994).

Peters, T.C., *Cherish the Word: Reflections on Luther's Spirituality* (St. Louis: Concordia, 2000).

Pettegree, A., *Reformation and the Culture of Persuasion* (Cambridge: Cambridge University Press, 2005).

Peura, S., 'The Church as Spiritual Communion in Luther,' *Lutheran World Federation* 42 (1997), 93-132.

—, 'The Essence of Luther's Spirituality,' *Seminary Ridge Review* (Winter 2000), 16-33.

Pinomaa, L., *Faith Victorious: An Introduction to Luther's Theology* (trans. W.J. Kukkonen; Philadelphia: Fortress Press, 1963).

Posset, F., 'Luther's Catholic Christology according to His Johannine Lectures of 1527' (PhD dissertation; Ann Arbor: University Microfilm International, 1984).

—, 'St. Bernard's Influence on Two Reformers: Johannes von Staupitz and Martin Luther,' *Cistercian Studies* 25 (1990), 175-87.

Preus, R.D., 'Luther and the Doctrine of Justification,' *Concordia Theological Quarterly* 48 (1984), 1-15.

Rahner, K., 'Why Does God Allow Us to Suffer?,' *Theological Investigations*, Vol. 19 (New York: Crossroad, 1983).

Raitt, J. (ed.), *Christian Spirituality II: High Middle Ages and Reformation* (New York: Crossroad, 1987).

Reid, D.R., 'Luther, Muntzer, and the Last Day: Eschatological Hope, Apocalyptic Expectations,' *Mennonite Quarterly Review* 69 (1995), 53-74.

Richard, L.J., *The Spirituality of John Calvin* (Atlanta: John Knox, 1974).

Rohrbough, F.E., 'A Lutheran Understanding of Prayer,' *Andrews University Seminary Studies* 38 (2000), 69-75.

Rupp, G., *The Righteousness of God: Luther Studies* (London: Hodder and Stoughton, 1953).

Sasse, H., *This Is My Body* (Minneapolis: Augsburg, 1959).

—, *We Confess Jesus Christ* (trans. N. Nagel; St. Louis: Concordia, 1984).

—, *We Confess the Sacraments* (trans. N. Nagel; St. Louis: Concordia, 1984).

Scaer, D.P., 'The Concept of *Anfechtung* in Luther's Thought,' *Concordia Theological Quarterly* 47 (1983), 15-30.

—, 'Luther on Prayer,' *Concordia Theological Quarterly* 47 (1983), 305-15.

—, 'Luther's Concept of the Resurrection in His Commentary on I Corinthians 15,' *Concordia Theological Quarterly* 47 (1983), 209-24.

Scaer, D.P., 'Santification in Lutheran Theology,' *Concordia Theological Quarterly* 49 (1985), 181-97.

Scaer, D.P., and R.D. Preus (eds), *Luther's Catechisms – 450 years* (Fort Wayne: Concordia Theological Seminary, 1979).

Schild, M.E., 'Praying the Catechism and Defrocking the Devil: Aspects of Luther's Spirituality,' *Lutheran Theological Journal* 10 (1976), 48-56.

Schlink, E., *Theology of Lutheran Confessions* (Philadelphia: Fortress Press, 1961).

Schwarz, H., 'Luther's Understanding of Heaven and Hell,' in F.W. Meuser and S.D. Schneider (eds), *Interpreting Luther's Legacy: Essays in Honor of Edward C. Fendt* (Minneapolis: Augsburg, 1969), 83-94.

Schwarzwaller, K., *Theologia Crucis: Luther's von Pradestination nach de servo arbitrio, 1525* (Munich: Kaiser, 1970).

Schwiebert, E.G., *Luther and His Times* (St. Louis: Concordia, 1950).

Seabright, R., 'Luther's Perspectives on Spirituality,' *Trinity Seminary Review* 8 (1989), 3-9.

Secker, P.J., 'Martin Luther's Views on the State of the Dead,' *Concordia Theological Monthly* 38 (1967), 422-35.

Senn, F.C., *Protestant Spiritual Traditions* (New York: Paulist, 1986).

Siggins, I.D., *Luther and His Mother* (Philadelphia: Fortress Press, 1981).

—, *Martin Luther's Doctrine of Christ* (New Haven: Yale University Press, 1970).

Siirala, A., *The Voice of Illness: A Study in Therapy and Prophecy* (New York: Edwin Mellen, 1981).

Soelle, D., *Suffering* (London: Darton, Longman & Todd, 1975).

Steiner, M., and S. Percy, *Day by Day We Magnify Thee* (Philadelphia: Fortress Press, 1989).

Steinke, P.L., *Preaching the Theology of the Cross* (Minneapolis: Augsburg, 1983).

Steinmetz, D.C., 'The Catholic Luther: A Critical Reappraisal,' *Theology Today* 61 (2004), 187-201.

—, *Luther and Staupitz: An Essay in the Intellectual Origins of the Protestant Reformation* (Duke Monographs in Medieval and Renaissance Studies 4; Durham, NC: Duke University Press, 1980).

—, 'Luther and the Ascent of Jacob's Ladder,' *Church History* 55 (1986), 179-92.

—, *Luther in Context* (Grand Rapids: Baker, 2nd edn., 2002).

Stephens, W.P. (ed.), *The Bible, the Reformation and the Church: Essays in Honour of James Atkinson* (Sheffield: Sheffield Academic Press, 1995).

Stephenson, J.R., 'Let Your Holy Angel Be with Me,' *Lutheran Theological Review* 9 (1996--97), 32-41.

Stevenson, K.W., *The Lord's Prayer: A Text in Tradition* (Minneapolis: Fortress Press, 2004).

Stolt, B., 'Joy, Love and Trust – Basic Ingredients in Luther's Theology of the Faith of the Heart,' *Institute for Luther Studies at Lutheran Theological Seminary at Gettysburg Colloquy Lectures* (31 October 2001), 1-16

Stott, J., *The Cross of Christ* (Downers Grove, IL, and Leicester: IVP, 1986).

Strange, D., 'A Sketch of the Thought of Luther on Martyrdom,' *Concordia Theological Monthly* 37 (1966), 6-41.

Strauss, G., *Luther's House of Learning: Indoctrination of the Young in the German Reformation* (Baltimore: Johns Hopkins University Press, 1978).

Strohl, J.E., 'Luther's Eschatology: The Last Times and The Last Things' (PhD dissertation; Chicago: University of Chicago, 1989).

—, 'Luther's "*Fourteen Consolations*",' *Lutheran Quarterly* 3 (1989), 169-82.

Strohl, J.E., 'Luther's Spiritual Journey,' in D.K. McKim (ed.) *The Cambridge Companion to Martin Luther* (Cambridge: Cambridge University Press, 2003), 149-64.

Surin, K., *Theology and the Problem of Evil* (Oxford: Blackwell, 1986).

Tappert, T.G., 'Meaning and Practice in the Reformation,' in Martin E. Lehmann (ed.), *Meaning and Practice of the Lord's Supper* (Philadelphia: Muhlenberg, 1961), 88-102.

Tappert, T.G. (ed.), *The Book of Concord: The Confessions of Evangelical Lutheran Church* (Philadelphia: Fortress Press, 1959).

Terry, D.J., 'Martin Luther on the Suffering of the Christian' (2 vols.; PhD dissertation; Ann Arbor, MI: UMI Dissertation, 1990).

Thielicke, H., *Death and Life* (trans. E.H. Schroeder; Philadelphia: Fortress Press, 1970).

Thiselton, A.C., 'Luther and Barth in I Corinthians 15: Six Theses for Theology in Relation to Recent Interpretation,' in W.P. Stephens (ed.), *The Bible, the Reformation and the Church: Essays in Honour of James Atkinson* (Sheffield: Sheffield Academic Press, 1995), 258-89.

Tinder, G., 'Luther's Theology of Christian Suffering and Its Implications for Pastoral Care,' *Dialog* 25 (1986), 108-13.

Torrance, J.B., *Worship, Community and the Triune God of Grace* (Downers Grove, IL: IVP, 1996).

Torrance, T.F., *The Trinitarian Faith: The Evangelical Theology of the Ancient Catholic Church* (Edinburgh: T&T Clark, 1988).

Trueman, C.R., *Reformation: Yesterday, Today and Tomorrow* (Bridgend: Bryntirion, 2000).

Vajta, V., *Luther on Worship* (Philadelphia: Muhlenberg, 1958).

Vander Zee, L.J., *Christ, Baptism and the Lord's Supper* (Illinois: IVP, 2004).

Vercruysse, J.E., 'Luther's Theology of the Cross: Its Relevance for Ecumenism,' *Centre pro Unione* 35 (Spring, 1989), 2-11.

—, 'Luther's Theology of the Cross at the Time of the *Heidelberg Disputation*,' *Gregorianum* 57 (1976), 523-48.

Voelz, J.W., 'Luther's Use of Scripture in the *Small Catechism*,' in D.P. Scaer and R.D. Preus (eds), *Luther's Catechisms – 450 years: Essays Commemorating the Small and Large Catechisms of Dr. Martin Luther* (Fort Wayne: Concordia Theological Seminary, 1979), 55-64.

Vogel, W., 'The Eschatological Theology of Martin Luther, Part I: Luther's Basic Concepts,' *Andrews University Seminary Studies* 24 (1986), 249-61.

—, 'The Eschatological Theology of Martin Luther, Part II: Luther's Exposition of Daniel and Revelation,' *Andrews University Seminary Studies* 25 (1987), 183-99.

Volz, C. (ed.), *Teaching the Faith* (River Forest: Lutheran Education Association, 1976).

Voragine, J. de, *Legenda aurea* (Heidelberg: Verlag Lambert Schneider, 4th edn., 1963).

Watson, P., *Let God Be God: An Interpretation of the Theology of Martin Luther* (Philadelphia: Muhlenberg, 1948).

Weborg, J., 'Pietism: "The Fire of God Which … Flames in the Heart of Germany",' in F.C. Senn (ed.), *Protestant Spiritual Traditions* (New York: Paulist, 1986), 183-216.

Webster, J., '"The Grammar of Doing": Luther and Barth on Human Agency,' *Barth's Moral Theology: Human Action in Barth's Thought* (Edinburgh: T&T Clark, 1998).

Wengert, T.J., '"Fear and Love" in the Ten Commandments,' *Concordia Journal* 21 (1995), 14-27.

Wengert, T.J. (ed.), *Harvesting Martin Luther's Reflections on Theology, Ethics, and the Church* (Grand Rapids: Eerdmans, 2003).

White, J.F., *Sacraments in Protestant Practice and Faith* (Nashville: Abingdon, 1999).

Wilch, J.R., 'Belief in Life beyond Death in Genesis,' *Lutheran Theological Review* 3 (1991), 57-66.

William of Ockham, *Summa Logicae* (2 vols; ed. P. Boehner; St. Bonaventure, NY: The Franciscan Institute, 1957).

Williams, R., *Christian Spirituality: A Theological History from the New Testament to Luther and St. John of the Cross* (Atlanta: John Knox, 1979).

Wilson, H. S., 'Luther on Preaching as God Speaking,' *Lutheran Quarterly* 19 (2005), 63-76.

Wingren, G., *The Living Word: A Theological Study of Preaching and the Church* (trans. V.C. Pogue; Philadelphia: Fortress Press, 1960).

—, *Luther on Vocation* (trans. C.C. Rasmussen; Philadelphia: Muhlenberg, 1957).

Wisner, D.A., *Prayers Based on Luther's Small Catechism* (Minneapolis: Augsburg Fortress Press, 1991).

Wolf, E., *Staupitz und Luther* (Verein fur Reformationsgeschichte 9; Leipzig: M. Heinsius, 1927).

Won, Y.J., 'The Work of the Holy Spirit and the Charismatic Movements from Luther's Perspective,' *Concordia Journal* 11 (1985), 204-13.

Wood, A.S., *Captive to the Word: Martin Luther: Doctor of Sacred Scripture* (Grand Rapids: Eerdmans, 1969).

Wood, S., 'Spirit and Spirituality in Luther,' *Evangelical Quarterly* 54 (1982), 14-24.

Zachman, R.C., *The Assurance of Faith: Conscience in the Theology of Martin Luther and John Calvin* (Minneapolis: Augsburg Fortress Press, 1993).

Zwanepol, K., 'A Human God: Some Remarks on Luther's Christology,' *Concordia Journal* 30 (2004), 40-53.

General Index